"*Straw* is the story of a guy who had two strikes against him in the middle innings of life and then hit one out of the park."

—Reggie Jackson

"Darryl Strawberry hit more than three hundred homers and shared in four championships, but he will be remembered as much for what he didn't accomplish as for all of the things he accomplished. In *Straw*, he tells you why."

—Buster Olney, author of *The Last Night of the Yankee Dynasty*

"Darryl has written a profound book on the meaning of celebrity, sports, and manhood. Reading his story, you follow an incredibly talented ballplayer who fell prey to his demons off the field. This is a riveting and memorable account of one man's pursuit of a meaningful life."

—David Cone

"*Straw* does have the virtue of sincerity and of seeming profoundly felt. Its narrator emerges as a real and complex man: humble in the face of his failures, palpably hungry for redemption, and yet still capable of myopia and self-righteousness. You feel for him in a way you never did—at least I never did—when you were merely cheering and/or booing him at Shea."

—*New York Times Book Review*

"If you're looking for an interesting book about a chaotically interesting life, *Straw* makes for good reading."

—*St. Louis Post-Dispatch*

"In an incredibly poignant moment in *Straw*, Darryl Strawberry writes, 'I really don't know what it is about me that has made fans so kind to me over the years.' . . . In major sections of the memoir, it is like watching the third base coach waving his arms frantically as Strawberry is ready to touch third base and barrel into home for the winning run. But the game isn't during the glory years in Shea Stadium and the coach is actually a conglomeration of the demons that have delightfully played with Strawberry for years."

—AtHomePlate.com

STRAW

FINDING MY WAY

Darryl Strawberry

with John Strausbaugh

ecco
An Imprint of HarperCollinsPublishers

HarperCollins books may be purchased for educational, business, or sales promotional use. For information, please e-mail the Special Markets Department at SPsales@harpercollins.com.

All illustrations courtesy of the Strawberry family, except those on insert pages 4, 8, and 9 courtesy of New York *Daily News*.

A hardcover edition of this book was published in 2009 by Ecco, an imprint of HarperCollins Publishers.

FIRST ECCO PAPERBACK EDITION 2010

Designed by Cassandra J. Pappas

The Library of Congress has cataloged the hardcover edition as follows:
Strawberry, Darryl.
  Straw : finding my way / Darryl Strawberry.
    p. cm.
  ISBN 978-0-06-170420-8 (hardcover)
  ISBN 978-0-06-170421-5 (paperback)
1. Strawberry, Darryl. 2. Baseball players—United States—Biography. I. Title.
  GV865.S87S87 2009
  796.357092—dc22
  [B]   2008054447

14   OV/RRD   10 9 8 7 6 5 4 3 2

For Tracy,
my amazing wife whom I love so very much.
You led me to finding my way through your faith, strength,
encouragement, and tough love when I needed it.
I cherish you for being the woman you are to me
and for who we are as one.

For my children,
Darryl Jr. (DJ), Diamond, Jordan, Jade, and Jewel.
You touch the depths of my soul and
I love you more than words could ever say.

For my mother, Ruby,
who always knew I would get it right someday.
I love you and I miss you so much!
Rest in peace, my angel!

For my relationship with you, God,
through Jesus Christ. Without you this book and
the life I have today would not be possible.
For your unconditional love, healing power,
never-ending mercy, and true gift of grace that I could
never be worthy of receiving, my love and deepest,
deepest gratitude.

Introduction

This is not a book about baseball. It's a book about life. I love baseball. It was and still is a big part of my life. It's a big part of this book, too. But baseball was not my life. In a lot of ways it was more like my escape from life. I was great at baseball right from the start. It's taken me a whole lot longer to get good at life.

Don't get me wrong. I'm not saying you shouldn't read this book if you're a baseball fan. I'm saying you don't have to be a baseball fan to read it. Because this is really a book about my struggles, how I endured them, and how I overcame them. It's about living the high life, and about falling as low as a man can get. It's about excelling as a baseball player, and failing miserably as a man. It's about being blessed with great talent and gifts, but hating and punishing yourself anyway. It's about running away from my responsibilities as a husband and father, and the terrible consequences of that for me and my loved ones.

And, in the end, it's about triumphing over all my personal demons and self-loathing, and, through the grace of God and with the help of others, finding peace. I endured and overcame, and I finally got my life in order. I'm in a position now to be a positive force in the world and help others, and it feels great.

I've written this book because I want to give hope and encourage people who are struggling to find peace themselves. Every life begins with great promise, and every life is filled with some kinds of trials and tribulations. How do you endure and overcome those troubles? How do you keep your faith and not give up when the troubles come along? This life is a journey, and for all of us there are going to be some pit stops, detours, and dead ends. I hope the problems you face, whatever they are, aren't as painful as mine were. And, whatever they are, I hope this book encourages you to keep going forward in your journey.

I've written a lot about my father in this book, because he was a huge and very negative influence on my life. My father was a raging alcoholic who whupped me all the time and told me I was never going to amount to anything in this world. That was just about all he did for me, and then he was gone. He never told me he loved me. He never showed me he loved me. He was never there to offer fatherly support or guidance. How does a boy learn how to become a man from a father like that?

I'm not blaming him for all the mistakes and stupid decisions I made, or for the pain and sorrow I caused myself and others. I take full responsibility for everything I have ever done. I know "My father beat me" is a clichéd excuse for bad behavior. I'm not using it as an excuse. There are no excuses. There are only explanations.

People have asked about me a million times, "What the heck was wrong with that guy? He was blessed with a phenomenal talent. He was paid millions of dollars to do what he did best and loved most. He had legions of adoring fans. Everything was available to him. Houses, cars, fans, and fame. He was everything Americans want to be. How could he throw that all away on alcohol and drugs?"

The explanation is simple: I did not love myself. I didn't even like myself. When you don't like yourself, you try to find ways to escape, to run away from yourself. That's what baseball was for me. I was great at it, it was fun, but it didn't make me like myself. No matter how well I did on the ball field, my father's voice inside my head told me, "You're no good. You'll never amount to anything." And I believed it. It was a poison in my life. I had to go through hell to get all that poison and sickness out of me and start to believe in myself. I had to hit bottom, the deepest pit, to understand that I wasn't the failure that voice in my head kept telling me I was. I was a good person and I had good intentions. I wanted to feel good about myself. I just couldn't figure out how, and so I filled in with some lousy substitutes like alcohol and cocaine. They only made me like myself less.

I'm telling that story now because I want other people not to have to wait as long as I did to find the peace I've found. Why it took me so long probably has something to do with professional sports, where you're always supposed to be strong, always a champion. You're not supposed to hurt. Things are not supposed to affect you. You play and produce no matter what.

And if you do that well, you're treated like a star. You never have to grow as a man. Someone's always there to manage your life for you. If you have aches and pains, you call the trainers. When it's time to negotiate a contract or do other business, you call your agent. If you get in some kind of trouble . . . you call your agent again, and he calls a lawyer. You live your life like a child, playing a game, while a team of professionals takes care of all your needs.

And all your desires as well. When you're a star athlete, a celebrity, you're surrounded by people ready to fulfill your every want. They turn your fantasies into reality. What do you want? Money, women, drugs, cars, constant parties, constant praise? They're all yours. You can indulge yourself without limits, without restrictions, and without responsibilities.

It felt like complete freedom to me. I thought I'd gotten out from under my father. No one was going to control me anymore. No one was going to dominate me. I was a man. I was going to do whatever I wanted, whenever I wanted. I was in complete control of my life.

Only I wasn't. The truth is I was completely out of control. The truth is that nothing in life is really handed to you for free. Sooner or later, you have to pay for everything you get and everything you do. Eventually, you have to face the consequences of all your actions and decisions.

Professional baseball let me put off that reckoning for a long time. I channeled all my energy out there on the field, and I was a champion there. But deep down inside, I was a very hurt young man. And all the home runs, all the World Series rings, couldn't take that pain away. All the cheering crowds in all the stadiums where I played couldn't drown out that voice in my head.

I think a lot of it comes back to where you grew up and how you grew up. Let's be honest, an awful lot of males in America, especially young black males, grow up now without a father figure around. You may have a mother who raises you with principles and values. But if a boy's father has left the house because of a divorce, or he's just a "baby daddy" to begin with, that kid is missing something vital—a man around the house to act as his guide and role model.

I didn't have that figure in my life, and it cost me dearly. I spent a lot of years trying to figure out on my own how to be a man. I made a lot of mistakes. I searched and searched to find who I was, and boy did I search in a lot of the wrong places.

I see a lot of young black men in this country looking for the same thing, and also looking in all the wrong places. Especially in poorer communities, the men who could be positive role models for black youth—the ones who become successful doctors, lawyers, businessmen, athletes—move up and out. The young males in these communities, often raised without a father figure at home, look around, and the only "success" stories they see are pimps and drug dealers. Trying to figure out what it means to be a man, all they see are macho stereotypes like gangbangers and rap stars. It's no wonder they grow up believing that money, sex, drugs, and violence make you a man.

One of the reasons I'm writing this book is to show young men an example of a guy who grew up in a very similar environment, who had all the same questions and confusion they do, and who struggled for a very long time to figure out who he is and why he's on this earth. I had all the money, sex, and drugs a young man could want, and none of it helped me become a real man. I know firsthand that none of that has anything at all to do with being a man, and I want to pass that knowledge on.

I don't believe you have to go through what I did, all that pain and confusion and humiliation, to find yourself. I don't believe you have to hit rock bottom before you can deal with your problems. I did, and I know many others have. But with a guide, someone who's been to hell and come back to life, maybe you can avoid some of the pits I stumbled into. Maybe think of this book as a road map to hell and back again. There is a way out. I'm living proof.

And that brings up the other story I want to tell. I was diagnosed with cancer. Twice. I was operated on three times. The last time was in 2000. I'm writing this in 2008. I'm still here. And I greet each and every day that I'm still here as a gift straight from God.

See, I believe God had a purpose for me on this earth, and I wasn't anywhere near fulfilling that purpose. That's why he kept me around, as sick as I was in my body, my mind, and my soul. God is very patient with us. He keeps faith with us even when we lose faith in ourselves.

I believe God has a role for each and every one of us. You never know what God is going to use you for. In my case, it definitely wasn't baseball. I went through the highs of being successful, and the lows of self-destruction. I always knew God was calling me to something, something greater than hitting home runs. But I kept missing that call for a long, long time. I kept chasing all the temptations of life instead. When I should have been surrendering to God, I was surrendering to the world. God had to take all that away from me before I realized how meaningless it all was.

I know now why God kept me around. He wanted me here to help others who are struggling, lost, in pain. He wanted me to be an example to others, to bring them hope. His purpose for me was never just to do well in the ballpark. It was to do good in the world.

If you accept that you're here for a reason, whether you believe in God or not, maybe it will help you survive and triumph over whatever problems and troubles you're struggling with.

Each of us has his own journey and his own story. But your story might help the next person who's struggling. And that's why I tell mine.

STRAW

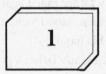

1

'LL KILL ALL y'all," the drunk with the shotgun raged.

"All y'all" was my mother, my two younger sisters, my two older brothers, and me. I was thirteen.

The drunk with the shotgun was my father.

This was not the first time I had seen my father in a drunken rage. Far from it. At thirteen, I could not remember a time when I did not live in fear of this man, my own father.

I used to see these families on TV. Dad comes home from work, and all the kids run to greet him, hug his legs, happy that Daddy is home. "Come here, you guys, give me a hug," he would say. "Give us a kiss. I love you."

Those people might as well have lived on a different planet from my house. When my father came home at night, it was exactly the opposite: We all hid. Because you never knew what kind of monster was coming home. Sometimes he was raging and violent. Sometimes he was just cold and sullen. But I don't remember him ever with a smile on his face, throwing open his arms and saying, "Come here, son, give me a hug." When my father raised his hands toward me, it wasn't a hug he had in mind.

We boys knew he sometimes was abusive to our mother, who was half his size. He'd been beating me and Ronnie for years. We had been hiding from him for a long time by this night.

What was special about this night was that we did not hide from him. We finally stood up to him. This was not the first time he disrupted our house, it was the last.

"I'll kill all of you," my father raged again.

Ronnie, who was fourteen, stood next to me. He had a butcher knife from the kitchen in his hand.

"Oh no," he said, matching my father's growl. "If anybody's killed here tonight, it'll be you."

I have thought long and hard about that night in the more than thirty years since. About how the Strawberry family came to such a point, and about the effect it had on all of us afterward. I think its roots reach far back to before I was born, to my father's own childhood. I know it threw a long shadow that still touches our lives.

MOST OF WHAT I know about my father's early years we heard from cousins, not from him. He was born in Mississippi, an only child. They called him Sonny Boy. They say his mom was a beautiful lady, but his dad was an evil man, a raging alcoholic, physically abusive to the mom. She died before her time. It might have been from the stress of living with this man, though there was some talk in the family that she died from the beatings he gave her. After that my dad was mostly raised by his grandmother. He and his father had no relationship to speak of.

I think that childhood explains a lot about why my father acted the way he did toward us. The rotten apple doesn't roll far from the tree. They say that alcoholism is a disease, a genetic disorder passed down within families from one generation to the next. I know some people dispute that idea, but I'm a believer. If you add other kinds of addictive behavior and abusive parenting to the alcoholism, I guess you could use the Strawberrys as a textbook example.

My father got out of Mississippi as soon as he could and came to Los Angeles as a young man. He met and married my mom there, and they had five kids right in a row, one each year for five years: Michael, Ronnie, me, Regina, and Michelle.

We started out in an apartment in Watts. I don't have any memories of Watts, but there are stories. My mom told me one about how she went to work one day and left my dad in charge of Ronnie and me. We were toddlers, still in diapers. She comes home and finds us on the kitchen floor, covered in flour. We had somehow gotten into one of the cupboards and covered ourselves in it, while Dad slept.

Another time, a neighbor called my mom at work and said, "Your two babies are walking up Rosecrans Avenue." Me and Ronnie, in our diapers, toddling hand in hand up this busy street. Dad had fallen asleep again, and we got out. We could easily have been killed. Rosecrans Avenue is six lanes wide with major intersections and cars flying in all directions.

Those stories say something about my dad's complete lack of paternal instincts. He just did not have anything like a normal father's care and concern for his children.

We moved to a small house in the Crenshaw neighborhood when I was seven or eight. It's in South Central L.A., but it wasn't like "the ghetto" or anything. It was all little stucco houses, filled with working-class families, struggling but getting by. Every house had a garage, and there were little front and back yards, most of them with some kind of fruit tree in them. Orange trees, lemon, grapefruit. We used to pick the fruit and eat it right there in the yard.

The neighborhood was mostly African-American. We had one white neighbor, a wonderful lady. The dads and moms all worked, the kids all went to school. We didn't see a lot of drugs or violence. It wasn't Beaver Cleaver's neighborhood, but it wasn't *Boyz n the Hood*, either.

My father was a clerk at the post office. That's a bit funny to me now, because if you could talk about anyone going postal, it was my dad. He worked the evening shift. He left the house around two-thirty in the afternoon and put in his eight hours. Then, lots of nights, he'd go drinking and carousing, gambling, chasing women. It'd be really late when he got home. We kids were in bed, and we'd stay there.

Some nights he'd be drunk and exhausted and just collapse in his bed. Those were the good nights. Other nights he came home drunk and belligerent, and that's when he'd get into it with our mother. We kids would lie in bed and listen to him screaming at her, yelling crazy nonsense half the time, angry at her, angry at us five kids just for ex- isting, angry about even having a family and having to be responsible for us. We'd lie there and listen to my mom trying to calm him down, crying, pleading with him.

The days weren't much better. My mom would go off to her job as a secretary at Pacific Bell. My father would usually wake up hung- over and grouchy. We tiptoed around, tried to stay out of his way. Don't even dare to ask him if you can go out and play. If you do, he'll just snap at you.

"Don't bother me, I'm sleeping. Don't come in here! Go back in your room, you don't need to go outside. For what?"

He was nicer with Michael and the girls than with me and Ronnie. Mike I think he respected. We all did. Mike was a great kid, level- headed, responsible. And the girls could get anything from my dad. They'd ask him for a dollar and he'd say, "My money's on the dresser. Go get it." Me, if I stuck my head in the door and asked for fifty cents, he'd growl, "Boy, get out of here. You don't need no money."

But even they got no real love from him. My father was very cold. He didn't have time for anyone but himself. He barely spoke to us. Looking back, Mike says, "For whatever reason, he just wasn't much of a dad. He really was never visible in our lives. He was there, but he wasn't there. He never supported anything we did regarding sports or anything. Basically we were afraid even to talk to him, because there was no connection, no bond there."

We were scared to death of him, the entire family. It does something to a little kid to actually be scared of his father, frightened every time he comes home. And my dad was a scary man. He was big—they called him Big Hank. That's where I get my size from. Too bad that wasn't all I got from him.

My mom worked very hard to put up with the man and keep up a stable household. She was a petite, pretty lady, but very strong in character and in spirit. She was a good Baptist, and she instilled Christian values and right conduct in all of us kids. My dad may have been big, but that little woman was the real strength in our family. She was as loving to us as he was cold. She dedicated her entire life to raising us right.

I never understood why my father was so angry with us all the time. He had a loving wife and good kids. We weren't noisy or troublesome. Later I came to realize that he just didn't want us—the loving wife, the five kids, the house, the responsibility, the burden. He wanted to drink, hang around with his friends, and go to the track. He liked the life out there. We found out later that he was messing around with a woman who lived around the corner. In fact, he later married her. But afterward he had to come home to five kids and a lot of responsibility he didn't want. We were growing and we needed things and he was supposed to provide for us. I think he had a hard time accepting that we were his responsibilities. He didn't want to be a husband and father. He didn't want to slave away every day at the post office to keep a roof over our heads and food in our mouths. I don't believe he ever accepted that your kids come first, before drinking and going to the track.

Not that he spent much on us anyway. He and my mom made decent money, but we lived like paupers, because my dad spent most of his earnings on himself. My mom begged him and begged him not to throw his money away on alcohol and gambling. He'd just scream at her, "It's my money! I made it and I'll spend it any way I want!"

We weren't in rags, but whatever nice clothes we had, for going to school or whatever, our mom bought us. And forget about cool toys or bikes. We built our own bikes out of junked ones we found lying around the neighborhood. We made our own version of dirt bikes. We'd ride them all over the neighborhood, popping wheelies and jumping the curbs.

My dad's other great love, besides carousing, was sports. He played softball on the post office team, the Wildcats. They had a softball league where they had great competition. They had nice, pretty uniforms, the whole thing. They were serious about it, and there were some wonderful players. And my dad was one of the biggest forces in the league. He had a big name, big reputation. Big Hank. Everyone knew and respected Big Hank. He was famous throughout this citywide league. On the mound he was an outstanding pitcher. Batters were intimidated by his speed. At the plate, he was a mighty long-ball hitter. He could hit that ball all the way to the next diamond.

All three of us sons inherited our love of sports from him. In fact, the girls did, too. Not because he did anything to encourage or mentor us. He wasn't the sort of dad who was going to take us to Little League games, encourage us to compete. He was too busy paying attention to himself. We just naturally had sports in our genes. We played football in the street, basketball on the raggedy old courts at school. Regina and Michelle played right along with us. The five Strawberry kids. A Strawberry posse.

We didn't play baseball in the street, because you might knock a ball through somebody's window, and that was a big no-no. Then Big Hank might come down on you. And you did not want that. Because Big Hank took great delight in beating us. These were not the sort of whuppings a parent gave kids to discipline them. These were out-and-out beatings. I know the difference. Whuppings were common in our neighborhood. Everyone's parents were decent, hardworking, Christian folks. They wanted their kids to grow up straight and respectful. They worried all the time that if they didn't discipline us we'd slide off into lives of crime and drugs. Whuppings were how their parents had disciplined them, and it was how they disciplined their own kids.

But with my dad it was more like he was taking out his rage and frustrations on us. The beatings started when I was around nine. He never beat the girls, and he rarely taxed Mike, but Ronnie and me he beat something fierce.

I guess part of what my dad thought he was doing was disciplining us, but it was way out of proportion to whatever we had done. Ronnie and I weren't wild. We were normal boys, doing what boys do. We got into a little trouble now and then. Maybe got sent home from school for some infraction, or thrown off the school bus for horsing around. We were kids. You're going to make mistakes. But every little thing we did, there was a beating behind it. He wasn't like, "You can't play ball in the street." It was always like, "I told you and I told you," and then the beating. He had this vicious way about him. Any little thing was all the excuse he needed.

He literally whipped us. He used the extension cord from the vacuum cleaner. We had to take our shirts off and lie across the bed, and he lashed us with that cord. He was a strong man, and his rage was powerful. We'd be flying all over the bed, trying to get away, and he'd lash us and lash us. It made me sick to see the huge welts he raised on Ronnie's back, and I had the same on mine.

It would happen for just little things. There was this old, raggedy telephone booth down the street, already broken and torn apart. Ronnie and I were out there one day hitting it with our bats. You know, the kind of thing boys do. My father saw us from a distance and called us over to the front lawn.

"Get your ass in here," he said. "You know what you're gonna get."

Yeah, we sure did. We couldn't run. We'd have to come home at some point, and he'd only be that much angrier. We couldn't fight it, either. We weren't strong enough to handle him. We just had to go into the bedroom and take it.

"You're no good, boy," he told me more than once while he was beating me. "You'll never amount to nothin'."

It got to the point where if I saw his car parked in front of the house when I walked home from school, I'd turn around and go hang out with friends somewhere. Just wait for him to go off to work before I set foot in the house.

Asked about all this by someone in the press years later, my mom said she didn't remember my father beating us all the time like that. I don't think she was in denial about it. She knew he was violent. He certainly hit her, more than once. I think she really didn't remember it, or maybe wasn't fully aware of it at the time. Then she said an interesting thing. She said it didn't matter whether she remembered it or not. What was important was that it was how we remembered it, and the effect those memories had on us.

I clearly remember one night after he beat us both, Ronnie and I were lying on our beds. His shirt was off and I could see the terrible welts on his back.

"I'm not going to live like this," he said. "We're going to have to kill him. We're just going to have to kill him, that's all."

Imagine a fourteen-year-old boy talking about his father that way. And me, thirteen, agreeing. Imagine hating your dad that much. We both hated our father, hated what he had done to us and what we became. We became monsters inside. I believe Ronnie especially was destroyed by my father. Ronnie was like a wrecking ball. He was torn up about life. He had no identity, no idea of who he was. After our father left, Ronnie just went wild. He flew out of control and spiraled down and down, and to this day he hasn't fully recovered.

I wasn't a bad kid, a wild kid, a rebellious kid. I wasn't out all the time running around and getting into trouble. In fact I was just the opposite. I was a good kid, quiet and sensitive. I liked school. I walked straight to school in the morning and straight home after. I was obedient in class. I did my homework and got decent grades. I didn't hang out on the street. I was too shy to chase girls. My favorite thing in the world was just to hang around the house with my sisters, just lie around quietly and watch TV. They were both like my mom, petite and pretty. Regina and I were especially close. We were just a year apart, and we were both quiet and shy. All through our lives, anything Regina has ever asked me for, she got, and she's been a huge help to me, too. Michelle, maybe because she was the baby and had to assert herself, was a lot more outgoing, funny, and talkative. She still is.

When my mom first saw me play baseball, she was astounded at my energy and skill on the field. She'd never seen me do much of anything physical. If I had any faults, it was that I was really lazy around the house. I never wanted to clean up or help with chores. My sisters used to complain to my mom.

"How come we have to do the dishes all the time? Why doesn't Darryl have to?"

"You get in that kitchen and leave your brother alone," my mom would say.

Maybe I always knew the world outside was full of troubles and temptations, and I was better off at home. As long as my dad wasn't there, anyway.

It's sad. I never had a real relationship with him. He never just sat me down and talked to me kindly, never gave me a word of fatherly advice or counsel, never taught me how to tie my shoe or hit a baseball. None of those things a father and son are supposed to do. He either ignored me or beat me, period.

I did learn one valuable lesson from him. My kids have never gotten a whupping from me. Their mamas used to say, "Why don't you whup them?" And I said, "I am not going to whup my kids." I think of the scars he left on me. I would not scar my children like that. Those are real scars. Ronnie and I hated ourselves. We thought, "I'm nothing." Even putting on a major league uniform and being the success I was, I still felt like nothing. When people praised me, I was still nothing. Because my dad told me I was nothing and I was always going to be nothing.

THAT FINAL NIGHT didn't start out much different from a lot of nights that had gone before it. My father went out after work, and when he came home after midnight he was in a drunken rage. The first thing I remember is being woken up by his screaming and shouting at my mom. It wasn't a big house, and you didn't have to shout very loud to be heard.

Ronnie and I sat up in our beds and stared at each other. Mike's bed was empty. We both got out of bed at the same time and went to see what the commotion was about this time.

It was a small house, with all the rooms on one floor. All us kids slept in two bedrooms to the right as you came in the front door. To the left were the living room and the kitchen and dining room. Behind the dining room, a step down, was my parents' bedroom.

When Ronnie and I walked into the dining room, Michael was standing there, near the open door to my parents' room. My father was in the bedroom, crazy drunk, yelling nonsense—"talking out the side of his neck," as we used to say. We watched through the door as he went to the bedroom closet and brought his shotgun out. He didn't aim it at us, he just held it at his side and said he was going to kill us all. Mom later told us that she'd taken the shells out of it, but we didn't know that at the time, and I don't know if my father did, either. When he showed us that gun and threatened to kill us all, that was it. Something snapped in all of us.

Mike, the oldest at fifteen, led the way.

"Get out of here and leave us alone," he said.

My father looked stunned. None of us had ever stood up to him before.

"What you say, boy?" he growled.

"You heard me. Get your things, get out of here, and leave us alone."

My father lunged toward him. Mike ran behind the dining room table and into the kitchen. Ronnie and I followed him, my heart banging in my chest. I saw Mike grab a skillet and Ronnie a butcher knife. I grabbed a frying pan. I know it seems a silly thing to grab at a moment like that, but it was heavy. And there was no question I would hit him with it.

We ran back to the table and stood side by side, the three of us boys. Our father stood across the table from us, looking like a crazy man. His eyes were wild and drunk, his chest heaving. He had that shotgun dangling in one hand and balled the other into a fist that looked like a sledgehammer.

"Come on, hit me," Mike said. "You hit my brothers all the time. Hit me. Come on, I'll bust your head."

My father narrowed his drunken eyes at Mike. Mike was a big kid—not brawny, but over six feet tall and very wiry and athletic. He held that skillet in both hands like a bat. Even in his wild state my father must have been able to see that Mike was deadly serious about using it.

"Come here, boy," my father growled.

"Come get me," Mike growled back.

"I'll kill all y'all," my father said.

"Oh no you won't," Ronnie said, hefting the knife.

By this time Regina and Michelle were awake, too, standing behind us, their eyes wide as saucers. My mom saw that we boys meant business and tried to defuse the situation before anyone was seriously hurt.

"You boys get out of the house," she said. "Go down the street."

"No. No way we're leaving you here with him," Mike said.

So there we were. My father on one side of the table, his three sons on the other. A showdown. A shotgun against a butcher knife, a skillet, and a frying pan. And our cold determination that one way or another, this was the last night our father would terrorize our family.

There was a movie in the 1990s that Mike and I have talked about, called *Jason's Lyric*. Forest Whitaker plays an abusive, out-of-control father who comes home in a rage and starts beating his wife in front of his two sons. The boys have had enough and confront the father. There's a gun, and they fight over it, and it goes off, killing the father.

"We could have had a situation like that," Mike says. "What if Mom hadn't taken the shells out of that gun? If I'd gotten my hands on it, I could've gone to that extreme."

I know what Mike means. Our father had pushed all three of us to the point where anything could have happened that night. We were serious. We really could have killed him. No question Mike and I would have hit him upside the head. Who knows what Ronnie might have done with that butcher knife. We were through. We had heard my mom crying and arguing with him for too long. Ronnie and I had taken too many beatings.

My dad ran his crazy eyes over our faces, and we stood our ground. And suddenly the most amazing thing happened: We saw all the fight go out of him. Big Hank just deflated before our eyes. We had never spoken back to him, never stood up for ourselves against him. He was just so stunned by it that he suddenly looked more confused than angry.

"Just get out of here," Mike told him. His voice was calm and firm. He sounded a lot more mature than he was. It was as though in that very moment he took over as the head of the household, and our father, who had always been a stranger to us anyway, was just an unwanted intruder. All of us, my dad included, knew at that moment that it was all over.

A couple of policemen showed up at the door. I've never been sure who called them. My father had been shouting loud enough for the whole block to hear him. The policemen told him it might be a good idea if he left, and my mom told him not to come back, and that was that. His reign of terror in our family was done. He was never again a physical presence in any of our lives.

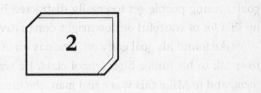

2

AFTER THAT NIGHT, my mom was left to raise us five kids and provide for us all by herself. She did an amazing job of it. She loved us so dearly, and we all loved her back. As Mike says, the six of us had already bonded as a family long before. It had been just us for a while. Our father didn't even seem like part of the family. He was out of our family a long time before he was out of our house.

Mike stepped up as the man of the house. "I guess because I was the oldest, and I just felt I had to help my mom," he remembers. "After our father left, we needed to get through it."

Mike was fifteen, Ronnie was fourteen, I was thirteen. All of us were just coming into our young manhood. And we had no father figure around to guide us, explain it to us, help us through it. We had never had that kind of father anyway, and now we didn't have one at all. All three of us had to figure out this manhood thing by ourselves.

Mike had the easiest time of it. It wasn't just because he was the oldest. Mike had always been the smart, levelheaded, responsible one.

He had a lot of poise and self-confidence. He was tall and handsome, with a big Afro. Girls liked him. Guys did, too. He had it going on. He was in sports in high school—football, basketball, baseball. People raved about his skills. Truth is, I always considered him a much better athlete than I was.

I'm a true believer that for young people to weather the struggles of growing up and becoming adults, they need goals in life, something to set their mark on and focus their lives on achieving. Without goals, young people get too easily distracted by nonsense and caught up in a lot of wasteful or downright destructive behavior.

Mike found his goal early on. One day an officer of the LAPD came to speak to his junior high school class. He was a black man, in uniform, and to Mike this was a real man, the kind of man he wished our father was. A black man doing good in the community and earning a lot of respect and prestige for it. He wasn't out there drinking and gambling and wasting his time like our father did.

Right then and there Mike was like, "That's what I want to be." He went up to the man after class and asked him what he had to do to become a police officer. The officer told him to focus on school, stay away from alcohol and drugs and bad influences, and if he still wanted to join the force after he got his education, the LAPD would probably be glad to have him. Mike set it as his personal goal, and he directed and focused his life toward it.

And then there was his other love, baseball. After high school, he went to Southwest Junior College and played baseball there. Michael was a great baseball player, but I think his girlfriend had other plans for him. He dated the same girl from junior high on. They ended up getting married and having three kids. He did eventually make it as far as the minor leagues. He was drafted by the Dodgers when he was in junior college, right about the same time I went to the Mets. I was kind of jealous that he was drafted by the home team. He made a lot of noise in the organization and turned a lot of heads, but he never got the chance to play at the big league level.

After that he did make it onto the force at the LAPD. He was a patrolman. He actually got shot during the Rodney King riots in 1992. He and his partner were driving down a street when some kid jumped out with an AK-47 and shot up the car. A bullet struck Michael's helmet. I don't even want to think about what would have happened if he wasn't wearing that helmet. To this day he says he doesn't know how he and his partner survived.

Ronnie, unfortunately, went the other way. After our father left, Ronnie just went wild. He went on a rampage of destructive behavior. He was full of rage. He got into fights at school, got expelled, and never went back. He just hung out in the neighborhood, and he became notorious.

Every time you looked up there was something going on.

He got in all kinds of trouble with the law. He went to court one time and my dad had to show up, because my mom couldn't leave work.

The judge said, "Well, Mr. Strawberry, what do you think we should do with him? Can you take him?"

And my dad, typically, said, "No, I don't want him. I can't do anything with him. You can keep him."

Ronnie broke into a house around the corner one time and stole a bunch of guns. Brought them home and laid them out on the bed.

I was terrified. "Ron, you gotta get those guns out of here," I pleaded.

"Shut up, you little punk," he snarled. "You don't know what you're talking about. You better say nothing."

Next day the police came to search the house. Luckily for Ronnie, he had gotten rid of them overnight.

My mom couldn't control him. She would tell him he couldn't leave the house, and he'd just climb out our bedroom window. He'd stay out all night, hanging with older people on the block. They used to sit out in front of this one house and carry on all night long. Drinking, smoking weed, and smoking these things called Sherman sticks, which were joints laced with PCP. They'd smoke that stuff and go crazy. Ronnie was right there with them. Later at night, when they got high enough, they started fighting. Whacked out of their minds. A guy from down the street would decide that the man next door was messing with his wife, and they'd get into it. Next morning I'd see them walking down the street together like nothing happened.

In my heart I wanted to be more like Mike. But my father had scarred me just as badly as Ronnie, and as soon as he was gone I started to act out, too.

At the start of the seventh grade, I was among some of the first black kids from the city to be bused out to Sutter Junior High in the San Fernando Valley. It was in Canoga Park, more than an hour away by bus, and to us it was as foreign as the far side of the moon. The Valley was just a completely different place from Crenshaw. It was my first encounter with white kids. I loved seeing their culture, and I have to say they were very friendly and welcoming to us. But they were so alien. They came from wealthy families with big homes and swimming pools. They wore great clothes and expensive watches and always had cash in their pockets. They came to school in brand-new cars, not a big old yellow bus.

I'll never forget stepping down off that bus the first day. The school looked humongous. I'd never seen a junior high so big, or so nice. And all the kids everywhere were white. White white white. I don't know how many thousands of students. And maybe a hundred or so of us black kids from the city.

I wanted to do well and get along, but my dad had beaten a lot of anger and resentment into me. Pretty soon I looked around at all those nice white kids and saw opportunity. I was a big black kid from the city. I figured it shouldn't be too hard to get over on some of these Valley kids.

So I just started to extort things from them. "How much money you got in your pocket?" I'd ask a kid. "Gimme some." Or I'd say, "Bring me a watch tomorrow."

It worked, and I started feeling like I was a pretty bad dude. The only problem was, they were going to the principal and complaining about this big black kid forcing them to give him money. I got called into the principal's office one day, and they showed me this big photo of me they'd printed up. It was like a wanted poster with my face on it. In the principal's office. White kids would come in to complain about this black kid intimidating them, and when asked if they could ID the culprit, they pointed at me. I'd had no idea this was going on. I thought I was skating.

So I got expelled from Sutter. My mom was not pleased.

The next year they sent me to another all-white school in the Valley. Again, the kids were nice, but by then I had a really bad attitude. I just didn't want to be there. I sassed teachers, guidance counselors, everyone, and they kicked me out of there, too. From there they sent me to a school in the city, Audubon Junior High. I didn't even go there. I just pretended. I went there to register, and I didn't go back for two months. My mom dropped me off at the bus stop every day, and as soon as she drove off to work, I turned around and walked back home. I'd stop along the way to buy a quart of beer, sometimes a nickel bag of weed, and just hung out all day. After two months the school finally noticed I wasn't coming to class and wrote my mom.

"What am I going to do with you?" she cried. I mean here she was, alone, struggling to raise five children, and both Ronnie and I are giving her heartaches.

Audubon expelled me in the middle of the eighth grade, and I was sent to Horace Mann Junior High. It was about a thirty-minute walk. The student body mixed together black kids from a bunch of neighborhoods, but we hung out in posses of kids from our own 'hoods anyway, and fought the posses from other 'hoods. I got into fights and other kinds of trouble. Got called into the principal's office on a regular basis. There'd be a big rumble between my gang and another, and a kid would get hurt, and I'd be blamed for instigating it. A lot of times I did.

I made it through the rest of that school year, but in ninth grade I really acted out. A bunch of us walked to school together—me and Regina, a girl she was friendly with, a crew who lived along the way. We'd smoke weed as we walked to school.

One morning I was just too wasted to go to first period. But I didn't want to get caught cutting class, so I came up with what seemed at the time like a brilliant plan. I went into the boys' room, pulled some of the insulation down from the ceiling, shoved it into the trash can, and lit it. Then I walked across the hall and took a seat in class. In no time the fire's burning really well and the boys' room is full of smoke. The fire alarms go off all over the school, and we're all evacuated. That was how I got out of first period.

That afternoon the inevitable happened: I got called into the principal's office. I'm standing on one side of his desk, he's sitting behind it glaring at me.

"Did you set the bathroom on fire?"

"No sir."

"Someone said they saw you coming out of the bathroom right before the alarms went off."

"Must have been some other kid, sir."

"Really? Because this someone knows you and swore it was you."

Eventually he wore me down and I confessed. They called my mother and we had a big meeting about what to do with me. In the end they decided I could finish the ninth grade, I guess because they just wanted to get me out of there, but I would not be allowed to attend the graduation ceremonies.

By then I was following Ronnie around, trying to act like him and hang with his crowd. There was an elementary school nearby where we all used to go shoot hoops. Ronnie's crowd were a bunch of lowlifes. After shooting hoops awhile, they went around the back of the buildings and shot craps all night. When I was maybe fourteen, I started shooting craps with them. Sometimes I'd bust a crap game, come home with $200 in my pocket. Give my sisters some money, buy a little beer and weed, and we'd celebrate.

I was living large, and I started to get cocky. Playing basketball, I'd be slam-dunking over other players' heads and talking trash at them. I was already well over six feet tall and very good at basketball, and I wasn't shy about letting them know it, even though these guys were mostly older than I was and some of them were true thugs.

They didn't dig my act. One afternoon they started complaining about me to my brother.

"You need to talk to your little brother, Ronnie. He gonna talk himself into trouble."

Ronnie got right up in their faces. "Hey man, ain't none of y'all fucking with my little brother, because you know what you got to go through."

Ronnie was like that. He was crazy. He would have taken them all on.

Then he whipped around on me and said, "Listen, you little punk, you stop talking that trash."

I said, "Man, what you talking about? We playing sports."

He and I got into an argument, and it started to heat up. And as it did, I got scared. Ronnie was not a big kid. He was short and wiry. But he had a vicious temper on him, and when he fought he went crazy wild. He would just go at you. He had no fear in him, no fear at all. He always threw the first punch, and I saw him knock bigger guys out flat with just that one punch. Everybody had mad respect for him.

Including me. But I tried to stand up to him.

"Go home," he said.

"Man, you crazy," I said to him. "We just playing."

"Go!" he shouted. He started to run at me. I was smart enough to run away. He chased me up the street. Actually picked up a trash can and hurled it up the street at me.

"Go home, punk!" he yelled. "And don't be coming down here talking that trash."

When I got home I told Regina and Michelle what happened.

"Man, Ronnie is crazy. My own brother running me off from down there."

Of course, later it dawned on me that he was looking out for me. I may have been bigger than he was, but to him I was still his little brother, and he was not about to have those other cats mess with me.

Even then, though, I wasn't cured of craps. That didn't happen until one night when a big crowd of us were shooting craps on the sidewalk down the street. Suddenly some guy drove up with a shotgun. *Boom!* He fires it off. Everyone scatters, scrambling in all directions. I ran around the corner and hid in a back yard. My heart was hammering so hard it felt like it was going to burst straight out through my ribs.

We all ran out of there so fast we left a pile of money on the sidewalk. That guy scooped it all up and disappeared with it.

That was it for me and gambling. I was done. I never went back down there again. I realized that it wasn't for me.

But Ronnie stuck with it. And worse. Gambling, drinking, drugs, crime. One time he and a friend were walking the friend's Doberman pinscher on Crenshaw Boulevard, and the friend sicced the Doberman on some guys he had a beef with. Not long after that, Ronnie was walking up the street by himself and those guys jumped him. One of them smashed his eye with brass knuckles. He came home with his face swollen and bruised like a rotten pumpkin.

But it didn't stop him. He continued to roll on with it. And he got deeper and deeper into the drugs. After high school, when I left Crenshaw to go play in the minor leagues, I called home all the time and spoke to my mom and sisters. Checking in, checking on everybody.

They'd say, "Ronnie's nuts."

"What do you mean?"

"He's high all the time, running around here with TVs on his shoulder, walking around with no shirt on. He's a mess. Stealing money, smoking dope."

Mom raised us to respect everybody and accept our responsibilities in life. She was very small, but she could speak very loudly when need be. You just didn't get out of line with Mom. It wasn't happening. She'd tell you straight up, "I don't care how big you think you are, you best behave." And you'd shrivel right up and slink away.

But she couldn't control Ronnie. She stayed on his butt and spoke to him over and over until she was blue in the face. He'd tell her he was going to straighten up, but he never did. He was hard to tame. He had gone through so much with our dad, and it left him wild and uncontrollable. His attitude was, "Nobody's gonna control me. I'm gonna control myself."

We used to say, "Mom, what are you gonna do about Ronnie?"

She said, "I'm just gonna love him, and I'm gonna pray for him."

SPORTS WAS MY refuge and my escape. From when I was maybe ten years old, I knew I had natural athletic talent. I was good at every sport I tried. I'm not bragging. It was just in me. I loved it. It was pure joy for me to play baseball, basketball, football. While I was playing I could almost forget my anger and my troubles. Almost.

Baseball actually came third for me, after basketball and football. I would play all three throughout high school. For a while basketball was my first love. I was so tall and gangly for a kid that it just came naturally. Until high school I never played it in an organized way. It was all just pickup games on lumpy old outdoor courts with no nets, just chains hanging from the hoops. But all the kids knew I was great at it, even those older friends of Ronnie's.

Football we played around the neighborhood, on the streets and in the parks. I was a left-handed quarterback. Young, skinny, throwing bombs. Four, five touchdowns a game.

The other kids started calling me Straw Dog. I asked one kid, "Why you call me that?"

"Because you be doggin' people!" he laughed.

I got into baseball when I was twelve or maybe thirteen. A bunch of us kids would follow our dads to the ballpark and watch them play softball. After the game, the dads would all head to a nearby bar, and we kids would take over the diamond. We played hardball. While they were getting drunk, we'd be at the ballpark playing. We'd play until it got dark and they finally stumbled out of the bar.

Like football and basketball, baseball just came naturally to me. Right from the start I could pitch, I could hit home runs, I could steal bases, I could field. I didn't think much about it, I didn't study the game, I just went out there and did it.

Michael, Ronnie, and I were all good. Some of the other kids were good, too, but they never pursued it the way we did. We got serious about it. All the other kids wanted us on their team. Pretty early on they decided they couldn't have more than one Strawberry on a team because it was unfair. So they'd split us up.

Here's something interesting: To this day, if you ask Mike who was the best of us three, he'll tell you, "Ronnie was a better athlete than either Darryl or me. He could run like a deer. He could pitch like Steve Howe. I remember us as kids having rock fights, and if you just peeked your head around a corner, he'd fire that rock right between your eyes. I think about how I had some success in professional ball, and I look at all Darryl's achievements, and I just have to wonder what Ronnie would have accomplished."

I agree. I always said that Michael and Ronnie were both better athletes than I was.

It was my friend Renaldo Owens, Rennie, who first got me into organized ball. I met Rennie when I was on the bus out to Sutter Junior High. He wasn't from my neighborhood, but the bus picked us up all over our area and then carried us out there together, a busload of black kids carried out to the white Valley every school day.

One day we were talking on the bus ride home.

"I play Little League at Rancho Park," he said. "The Padres."

"I can play baseball," I said.

He looked skeptical.

"You can't play. What position?"

"I'm a pitcher."

"Uh-huh. Well I'm a catcher. Bring your glove tomorrow and we'll see how good you pitch."

So we met up the next day. He squatted with his catcher's mitt.

"Let me see what you got," he said, still skeptical.

I was angry with him for being so skeptical, so I threw him a curveball with everything on it. Then another and another. Most kids my age couldn't do much with the curveball. It takes time to master. I threw Rennie curveballs that slid and popped like I was yanking them on a string.

After a few he jumped up and threw his glove down.

"You're the greatest!" he said, with a big grin. And he hadn't even seen me hit yet. "They're holding Little League tryouts over at Rancho Park. We're gonna go over there together and I'll introduce you to my coach."

We did that. The coach put me through a few drills, hitting, pitching, and I could see he was very impressed.

"Come over here," he said. He put his hand on my shoulder and walked me a short way away from the other kids. A draft was coming up in one week, when each team in the league would choose one player they wanted.

"You're not going to be in that draft," he said. "We're gonna keep you over here to one side. You're already on the team. You're on the Padres."

He didn't want any of the other coaches to see me and try to draft me out from under him.

So that's how Rennie got me on the Padres. We became good friends and a dynamic duo on the field, me pitching and him catching. We helped the Padres beat their biggest rivals, the Dodgers. I was hitting home runs over to the next diamond, and I was a smokin' left-handed pitcher, too. People said I had amazing speed and control for a kid so young.

I loved Little League. It was such a relief from all the anxiety at home. It was really good for me to be around other kids. I felt like I was worth something out there.

Renaldo and I played in Little League and Junior League together. We were very competitive with each other, and at the same time proud of each other. He was a baseball fanatic. He knew all sorts of baseball history and I knew next to none. I'd never studied up on it before, I just played it. And I kept on playing while he didn't. He stayed in sports, but as a journalist, not a player. He was not big enough. He was a small guy with a lot of guts and determination, but he couldn't compete on the professional level. With his knowledge of the sport, it made sense that he eventually became a sportswriter.

Renaldo got me started on learning about baseball, watching the majors. In fact, I got addicted to it. The Dodgers were my team, of course. What a great team. Ron Cey, Davey Lopes, Dusty Baker.

I followed their battles against the Big Red Machine, the Cincinnati Reds. I watched them on TV all the time.

Meanwhile, Mike was playing in the Babe Ruth League for a coach named John Mosely. Mr. Mosely was a neighbor of ours. He also coached baseball at Compton College. He was another solid, successful black male who seemed like the opposite of our father. Mike was always saying to him, "You think I'm good, you should see my little brother."

So Mr. Mosely watched me play, and he saw something in me. He saw a great deal in me. I mean, all the coaches who saw me already recognized that I had some kind of special talent for the game. I could pitch, I could hit, I could steal bases, I could play outfield. But Mr. Mosely was the one who saw that with discipline and focus, this gangly kid could go all the way to the majors. He wasn't the last coach to see I needed discipline and focus, but he was the first.

He came over to the house one day, when I was lying around as usual watching cartoons or whatever on TV with Regina and Michelle, and told me he wanted to help me work on my game. I was a lazy kid. I didn't want to work on anything. When it came to baseball I just wanted to go out there and play the game and have fun. But he took me under his wing, and he began teaching me the fundamentals. I became a personal project for him, and he became a father figure for me—the first of many men who would play that role in my life, filling in for my father. He brought fatherhood, leadership, and stability into my life, and Mike and Ronnie's, too. He taught us everything about baseball.

I didn't make it easy on him. There'd be days when I just didn't feel like practicing, so I wouldn't show up at the park. Mr. Mosely wasn't having that. He'd drive right over to the house and yank me out. Some days I just wanted to lie around, and I knew he was coming for me, so I'd tell Regina and Michelle, "When Mr. Mosely comes, tell him I'm not here."

So Mr. Mosely rings the bell. The girls answer the door.

"Darryl's not here," they say.

Mr. Mosely is no fool. "Girls, is he in there sleeping?"

They'd cave and let him in. He walks straight into the bedroom and pulls the sheets off me.

"Straw, get up. I'll be waiting in the car. We're going to practice."

Yes, he was a true enforcer. He pushed me, pulled me, made me see in myself the potential he saw in me, made me believe in myself and my worth at a time when all I'd ever heard, all my life, was that I was worthless. He told me that with work and focus I could be great, when all I'd ever heard was, "You'll never amount to nothin'."

I owe him so much. If Mr. Mosely hadn't come into my life when he did, there's a good chance that I really never would have amounted to nothin'. He set a goal for me and had faith that I could reach it. Once I took it on as my goal, I never stopped believing it and working toward it. Without someone like him I probably never would have found a path, because I had no guide. Or I would have taken a wrong path, like Ronnie did.

Little by little, I began to believe that what Mr. Mosely said was true. I really could be a success in baseball. One day, I made a little sign and stuck it on the door of the bedroom: I AM GOING TO THE MA-JORS. My sisters thought I was crazy. Mike and Ronnie didn't pay it much mind.

My mom didn't pay it much mind, either. She saw that I was happy playing ball, and that made her happy. She didn't realize how good I was at first. Not until she came to a Junior League game, where I was on one team and Ronnie was playing center field for the other team. I came to bat and hit a huge home run, way out past his head. He's shagging for it, my sisters are laughing and laughing.

My mom was surprised. The Darryl she knew just lay around the house all the time, moping, doing nothing. She had never seen me so energized.

She supported my ball playing, but she was never like a backstage mother about it. She never pushed. In fact, she was kind of the opposite. I used to wear my ball cap around all the time. You couldn't get it off my head. I'd wear it to the dinner table and she'd say, "Boy, take your hat off in this home."

Later, when I played baseball and basketball in high school, she came to the big games with my sisters. She still couldn't get over how different I was in the field and on the court. She used to say, "I can't believe that's my son running up and down that court like that, as lazy as he is. He won't do nothing around the house." I'd come home, full of pride, and she'd just say, "I didn't know you had that in you, lazy as you are around this house."

It wasn't that she tried to discourage me. She just didn't want me to get too full of myself.

Through Little League I met the kid who would become my best friend in life, Eric Davis. We played on different teams. When our two teams played each other, I watched him hit and play shortstop and said, "This guy's gonna be a great player." He had style. He had it going on.

Eric had already heard about me. Apparently the whole Little League was buzzing about this big left-handed kid who could do everything—hit, pitch, steal bases, field—and on top of all that, had this unforgettable name, Strawberry. The first time Eric saw me he could tell it was all true. He later said I was like "a freak of nature."

We lived in different neighborhoods and went to different schools, but from that summer on we have gone through our whole lives together.

3

AFTER BOUNCING AROUND to all those different junior high schools and finally squeaking out of Audubon, I went to Crenshaw High School. It was a good two-mile walk from home. Crenshaw was an all African-American school. It had a great reputation in sports. And a lot of pretty girls, all kinds. But I wasn't interested, never paid attention to them. In the tenth grade, when I first got there, I thought, "Oh this is fun, this is different." But at the same time I still had some Ronnie traits in me, too, not wanting to go to class, ditching whole days just to lie around the house drinking beer and smoking pot.

But I found out right away that if I didn't go to class and make good grades, I couldn't play on any of the teams. And I wanted to play on all the teams. Crenshaw's basketball, football, and baseball teams were known and respected throughout Los Angeles. And beyond. Scouts from the professional leagues came to watch our varsity teams. A lot of guys from Crenshaw went on to play professionally. They'd graduate from Crenshaw and go straight into professional ball, not stopping to go to college. A lot has been written about how baseball was "the ticket out" for us. It's true in a sense, but I have to say we didn't necessarily all think of it that way. Most of us considered going on to college and getting a good education. In my senior year, with major league baseball scouts from all over the land telling their bosses about me, I still thought long and hard about going to college instead, and at least getting a few years of a college education before heading to the majors. I never did, and I don't regret it, but I have often wondered how my life might have been different if I'd waited a couple years, matured some, learned some more about the world, instead of being whisked straight from high school into professional ball. My boy Eric will tell you the same thing. He didn't see playing major league baseball as the only way out, either. He had a lot of offers from colleges and took them seriously before choosing to play baseball.

But in tenth grade that was all still ahead of me. I just knew I wanted to play, and the school wouldn't let you play unless you were going to class and getting good grades. So I did. I settled down a lot so they'd let me play. I still had wildness and anger in me. I could still be sullen and stubborn. But I soon found that my coaches at Crenshaw were all men who wouldn't put up with that. You showed respect, you played their way, or you didn't play.

The baseball coach at Crenshaw was a man named Brooks Hurst. He was a great man. A white man coaching baseball at an all-black school. We called him the White Shadow from that TV show. He taught phys ed, and then when sixth period came, he coached baseball. He was tough. He was the bad, bad white dude at an all-black school. He had a lot of respect around there. Brooks Hurst was a baseball fanatic, a baseball guru. He had played pro ball himself. He loved the game passionately and had deep knowledge of it. We used to see him out there all the time working on the field, being his own groundskeeper. Cutting a line, cleaning up. He kept that field up. For a black high school we had a field that looked good. He paid out of his own pocket for a lot of things the school couldn't afford. And he was on a teacher's salary, so you know his pockets weren't deep. He just loved the game and loved his team that much.

He was a huge influence on all of us. He had a group of young black athletes who could be real knuckleheads. Good athletes, but hardheaded. Determined to do everything our own way. And he was just as determined to teach us discipline and the fundamentals. Practice, practice, and more practice. You were going to play the fundamentals his way or you were going to sit your behind on the bench.

Mr. Hurst saw that he had a lot of talent on his team. Talent all up and down the line. But talent alone wasn't enough. He demanded that we be as passionate and focused about it as he was. He was a big believer in hustle. You always had to be hustling. End of an inning, you didn't stroll in from the outfield, you hustled. He had very firm ideas about how to take a bunch of talented young athletes and mold them into a winning team. He understood that one thing young athletes need most—especially cocky, hardheaded young athletes—is discipline.

In the tenth grade I was coming from being a big-time star in Little League and kind of had my own style. I didn't think I had to listen to no coach tell me how to play. I didn't think I needed to hustle. All he had to do was get out of my way and watch me be a star.

One afternoon I came trotting in from the outfield, and as I got near the bench I slowed down and walked the last few steps. You never walked around Mr. Hurst. You hustled, all the time, everywhere. He jumped up at me, shouting, "Who told you you can stroll over here like that?"

He was truly angry. Mr. Hurst was a big guy, well over six feet tall and solid as an oak. He grabbed the brim of my ball cap and yanked it down over my face.

The rest of the team giggled and snickered. A hot flash of anger and embarrassment swept through me. Didn't this man know who I was? Nobody humiliated me that way! I threw down my glove. Then I pulled my jersey up over my head and handed it to him.

"Forget this," I said. "I quit. I'm done. I ain't playing for you."

We stared at each other for a few seconds. We were both angry. I don't know if I expected him to back down. If I did I was a fool.

So I turned and stalked off the field. Walked my way right off the team, feeling all their eyes on me as I did.

When Michael heard what happened, he said, "He can't go treating my little brother like that. I don't care who he is."

So he quit the team, too, in family solidarity.

The team ended up going into the playoffs, but they lost. And all the other players said, "Man, I wish we had you and your brother. We would have won."

So it was a big loss to the team—but it was even a bigger loss to me and Mike. Because of my stubbornness and hot head, neither of us played. It really hurt us both not to be out there playing with the rest of the team, but I was young and dumb and I wasn't gonna let anybody tell me what to do. Forget it, I'll just play some other sport. I'll play football, I'll play basketball.

But I missed it something awful, and in eleventh grade when baseball season came around, I went back to Mr. Hurst and told him I was ready to come back and do things his way.

"Darryl, you've got tremendous raw talent," he told me. "But you still have to work at it. I've watched you play basketball. If you put that kind of energy into your baseball, you'll be great at it."

This time I understood what he meant. I knew that one of the reasons I'd done well at basketball was because the coaches were such hardcore disciplinarians. If you screwed up in a game, you'd be at practice all next day running suicides. Running suicides is when you have to sprint back and forth across the court, oh, maybe twenty-five times at top speed. You start running half the court and back, and then three-quarters, and then the whole court. I don't care how young and fit you are, it's exhausting, and whatever you did to earn it, you'll think twice about doing again.

If you cut a class, talked trash to a teacher, anything like that, the coach might bench you the next game. At home, in front of your home crowd. Boy was that humiliating. One time I mouthed off at a teacher and got benched. A friend of mine, who was also on the junior varsity team, got caught with his girlfriend in the bathroom and got benched, too. We sat together through the first quarter, second quarter, into the third quarter. We were stars of the team. Everyone was wondering why we weren't playing. It was mortifying. We sat there fuming.

Finally I said, "If he doesn't put me in before the end of the third quarter, I'm walking off."

"I'm with you," he said.

Third quarter ended and we were still sitting.

"That's it," I said. We both walked off the court. The coach didn't say a word. He just watched us go.

Oh, did we ever pay a price for that. Next practice, the coach said, "Y'all think you're something, don't you?" He had us running suicides until we really did practically die. That man nearly buried us.

"I'm about to quit this," my boy gasped. "Forget this, man. I'll check out and go to another school."

"No, we gotta stay, man," I said. "We gotta do this and suck it up."

Finally we both collapsed on the court. We were limp as wet laundry, gasping for breath. My shins and calves were on fire.

The coach stood over us. "Y'all will never walk off on me again. Y'all ain't gonna embarrass me. Y'all think you something? You got nothing."

And off we go running some more. Oh, it was murder.

But we learned. The hard way. It didn't matter how good you were. If you were disrespectful or undisciplined, they weren't going to let you play.

I brought those humbling lessons with me to Mr. Hurst when the basketball season ended. I was a year older, and some wiser. And thankfully he let me back on the team.

BY THAT YEAR, '79, word was out that this black high school in L.A. had some phenomenal players and the coach had built an amazing organization. I mean, the word was out. Sportswriters from all over came to watch us play. Scouts from all the major league teams came.

We'd go out on the field, there'd be twenty, thirty professional baseball scouts standing there watching us, taking notes. And we put on
quite a show for them. Even today, if you ask scouts who were around
then what was the best high school varsity team they ever saw, nine
out of ten will say, "The '79 Crenshaw Cougars. Hands down. I have
never seen another team like that."

Most of the guys were seniors, a year ahead of me. Chris Brown
was the star. He was the best player on our team, and we all acknowl-
edged it. But he was a prima donna, too. He was stubborn as a mule
with Mr. Hurst—even worse than I had been. When he didn't want
to practice he stood over on the side, put his glove on his head, and
talked trash about everybody. Hurst couldn't control him. But when
game day came? Nobody could touch him. He crushed his senior year.
He ended up a second round draft pick for the San Francisco Giants.
After a strong first year with them, he began to have injuries that cut
his time in the majors short. He had a little success, but he should have
had more. He worked different kinds of jobs after he left baseball. At
one point he was in Iraq driving a truck for Halliburton, supplying
fuel for our military vehicles there. He's gone now—he died horribly,
after a mysterious fire in his home in Texas, in 2006. He was only
forty-five. A bunch of us attended the funeral. It was so sad. He'd had
so much potential and promise.

Other great players on that team included Carl Jones, Cordie Dil-
lard, Reggie Dymally, and the McNealy twins, Darryl and Derwin.
They were as identical as salt and pepper shakers. Most of the time we
didn't even bother to tell them apart. We just called them both Twin.
A bunch of guys on that 1979 varsity team—a dozen, I think—would
get drafted by major league teams. For whatever reason, only Chris
and I would make it out of the minors.

We were a great team, but we used to give poor Brooks heart attacks and ulcers, because we let a lot of teams jump out ahead of us in
the early innings. Then we'd get our fight up and come back big, just
explode in the fifth inning, seventh inning, crush the other team. It
made Brooks crazy.

"You know, you guys need to stop thinking you can turn it on every time you want to."

We didn't listen, but he was right. It caught up with us in the championship game.

Scouts from all the major leagues watched our every move. They drooled over Chris. And they asked Mr. Hurst, "Who's the tall, lanky left-hander?"

"Oh, Strawberry? You can't touch him yet. He's a junior."

"What?"

"Yeah. He plays great basketball, too."

Somewhere in there my dad heard some of the buzz about me and called Ronnie.

"Boy, is your brother that good?" he asked.

"Yeah, he is," Ronnie told him.

But he never called me. After that, he came and watched me play a few times, but he kept his distance. He'd heard that I was good, and he came to see for himself. And what he saw was all these major league scouts who came to watch me play. He must have felt something. He was such a great athlete himself. He knew I got my talent from him. But he never came over to me afterward. Most of the time he didn't stay for the whole game.

We roared into the citywide playoffs. We won our first couple games 12–1 and 11–3. When we got on the bus to ride to Dodger Stadium for the championship game, we were so high on ourselves it's a wonder the bus didn't float off into the sky. We were positive we were the best team in the city. Nothing was going to stop us.

All we had to do was beat Granada Hills, an all-white team from the Valley. They looked great, really professional. We were a bunch of black kids from a penny-pinching inner-city school and we were intimidated. I think playing in that gigantic stadium made us self-conscious, too. We had so much to prove that day, and it put us off our game. We should have beaten them. They were good, but they weren't great. Except for this one tall blond kid named John Elway. He started the game at third base, then the coach switched him to the mound. He pitched well. And we fell apart. We made dumb errors, our bats went limp, and even Mr. Hurst made a few bad decisions, which was really rare for him. He was as rattled as we were.

When the game was over and we'd lost, I couldn't believe it. I stood in the outfield and cried. I felt so bad. We all did. We wanted to show the whole city of Los Angeles what a great team we were, but we choked and blew it. The pressure got to us.

THAT SUMMER BETWEEN eleventh and twelfth grade I played in the Connie Mack Summer League. Summer League is for high school players. You're too big to play Little League anymore. When school gets out, you go play Summer League. Our team was the Compton Moose, playing out of Gonzalez Stadium under coach Earl Brown. When we took the field the fans would cheer, "Moose on the loose!" Mr. Brown brought together all the great high school players around our part of the city. Me, Eric Davis (who was at Fremont High), Chris Brown, all of us. Eric was the shortstop, Chris played third, I played right. Eric was the leadoff hitter and I batted cleanup, and I never had to bring him in because he always led off the games with home runs.

Eric and I became the best of friends. I called him E.D. My boy. And I was his boy. Straw. Coach Brown used to kid us both, trying to get a rivalry between us.

"You can't play with Eric Davis," he'd say to me. Then he'd say to Eric, "You can't play with Darryl Strawberry."

We won the citywide championship at the end of that summer and went up to Seattle to play in the big tournament there. None of us had ever been outside Los Angeles. We made second place in the tournament. Scouts from all the major league teams were there watching, taking notes. Something like eight or nine guys from that team would go on to be drafted by the major leagues.

SO NOW IT was senior year, 1979/80, and I played on the varsity basketball team. A great team. Professional basketball scouts watched us all season. They'd ask the coach about me and he'd say, "Strawberry? Forget about it. He's going to major league baseball. He's going to be a first round draft pick." He knew.

We won the citywide championship for the third year in a row, but got eliminated in the statewide playoffs up in Oakland. I had to rush back to L.A. right after that game, because baseball season was about to begin. I only got in one day of practice before the first game.

Mr. Hurst said to me, "You know, I've been coming to all your home games, and cringing every time you went up for a slam-dunk." He was worried that I'd injure myself for baseball.

The '79 team had gotten so much attention that it just carried over into '80. We had TV cameras, sportswriters, and twenty or thirty major league scouts at all our games. Since Chris Brown and the other great players from '79 had all graduated, everyone was there to see this kid Strawberry. It was amazing. I'm eighteen, a high school senior, and all of professional baseball is staring at me. I did not know it at that moment, but it was the kind of pressure I was going to be under for years and years to come.

I didn't show them much at first. I had practically no time to practice. I was rusty, still in basketball mode. All the attention made me self-conscious. I'd go up to bat, and *whhhft. Whhhft.*

But then there was the time I came up to bat with the bases loaded. I was settled in now. I didn't think of all those eyes and cameras staring at me. I relaxed. The first pitch comes and it's a beauty and I am totally focused on it. I swing, easy, not pushing. My natural swing is back.

Pow.

I feel the bat and ball connect and I know it's a home run. You can feel it. You just know.

A grand slam. On the first pitch. And it was a long one. It sailed up and up over everyone's head and out of there, and who knows when it finally came back to earth?

That was the moment it all connected. I'm rounding the bases, the TV cameras are tracking me, the scouts are all standing there nodding, nodding.

Pretty soon I was in *Sports Illustrated*. They labeled me "the black Ted Williams." The writer had heard it from the scouts: "This kid out of Crenshaw, this Strawberry kid, has a swing like Ted Williams'. You never seen nothing like it. He's lanky, he's long, he's smooth, everything he does is graceful. Just like Ted Williams."

So that's what they wrote in *Sports Illustrated*. Somebody asked me at the time, "Do you even know who Ted Williams is?"

"Nope," I said. Rennie would have known, but I still hadn't really studied the history. I knew the Dodgers that year, some of the other current teams, but my knowledge of the history was real sketchy. Later I would meet Willie Mays, and it was the same way. I mean, I was aware that he was one of the greats of baseball history, but I was pretty vague on why.

Here's an interesting thing about that *Sports Illustrated*: Keith Hernandez was on the cover. In a few years we'd be together on the Mets, and he'd be like a big brother and mentor to me. We'd go through a lot together—including some infamous spats.

Most folks thought my going to the majors was a foregone conclusion that season, just like my basketball coach had said. Scouts came up to me all the time. One guy told me, "Darryl, I just want to tell you you're going to be a great ballplayer. We're not gonna have a chance to draft you, so I'm not even going to try. You'll be snapped up before we even get close. I just wanted you to know that I've been watching you and you have a great career ahead of you."

I think the only one around who wasn't impressed with me was me. In spite of all the praise and attention, my image of myself was still pretty low. Even when the crowds cheered, I still heard a voice in my head, a bitter, sullen man's voice, telling me, "You think you're something? You're nothing, boy. And you ain't never gonna be nothin'."

I'm not looking for excuses. I'm not blaming my dad for anything I ever did. But I was missing something. I didn't have a father who

supported me, was proud of me, encouraged me to succeed. I had surrogate fathers in my coaches. Mr. Mosely, Mr. Hurst, Mr. Brown, and
the others. Those men were great to me. But they were replacements.
They were father figures, not the real thing. Maybe another kid would
be able to get over that. I sure wasn't the only young black male who
didn't have a dad around the house. I don't know. I just felt that loss
deeply. It hounded me. It damaged me, like it damaged Ronnie.

Mom was happy for me when I was in *Sports Illustrated*, but she
was still Mom. It was still, "Take that hat off in my house."

When it came time for the major league draft picks that June, I
think she was as nervous as I was. We both knew I was going to be
picked. If I decided to go, it was going to bring huge changes. I was
wondering if I should go straight to pro baseball, or go to college.
Oklahoma State was hot for me to come there, play baseball and basketball while I got a college education. I knew my mom preferred that.
The lure of major league baseball was strong on me, but I thought
maybe I should get the education.

She drove me to school on the day of the draft, and we were both
so anxious and thoughtful we hardly spoke.

What a day that was. I went to all my usual classes, but I was completely preoccupied. Then it happened. The principal personally came
into my classroom and pulled me out. All the other kids staring. Out
in the hall, the principal said, "Mr. Hurst has some news for you."

We go to see Mr. Hurst. He's so excited he's vibrating. But I played
it cool.

"You got drafted!" he says.

And I'm like, "Oh yeah." I mean, I knew I was going to be drafted.
The only question was which team.

And he says, "You're the number one draft pick in the nation!"

Well, that got my attention.

"The New York media wants to speak to you on a conference call,"
he said, still bubbling over.

And we held a press conference right there in his office. There's a
TV crew, and they unfurl a Mets jersey for me, and I'm on the tele-

phone with a bunch of New York sportswriters. It was all surreal. I didn't know much about the Mets. They weren't a team a kid in L.A. would follow. I knew they usually finished in the bottom of their National League division. It had been a long dry spell since the Amazin' Mets won the World Series in 1969.

But I liked their scout, Roger Jongewaard. He had first introduced himself to me when I was still in the eleventh grade and then came to every single game during senior year. He was a wonderful man. He knew I was a nice kid, he knew my background, he saw I was raised by Mom to be a good person. It was Roger who convinced the Mets to make me their first pick. They had another scout down in San Diego who lobbied just as hard for a kid there, Billy Beane. It was neck and neck which one of us would be their first-round pick. Roger convinced them it should be me. (Billy would go on to play for the Mets and others, then become general manager of the Oakland A's.)

I remember one reporter asking me if I was excited and I just said, "I guess I'm a little excited." I really didn't know what it all meant yet. It hadn't really sunk in. I just knew I was drafted, and maybe going to play pro ball. I still wasn't positive it was what I should do.

Michael and Ronnie were more excited than I was. And my sisters and friends and everyone in the neighborhood. Because it was huge news in L.A. The number one draft pick in the nation.

I think my mom was more like me. She wasn't sure what she thought about it all, either. When I got home that afternoon, the phone was ringing off the hook. People wanting to cheer for me, reporters wanting interviews. It was bedlam. Mom stood there, this tiny woman in the middle of all this excitement, and just said, "Congratulations. Let's eat."

I think she knew everything was about to change, forever, and like me, she wasn't sure what to make of it.

For me, all the attention just made me feel shy and uncomfortable. I wasn't in it for the glory. I just wanted to play baseball. I hated being the center of all that attention. That may sound crazy or just untrue, but it is true. I hated all the hoopla. My life changed at that point. In a lot of ways it's never been my life since. It became the property of the media, the ball clubs, the fans. I know—you hear famous people complain about all the downsides of fame and you just think, "Oh shut up. You wanted the attention, now live with it." I'm just telling you I never wanted the attention. It comes along with being a talented athlete, but it wasn't what I played for, and I didn't like it. I was still so shy, still so full of self-doubt and even self-hate. The last thing I wanted was all those people staring at me.

AFTER THE DRAFT came all the business of negotiating and signing the contract. My agent was Richie Bry. He'd seen the article in *Sports Illustrated* and flew out from St. Louis. He took the family to box seats at Dodger Stadium, where the Cardinals were in town to play the Dodgers. He represented a few Cardinals and introduced me to them in the clubhouse after the game. Then he took us all out to a fancy dinner. He had to lend me a tie for the restaurant.

A few other agents pursued us, but my mom liked Richie best. She said he took more of a personal interest in me than the others. So we let him represent me.

The Mets and the New York media put tremendous pressure on Richie to get me to sign a contract right away, but he resisted. He negotiated. That's what agents do. And the truth is I was in no hurry, either. I asked my mom whether I should go to the Mets or go to college.

"It's your decision to make," she said.

Richie asked the Mets for a signing bonus to convince me not to go to college. It's a standard negotiating ploy for high school players. But as the summer dragged on, I got my first little taste of how the media can turn on you. Who does this kid Strawberry think he is? Why is his agent holding out? Why don't they sign already? What, the Mets aren't good enough?

Wow. We weren't talking huge dollars. Nothing like the millions the "bonus babies" get now. I think it was a $200,000 signing bonus they haggled over until late summer. It'd be $5 million now. I mean, $200,000 was a lot of money at that time. Especially for me. I'd never even gotten a paycheck before. But still, it wasn't a fortune. You bought something your mom needed, something you needed. I bought us each a car.

In retrospect it's ridiculous that they went back and forth over it the way they did. The Mets wanted me. I was a very hot young property. The Mets had been the laughingstock of the National League for years. They finished in the basement three years in a row. Attendance at Shea was miserable, and the folks who did show up for games just came because they had a perverse affection for underdogs and losers.

Frank Cashen, the Mets' new general manager, had a five-year plan not just to rebuild the team, but to build a great team. He wanted to create new excitement, get the fans back in the seats. Signing up "the black Ted Williams" should have been a no-brainer. Why they took so long I'll never know.

One great thing that happened was that E.D. got drafted, too, by the Cincinnati Reds. Man, we were so proud of each other and pleased for each other. We were both going to the majors!

I remember us sitting together in the stands at Gonzalez Stadium early that summer, in the midst of all the uproar about my contract negotiations, watching the kids who were coming up right behind us play Summer League.

"Straw," he said, "you hold out as long as you want. You do what you gotta do. But me, I'm ready to sign right now. The Reds want me, I'm going. I'm out of here, dawg. Getting out."

He'd been in the same boat I was, trying to decide between going to the major leagues or going to college on a basketball scholarship. It was a harder decision for him, because he had a lot of colleges waving those scholarships in his face. I was good at basketball, but he was great. Now that he made his decision, though, he was full steam ahead, which was typical. My boy had the heart of a champion. We both did. We decided right there and then we weren't just going to the majors, we were going to eat the majors alive.

So he went off to play for the Reds and I went off to the Mets. I later graduated into the big show from the minors in '83, and he made it in '84. Over the years we often were on opposing teams in the park. There was a series at Shea in '88 where he snatched a hit of mine that was headed out of the park one day, and then he threw me out at third base the next. I would have been angry if it was anyone else, but he and I just laughed about it afterward. He made two great plays and I was proud of him. It wasn't until '92 that we got to play on the same team, the Dodgers, but by that point we both struggled with injuries and neither had his best year.

4

ONE DAY LATE that summer of 1980, my mom drove me out to Los Angeles International Airport. Roger Jongewaard met us there. The contract was signed. My bag was packed. He had our two tickets in his pocket. He and I were flying off to Kingsport, Tennessee, where I would enter the Mets minor league system, playing for the Kingsport Mets in the Appalachian League.

I was eighteen. And I was so nervous and scared I thought I was going to throw up. Except for a couple of team trips up the West Coast, I had never set foot outside Los Angeles. Shucks, there were still parts of Los Angeles I'd never set foot in. I sure never had any intention of going to Tennessee. To me, Tennessee was somewhere in the South where no young black man went if he didn't have to.

When it was time to board the plane I kissed my mom good-bye and hugged her and didn't want to let go. I wanted to tell Roger, "Forget it. Rip up my ticket and the contract. I've changed my mind." I may have been a big, tall, strapping lad, but inside I was one scared little rabbit.

I wasn't any happier when I got there. Kingsport was like a foreign country to me. A very small, very white city. I looked around and saw nary a black face except in the mirror. I had no problem with white people per se, I was just used to a more mixed society. Here I stood out like a big, brown thumb. I would go straight from the ballpark to my room. And call home to my mom every single night.

The hype and media circus followed me there. There was this "Strawberry is here!" frenzy. The ballpark ran promotions like Strawberry Sunday. If you brought a strawberry to the park you got into the game free. They loved that I was bringing national attention to their city and their ballpark.

The first day I walked into the clubhouse, there must have been fifty reporters and cameramen there.

"Hey Darryl, are you as good as they say?"

"Did the Mets pay too much for you?"

"How long will it take you to reach the majors?"

"What you think of Kingsport?"

I didn't know what to say to any of them. I tried to be polite and respectful, because that's how my mom raised me. But really I just wanted them to go away and leave me alone.

The hype didn't endear me to the other guys on the team, though I have to say most of them were all right about it. The Appalachian League was what they call a rookie league, a mix of new drafts like me and guys who were in their second year. It was the lowest rung of the farm system. Everyone wanted to get up through the minors into the big show. That can take years, and a whole lot of guys never make it at all. They bang around in the minor leagues for years until they give up or are dropped. And here's Strawberry, the black Ted Williams, and the media are wondering aloud how long it's going to take him. Two years, three? So my teammates were very curious to see this big shot everybody was raving about.

The manager, Chuck Hiller, was a good guy. He was funny. He called me Turkey Neck. It was his way of helping me cut through all the hype. He stayed on my behind, too.

"Making it to the big leagues takes a lot of work, Turkey Neck. But if you focus on your goal and train for it you might get there."

Since the contract negotiations took so long, I joined the team in the middle of their season. I played forty-four games. Which was plenty by me. I just wanted to get it over with and get the heck back home. There's nothing glamorous about the life at that level. It's a grind. Lots of long, long bus rides—fifteen, twenty hours—from one little hillbillyish town to another to another. Most of the time I had no idea where we were or where we were going. Danville, Greeneville, Johnson City? Never heard of them, and never in my wildest dreams thought I'd go to them. Playing in rickety little ballparks for crowds of four, five thousand people who were almost all white. A few black faces around the edges of the stands, but in the South, at least in the minors, baseball was a white people's sport.

And those people did not exactly welcome me with open arms, not when we were on the road, anyway. They all had an opinion about this big, tall, black kid who was supposed to be such a star, and that opinion wasn't good. They yelled stuff at me through the whole game.

"Strawberry, you're not so hot!"

"You overrated, kid!"

"You suck!"

That took some getting used to. I had never played ball in front of bunches of angry, shouting white folks. Welcome to the minor leagues, kid. Welcome to the South.

So I struggled, just trying to do my best, learn the ropes, listen to Hiller and the other coaches, just get through this experience. And the media are following us around everywhere, and already they're disappointed in me. I'm not smacking grand slams every time I'm at the plate. I'm doing all right, but that's not what they want to see. They want to see the freak-of-nature superstar. It was crazy. They were the ones who built up all these expectations. I didn't call myself the black Ted Williams. And here I'm in the minors a few weeks and they're already disappointed. "This kid's not such a big deal. He'll never make it. He can't adjust. Who said he was going to be a star?" Well, sir, you did.

They were all over Mr. Cashen, too. Are you satisfied with the way

Strawberry is performing? How long will it be before you bring him up to the big show? And Mr. Cashen, correctly, is saying, "He's a kid. It'll take time. He needs to develop and mature. We're not going to rush him."

Oh, I was not happy. I spent a lot of time alone in my room, feeling lonesome and homesick. Daytimes I lay on my bed and hid until it was time to head to the ballpark. After the games I did not explore whatever Kingsport or Danville or Greeneville had in the way of a night life. I was not going anywhere I didn't know.

I didn't chase after any girls, either. Plenty of them hung around the ballpark, wanting to get next to the players, but I had nothing to do with them. I was still on the shy side. And I felt like I really needed to focus on baseball. I used to watch Michael and his girlfriend argue and fuss. He wanted to play ball, and she didn't want him to. So I thought of girls as a distraction and pain in the neck more than anything.

I just went to my room every night and called home. Finally, my mom said, "Darryl, you keep calling like this, you're going to spend all the money the Mets gave you."

WHEN THE SEASON ended, the jet to L.A. could not fly me there fast enough. But I was only home maybe two weeks when they sent me to the Mets Instructional League camp in Port St. Lucie, Florida. The Instructional League was where they sent talented prospects to get some intensive training and keep developing their skills over the winter. I liked it better. It was mostly rookies from a lot of major league farm systems playing one another in parks all around Florida.

But it didn't prepare me for the Carolina League, where I went that spring, on the Lynchburg Mets, an A team in Lynchburg, Virginia. I struggled a lot that season, and the media came down on me really hard. The consensus was that the Mets made a mistake picking me. I wasn't going to cut it.

I wasn't sure I was, either. I didn't like Lynchburg any more than

I'd liked Kingsport. The fans booed me and sometimes yelled racial slurs at me. I was beginning to agree that the Mets had made a mistake, and so had I. I didn't need the pressure, I didn't need the abuse. I could just quit, go to college, play basketball. Lying around my room at night that season, I seriously considered it. Shoot, I was only nineteen. A good time to change the course of my life.

One day I woke up so depressed and so dreading another afternoon of booing fans that I could not get myself out of bed and drag myself to the park. The heck with it. I was done. I just lay there and let the Lynchburg Mets play without me.

Playing hooky from a game was, of course, a major infraction. But manager Gene Dusan didn't come down on me. Just the opposite. He sat me down and gave me a good, long talking-to. He said he felt for me and understood what I was going through, but he and the entire Mets organization had a lot of faith in me. If I just stuck with it, developed my skills, ignored the press and the heckling fans, I had great potential.

He got me back on track. My playing improved, and my attitude toughened. I got 13 home runs, 70 or 80 RBIs, and a whole lot of stolen bases. I ended that season much happier than I'd started it.

I went back to the Instructional League in Florida that winter, and things were definitely on the upswing. From there I graduated to the AA Mets team in Jackson, Mississippi, playing in the Texas League. And that's where I finally found my groove. I became a complete player that year, 1982. Hitting, fielding, stealing bases. I saw the light in myself, and then I started to see why the Mets organization believed I could play. I tore that Texas League up. I led the league with 34 home runs, knocked in 97 runs, and stole 45 bases—all new records for the team. I won the league's MVP award.

The pressure was off. I finally delivered like everyone expected me to. The press was like, "Okay, we're convinced. The Mets made the right decision. This Strawberry kid has the potential for greatness."

· · ·

IN FEBRUARY 1983, just before my twenty-first birthday, I went to the Mets spring training camp in St. Petersburg, Florida. Not the minors. The major league Mets camp. Guys like George Foster, Hubie Brooks, Eddie Lynch, Dave Kingman, Jesse Orosco, Rusty Staub, Ron Hodges . . . and me.

Man was that exciting. And intimidating. Mostly the other guys were older. It was a team of veterans. Frank Cashen was just starting to bring the youngbloods in. They looked at me as a young rook coming to spring training with all this hype. I kept my mouth shut and my eyes and ears open. I wanted to learn. And I wanted to show that I deserved to be there. I hit a few bombs, and the veterans were like, "Well, okay. This guy can hit. Let's take him with us."

But Frank Cashen wanted to use caution. In '81 they'd brought a promising young pitcher, Tim Leary, up from the minors after only a year. It was too soon. He injured his elbow in his very first start, and it ruined him for the entire season. In fact, it would dog him for years, and he never really got to play to his full potential. Mr. Cashen believed it was because they rushed him, and didn't want anything like that to happen to any other young players. He thought I was almost ready, but I could use a little more seasoning.

So after spring training with the major league Mets, I went back to the minors—the Triple A Mets franchise in Tidewater, Virginia. Triple A is the highest level of the minors.

I got off to a good start. The Mets did not. By the first week of May they'd won six games and lost fifteen. I'd only played sixteen games at Tidewater when Davey Johnson, the Tidewater manager, called me into his office.

"I'm taking you off tonight's lineup," he said. "Take the night off."

"Okay. Why?" I was confused. Did I do something wrong?

He grinned. "Pack your bags. You're leaving us. They're calling you up to New York tomorrow."

I called home to let my family know it was finally happening. I was going to play in the big leagues. I tried to sound casual about it. I tried to feel casual about it. I didn't want to get overexcited. I knew it was my time, my chance. I wanted to stay cool, not overreact. I think partly I was hoping that if I stayed cool, everyone else would, too. I didn't want the press and fans to make a huge deal out of my being called up. I didn't want them to think I was coming to New York as the Mets' savior. But I knew they probably would. They'd been waiting for this moment as long as I had, since the Mets first picked me in 1980. They'd been following my progress through the minors for three years, asking, "When is Strawberry coming? When is Strawberry coming?" My appearance at spring training had really fanned the speculation.

THE NEXT MORNING, May 6, 1983, I got on a flight to New York. With butterflies in my stomach and cotton in my mouth. It turned out to be another surreal day. Mets staff met me as I stepped into the terminal at LaGuardia. They hustled me over to the airport Holiday Inn, where I barely had time to drop my bags before they whisked me into a limo and we drove straight out to Shea Stadium in Flushing Meadows. Jay Horwitz, the public relations director, was waiting for me there.

"Hi Darryl. Welcome to Shea. You're going to hold a press conference."

"I am?" My heart pounded. A press conference was exactly what I had hoped to avoid. "When?"

"Right now."

Oh man . . .

He leads me into a room filled with media. Bam, the TV camera lights blind me. The whirring of newspaper and magazine photographers' cameras is like a field of crickets. Dozens of microphones point at me.

What an ordeal. It was nerve-wracking.

"Are you ready for the big leagues?"

"What do you think you're capable of doing?"

"What do you think the Mets' chances are this year?"

"How do you like New York so far?"

So far? I just got here an hour ago.

When that's done I'm led straight to the clubhouse, where there's a locker waiting for me. With my name on it. And a uniform hanging there. My uniform. I just stood there staring at it for a second as it sank in.

I am a major league ballplayer.

A second was just about all I had to savor the moment. It was time for batting practice. There was a game that night, and I was going to be in it.

All the other guys were there, getting suited up. They were really nice to me. I got a lot of warm greetings. "Have fun, kid. Enjoy yourself out there today. You made it." They'd met me in spring training and were happy I was on board. I got no sense of jealousy or bruised egos. Not yet anyway. The Mets were a losing club. A very losing club, in last place. No athlete likes to be on a losing team. If the kid could help win games, bring him on.

Stepping out to the field for batting practice, I was awestruck. Even the biggest, best Triple A ballparks are like sandlot fields compared to a major league stadium. Shea looked enormous. Ten times bigger than any Triple A park. Minor league fields had potholes in them. In major league ballparks the grass is level and manicured. In minor league ballparks the lights were bad, the clubhouse was a dump. The lights at Shea were great, and the clubhouse looked like a palace to me. I felt like a kid back on the Crenshaw Cougars that day we stepped into Dodger Stadium. I hoped I wouldn't blow it here today the way we did back then. A young gladiator stepping into the Colosseum of Rome for the first time couldn't have felt more nervous than I did. Victory or death!

Unfortunately, I died out there that night. We faced the Cincinnati Reds and their strikeout king, Mario Soto. He struck me out, all right—three times. Darryl Strawberry, the young phenom the fans and press had clamored for since 1980, went 0 for 4 that night. A stunning major league debut. My only consolations were that Soto had a dozen strikeouts that night, and the Mets won anyway.

The fans were great about it. They applauded and called out my name when I stepped up to the plate. They were just happy finally seeing me on the team.

I didn't give them much to cheer about in my next several games. No matter how prepared you think you are, stepping up to the big leagues is one giant leap for a young ballplayer. You're nervous and self-conscious. And you should be. The level of play and competitiveness are also a giant leap up from anything you've experienced. This is the big leagues, kid. These guys are all pros.

I went something like 0 for 11 before I got my first hit, and in about a month or so I began to settle down and settle in. Jim Frey, the batting coach, took me under his wing and helped a lot. He sat me down and said, "Kid, this is what you're going to have to do. You got a world of raw talent, but you have to make up your mind that you want to work on it and refine it. You be at the ballpark early and we'll get down to work, taking ground balls, fly balls, taking batting practice every day. Get your mind set and work on your fundamentals. Focus. There are a lot of distractions up here. I've seen a lot of players come up here and lose their concentration. If you do that you're dead. But if you focus and work hard, it'll pay off."

I worked with Jim that whole season, and boy did it pay off. I found my swing and my stride. Part of it was learning not to be intimidated by the pitchers. They saw this youngblood who was supposed to be a star long-ball hitter, and they were out to trim my wings a bit. They'd whip a ball up and at my head now and again to brush me back from the plate. Or get me to swing at trash. I had to learn to stand up to them, and to lay off those bad pitches. Every time you're out there you gain a little more experience. You log it and keep growing as a player.

I did well. Twenty-six home runs, 74 RBIs, 19 stolen bases. Once I got on a roll, the crowd roared every time I was announced at the plate. And the crowds, like the stadiums, were ten times larger than any I'd ever played for. The Mets still did terribly that year—we finished in last place again—but the fans started coming back anyway, to see this guy Strawberry knock one out to the parking lot. They'd waited a long time for this. The more I produced, the more fans showed up.

I GOT MY first taste of what the big league life was like off the field, too. It was a little wild, but nowhere close to the way the Mets would cut loose in a few years. I mean, we weren't winning. We were in last place. It wasn't anything to party and be wild about. If we'd been partying a lot, the other teams would just bury us even deeper.

Still, being a ballplayer, you had to have some kind of outlet. Drink some beer, smoke some cigars, play some cards, hang with some women. In '84 and '85, as we began to turn things around and became a winning team, we partied more, celebrated more. And in '86, when we were the winningest team around, we became party animals.

We were nowhere near that out of control my rookie year, but looking back, I can say that was the year I got initiated into the big league celebrity ballplayer lifestyle, and began to sow the wild oats of my own later destruction. To put it bluntly, I took my first steps that year toward becoming an alcoholic and drug addict. Some of the veteran players took it upon themselves to take me around, show me how it was done. Drinking in bars, drinking in nightclubs, partying with the hotties who are drawn to major league ballplayers like moths to a flame. When you get to the big leagues, you hit the bars and the clubs, and the women are all tens. And you don't have to chase them. They are chasing after you. I began to think maybe the ladies weren't such a pain in the neck after all. Though they sure were a distraction.

The sportswriters voted me Rookie of the Year. It came down to me and Mel Hall of the Cubs, who had a great year, too.

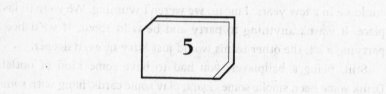

5

AT THE END of the season I went home to Mom's house in Crenshaw. I got quite the reception not only in the 'hood, but all over the city of Los Angeles. I was a homegrown star in the major leagues. Our neighbors loved that they had a real star living on the street.

Mom was proud of me, but as usual it was not in some "My son Darryl is special, he's a star" sort of way. She was proud of all her kids—well, except that Ronnie gave her heartaches—and I was just one of them. Just like she'd never pushed me before, she didn't puff me up much now. She was happy that I was happy. My brothers and sisters were proud of me, too, of course. Even Ronnie went around the neighborhood with his chest out.

I was happy to be back home on familiar territory. But everything had changed. Now, wherever I went in L.A., people knew me. They wanted to talk or get my autograph. I couldn't sit in a restaurant or walk into a store without attracting fans.

That I wasn't crazy about. I was always polite about it with anyone who came up to me, but I didn't enjoy it. In fact I kind of hated it.

I would have preferred to have my old self back, no attention or notoriety, no focus on me all the time. My life had moved on to a different place. You can't be a major league ballplayer and Rookie of the Year and expect to go back to your normal, quiet life at the end of the season. You're a celebrity now. Everybody wants a piece of you, everybody wants your time, everybody wants you to come to this party and that party. They want you to endorse this jacket and these shoes, they want you to do commercials, they've got a business they want you to invest in, all that stuff. So you hire people to refer them to, and then you've added all those people to your life. You've become a small business without trying or wanting to be, but just because you have to be.

It did make me think that maybe if I'd gone to play somewhere besides New York, the media capital, the fame and all that came with it might have been less intense. Everything that happens in New York is national news. I was covered from coast to coast. If I'd played for some smaller franchise in some less connected city, maybe the hoopla about every little thing I did or said would have been smaller.

I remember once I was walking in New York City with my mom. I think this was in that first season, or maybe the second. We passed a homeless guy huddled on the sidewalk, and I told my mom I envied him.

"Why on earth would you say that?" she asked.

"Because if I was like him, I wouldn't have to worry about everybody pulling at me," I said. "Nobody would pay any attention to me at all."

That's how I felt. The notoriety is a pain. You can't go anywhere without people tugging at you.

I never let myself become standoffish about it, though, not with the fans and not with the press. I was always available. I always thought we're all human. I was no better than they were. Who was I to act superior? I'd become someone who had an effect on people's lives because of what I did on the field. I saw that as a responsibility.

But at the same time, I still had a lot of growing up to do. Going from high school straight to the minor leagues, I'd missed good parts of growing up. I kind of skipped over eighteen, nineteen, twenty. Instead of growing up normally I grew up in public, and I had to grow up fast. Grow up being patted on the back everywhere you go or taking abuse, grow up with people cheering for you or angry at you and envious of you, grow up with people wanting to take things from you and take advantage of you.

Back then, there were no structures in pro baseball to help young players deal with all that. Nowadays the system is better about educating them, providing classes on how to handle their money, how to handle fame, all kinds of do's and don'ts. Nobody advised me about all that. Those were lessons I had to learn the hard way.

MEANWHILE, RONNIE WAS struggling much harder than I was. His behavior just kept spiraling down and down. People in the neighborhood told my sisters, "Tell your brothers to come get Ronnie. He's living down here in this rat hole of a crack house. He's got no business down here."

Mike and I went to look in on him. Mike was an LAPD patrolman by then. We drove the part of the neighborhood where Ronnie was supposed to be living, Mike in his patrol car, me following in my car. Mike didn't want to make a scene, rolling up in front of the crack house in his patrol car, so he parked around the corner while I pulled up in front of the house.

A guy was standing outside the house. He said Ronnie was inside.

"Go tell him to come out," we said. Mike didn't want to make trouble for Ronnie by going in there in his uniform, and I wasn't going to go into that rats' nest alone if I didn't have to.

We stood on the corner and waited. A few minutes later Ronnie came out, and he looked awful. He was raggedy, all skin and bones. His face was sunken, his eyes bugging. He was so strung out. It was an actual physical shock to me to see him, like I was slapped in the face. I started to cry. Mike did, too.

Ronnie was angry with us for being there, and I think embarrassed and ashamed, too.

"What y'all want?"

"Ronnie, come out of here," Mike said, tears rolling down his cheeks.

"Y'all ain't me," he said. "Look at you, big-time ballplayer. Look at you, cop. Who am I? I'm nothing. I'm nobody. This is who I am. Y'all don't know me. Go away and leave me alone."

Mike and I were bawling like mad now.

"Ronnie, you're our brother," Mike said. "We love you. We're not going anywhere. We're gonna take you from here. We're gonna do whatever we have to do to get you some help."

We talked to him for a long time.

"Why don't you just go with us, man?" I said. "Please."

He kept telling us to go away and leave him alone.

I said, "Ron, we're not leaving. You gotta go with us. We're not leaving this corner. We're gonna stand here and wait till you come with us."

Finally he realized we weren't fooling.

"All right," he said. "Just give me five minutes."

He went back inside, and we didn't see him for another forty-five minutes. He was in there smoking crack, with us standing outside waiting for him. When he came back out he was high as a kite, all jacked up, beaming, his eyes wild and shining.

"All right, let's go."

We got him in my car and drove him back to our mother's house. It was one of many times when Ronnie promised Mom and the rest of us he'd get straight, and he did try, but he failed. He was too damaged. The scars of his childhood ran too deep. I don't blame my father for any of the bad decisions I made in my life, but I do blame him for Ronnie.

ONE GREAT THING about being back in L.A. was hooking up with my boy E.D. again. At the end of every season for our first several

years we'd both come back home to South Central and hang out together until it was time to leave again for spring training. We always
went back to the ghetto, back home, even though we were making
mad money and could have hung out anywhere. We went back to the
'hood.

We did everything together. We had a workout that we did every
year to keep ourselves in shape. Not just us, but Chris Brown and the
whole bunch of us who'd grown up playing ball together and then
went off to different professional clubs, maybe twenty of us. We'd all
meet up again back in the 'hood between seasons and work out together, keeping in shape and keeping our skills sharp. The Program,
we called it. We started in January. We could've gone up to UCLA or
USC to work out on those beautiful diamonds they had, but we went
to Harvard Park on West Sixty-second Street not far from Crenshaw,
in the heart of South Central, right in the ghetto. Most people knew
it because it was a place where local street gangs met up to have their
turf wars, because it was right in the middle of their territories. Local
kids couldn't even play ball there because there was so much gang
violence, their parents wouldn't let them.

We decided to do the Program right there, right in the heart of it,
to take the park back at least for a couple months out of the year and
show kids another way. We wanted the kids to know that this was
where we came from. We made it, we were in the big leagues, but this
was our home and our park. If we could get out, so could they.

We'd bring out some old bats, balls, and gloves. We set up a trash
can behind the catcher, because we didn't have any fancy screen or
anything. We wanted to keep it like we always had it growing up, real
sandlot, like when we were kids. It was just a joy. We hit, we run, we
shag, we talk, then we hang out afterward. Use one of the trash cans
to light us a fire and stay out there till it gets dark. We'd drink beer
and talk trash awhile, and then we would jump into our sweat suits
and form a caravan and drive to the Forum to watch the Lakers.

Oh, we were the talk of the town, that posse. E.D. and I each drove
a brand-new Mercedes-Benz, and we'd drive at the lead of maybe a

ten-car caravan. When we came to an intersection, he'd block one side and I'd block the other to hold back the traffic while our caravan blew on through. We were young and wild and enjoying life. When we got to the Forum, everyone else in the place would be all dressed up, and we'd roll in there in our sweat suits. Nobody minded. We were big-time celebrities in L.A., all us guys. We were born and raised there, and we made it. We weren't just successful, we were great baseball players. Homegrown heroes. Afterward we'd hit the clubs with our crew and just turn them out. We did everything together. We even had our own bowling team with our girlfriends and buddies.

He and I bonded for life. It's like we have the same heart. We grew up together having a dream. We knew we were going to make it. We were determined. We weren't just going to get to the major leagues, we were going to dominate the major leagues. We encouraged and supported each other, we worked together to make that dream a reality, and we made it. And we're still best friends to this day. He's the only person I could ever say has walked the whole journey with me, the one I've always trusted, the one who has believed in me through it all, just like I have always believed in him. We believed in ourselves from the time we were boys.

The one thing we never did together was the drugs. He never got caught up in that the way I did. And he stuck with me through all that, too. It crushed him to see me go through it, because we were like brothers. It made him feel helpless. He used to say, "That's my boy, that's my only boy. I got a lot of friends, but that one there—that's my boy. I don't want him to lose his life. But I feel like I can't do anything to help."

Because he knew I would never ask him for help. If I asked he would do anything for me, he would die for me, but I never asked. That's who we were and how we grew up. We were athletes. Athletes are supposed to hide their pain, work through it. Whether it's physical or emotional. You grit your teeth and suck it up and get through it. And no matter how bad he feels for you, even your best friend won't push his help or advice on you. He'll do anything if you ask, but if you don't ask, he won't pry. He'll let you do what you got to do. He knows that it's your path and you have to travel it your own way.

"He's going to walk through it alone," Eric would say when he saw me really struggling. "He's a survivor. He's strong."

Growing up, we always knew we were going to make it no matter what. He knew that I'd come through it eventually.

THAT WINTER AT one of the Lakers games my friend Duane Franklin introduced me to Lisa Andrews. Duane and I had played basketball together at Crenshaw. He was in junior college now, and still loved basketball. He went with me to games and to the Forum Club afterward, where I met Magic Johnson and all those guys.

I will always remember the moment he introduced me to Lisa, if only because it was the start of what ended up being such a nightmare for both her and me. I saw him talking to this beautiful girl. She asked him who I was.

"Oh, him?" Duane said casually. "That's my boy Darryl. He plays baseball."

He came back over to me and told me I should go say hello. She was really pretty, so I did. We made small talk. She told me she lived in Pasadena with her mom. I didn't come on to her like, "Hey baby, I'm Rookie of the Year." My mom didn't raise me that way. Besides, I thought she was a lot more interested in basketball than baseball anyway. We talked, I got her number, and a few days later I called. We started to go out on dates. I drove out to Pasadena to pick her up. Met her mom, who was nice. We went to the movies, dinner—the usual sort of things. And I fell in love. It didn't take long. A few months.

At first she just seemed to be a sweet, beautiful young lady. But as we got serious about each other, we also started to argue and fight. Behind that sweet façade, she had an explosive temper. I later read some writer calling Lisa "a tempestuous beauty." That was a major understatement. When Lisa got angry she wasn't a tempest, she was a full-on hurricane. She wasn't just a firecracker, she was a stick of TNT dynamite. And it didn't take much to light her fuse.

For one thing, she turned out to be extremely jealous of my fame and the way people reacted to me in public. Especially the way girls reacted to me in public. She always thought girls were after me. A girl would just look at me and Lisa would go off.

In a way I can't blame her. Girls were coming on to me all the time. I was a rising young star in major league baseball. I was known everywhere she and I went in L.A. The hometown hero who made good in the big leagues. People came up to me to say hi and ask for autographs all the time. Some of those people were pretty girls. They had no trouble flirting with me right in front of Lisa. And she would fly into a rage.

"What do you want me to do about it?" I'd say. "I have no control over the way people look at me."

I wasn't making dates with any of these other women. I wasn't seeing them behind her back. Not that she believed me.

I'm not saying she was the whole cause of our problems. It takes two to tangle. And boy did we tangle. We were very young. Looking back, I don't see how either of us could be expected to handle all the fame and attention I was getting.

I began to have some serious doubts about this thing—and so did many of my friends. They saw me and Lisa arguing all the time.

But at the same time, the relationship felt like it had a momentum of its own, like a current that was pulling us along. I don't know if you've ever been in a relationship like that, where you're fighting a lot, you have serious doubts about it, and yet at the same time it has a life of its own and it's carrying you both where it wants to take you. It's like fate has somehow doomed you to be together.

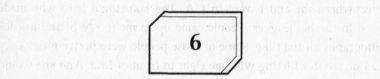

6

WHEN I GOT to St. Petersburg for spring training in February '84 I was just shy of twenty-two years old. Even though I'd done well personally in the '83 season, the team had a dismal season, finishing twenty-two games out, in last place. Now the general feeling was that in '84 the Mets were going to start on our road to victory. There were some big and hopeful signs at the spring training camp. They had me, Rookie of the Year. Dwight Gooden, the superstar young pitcher, arrived for the first time. Davey Johnson came up to be manager. We had Mookie Wilson, Ron Darling, all these great players.

Keith Hernandez had been planning to leave at the end of our lousy '83 season. The truth is, he hadn't even wanted to be on the Mets from the start. He'd come over in the middle of the season from the Cardinals. Even though he'd help lead the Cards to the World Series the year before, he and manager Whitey Herzog had never gotten along. Keith was a very smart guy and a bit of an eccentric, and I think Whitey just never got him. Also, for a while there Keith had some trouble with cocaine, and Whitey just was not down with any of his players using drugs. So Keith got traded away from the best team in baseball to one of the worst, and at first he hated it. But then, by the end of the season, he began to feel good about our potential, so he decided to stick around for '84.

I was really glad he did. I loved Mex, as he was known. He was about ten years older, had been in the majors since the mid-1970s. He was a very intense player, a great left-handed hitter, and he had a great knowledge of the game. He went about it very professionally. He became one of the Wise Men of the team, and taught me a lot of things.

Doc Gooden and I were pals from the start. He was nineteen, I was twenty-one. We were the babies of the team, the young hotshots playing at a level of competition that looked far beyond our years.

And we were all excited to be playing for Davey. We related to him. A lot of us had played for him in the minors. He was younger than the previous managers, George Bamberger and Frank Howard, which helped us feel like he just got us more than they had. And he was a former ballplayer himself, which made him a players' manager. His philosophy was basically, "I'll let the guys play. I've got younger players, I'll let them play, let them learn what this is all about. They're gonna make mistakes, and I'll get on their behind when I need to, but they can only learn by doing." He didn't hammer us.

He didn't nag at us about our behavior off the field, either. He did not see it as part of his job description to act as our hall monitor or chaperone off the field. What we did in the ballpark was his business. What we did elsewhere was ours. It was a sore point between him and Mr. Cashen from the very start. Mr. Cashen was a quiet, clean-living man himself, and he would have much preferred if everyone in the ball club was like him. He did not feel comfortable around loud, cocky, rowdy jocks. And he felt it was bad for the Mets franchise.

We were loud, cocky, rowdy jocks. Including Davey. We weren't so bad yet in '84, but over the next few years Davey would allow our behavior off the field to get completely out of control. He was a believer that the team that parties together bonds as a family and goes on to win ballgames together. For a while, much as Mr. Cashen hated it, Davey seemed to be right. We went from last place in our division in '83 to second place in '84.

Still, it was a rocky season for me, and it started at spring training. A reporter asked me if I thought I had to step up and become a leader if the team was going to go all the way that year. I gave what I thought was a careful answer. I said I wanted to lead by example on the field, but I didn't see myself trying to be the voice of the clubhouse or speak for all the older, far more experienced veterans on the team.

I got an early lesson in how the press can twist your words. When the article appeared, it had me saying I'd have to be the team leader if we were going to win. Pretty much the opposite of what I meant—but it was what the reporter wanted to hear, I guess.

Let's just say my older teammates were not pleased. A lot of them, I think, already had some resentment against me and Doc, the baby superstars who were getting all the press and fan mail, with everybody acting like the two of us phenoms were supposed to carry the whole rest of the team to victory. Rusty Staub in particular took it the wrong way. Rusty was a veteran to the veterans. He'd been in the majors since I was one year old, and was getting toward the end of his career—he'd stop after the '85 season. When he read that this kid Strawberry wanted to be the team leader, he made a statement of his own to the press, which boiled down to: Who does this kid think he is? You can't just say you're a leader. You have to do something and earn the respect of your teammates to be a leader.

If Rusty had come to me instead of the media, I could have told him what I really said. But this was the beginning of a period when the Mets, including me, would do a lot of our bickering in public, airing out our dirty laundry in the newspapers—which the reporters fully encouraged, of course. We would lash out at each other through the press, which caused a lot of unnecessary confusion and hurt feelings, but made for a great show in the newspapers. We were like the precursor to those dysfunctional families you see all over reality TV these days, living out our little trials and traumas in the full glare of the media lights.

Mex stuck with me through the incident. He, and starting in 1985 Gary Carter, were our natural team leaders. He knew I would never try to step in and take that role from them. They were veteran players. They'd been there, they knew what it was like. I just considered myself a key player who'd perform at a high level for the club and be productive.

Mex took me aside and warned me to be more careful about what I said to reporters. Sometimes just by the way they framed a question there was no way to answer it without getting in trouble. The old "When did you stop beating your wife?" trick.

AROUND THEN, LISA came to live with me in Port Washington, the little town on Long Island where a lot of the Mets rented or owned homes. It's a nice, quiet spot and an easy drive to Shea.

In retrospect, having her live with me there was probably not the best idea. Maybe we would have fought less if she'd stayed in L.A. Everything with that girl was drama, drama, drama. She loved a good fight. Anything was an excuse for a fight.

I know I would have played better if she wasn't living with me. I denied it for a long time, but looking back, I have to admit that my stormy relationship with Lisa did not help my performance on the field that year. I had a decent year in '84, but I didn't have a great year. And what everyone in the universe expected of me was a great year.

I knew I was supposed to leave all the personal stuff behind when I went to the ballpark. I just didn't know how to do that. We'd get into one of our fights over nothing in the morning, then I had to drive to the park and play. If she came to the game she'd come separately, roll in around the fourth inning, make an entrance in the nice, expensive outfit I'd paid for . . . Let's just say my mind sometimes wasn't clearly on my job like it should have been.

I had a slow start. That by itself wasn't too worrisome. I'd always been a slow starter. I always took a while to find my rhythm and came on stronger as the season went on. But this season the slow start turned into a slump. A slump was not what the fans or the media wanted from Darryl Strawberry. The sportswriters criticized me something fierce. The fans started to boo me every time I struck out or flied out. And then some of my own teammates carped about me to the press behind my back, saying that I wasn't trying hard enough or that I was letting my personal life affect my playing.

I was trying hard. I was just struggling. But this is where being blessed with great natural talent could also be a kind of curse. When you're a natural athlete, you make it look easy. People always said that about me. "He makes it look so easy out there." My "sweet" swing. The way I "loped" like a "gazelle" when I stole a base or ran down a line drive. I made it look like it wasn't work. Everyone praised me for it when I was doing well. "Look at that swing! He makes it look so easy!" But if I struggled, suddenly it flipped around to everyone complaining. "Look at him! He's not even trying."

I took all the criticism to heart. Later I'd be better at shielding myself from the critics and shrugging it off when fans booed, but I was twenty-two years old, and I'd always been someone who felt his emotions intensely. With everybody telling me that I was letting the team and the fans down, my feelings got intensely hurt. Midway into that season I was dragging myself reluctantly to the park. I didn't feel like taking the abuse again. I tried to rally and punch my way through, but it just made things worse. My concentration was shot, and baseball is all about intense focus and concentration. If you're preoccupied in the outfield, you're not going to make the plays. If you're tentative and self-conscious at the plate, the pitcher's going to see it and eat you for lunch.

THERE WAS ANOTHER factor affecting both my mood and my play, although I would never admit it back then: alcohol. At twenty-two, I had already learned that drinking was one way to cope with my problems. I just hadn't learned yet that it was one terrible way to do it.

In '84, the Mets were not yet the infamous rolling frat party we became in a couple years, but we were on our way. Lots of guys on the team drank and partied as hard as they played. Drinking, drugs, fights, gambling, groupies—it all broke into the open and made scandalous headlines in the eighties.

The Mets did not say, "Let's go home and get our rest. We got a game to play tomorrow." We were just becoming a family at that point, and part of that process was not just playing together, but hanging together after the game. When we were at home, we'd drink in the bars in Port Washington. On the road, we hit the local hot spots.

I'd started drinking with some of the boys in my rookie year, trying to fit in and be one of the guys. This year I started to drink more heavily. Now I wasn't drinking just to party. I was drinking to try to feel happy about myself for a few hours, drinking to forget my frustrations at home and in the ballpark. Anybody who's been there can tell you that's a different kind of drinking, and more dangerous. But I didn't know that yet.

And anyway, most of the other guys were doing it, too. We'd play a game, go out drinking, get up the next day, and play another game. Most days it wasn't too hard to bounce back. We were young athletes in peak condition. Getting out of bed and playing through a hangover was a piece of cake in those days.

Oh, who am I kidding? We also had help, in the form of amphetamines. We called them beans, greens, or greenies. And they were as routine a part of our equipment as bats and balls.

Are you shocked? No, you're probably not. Not anymore. Back in 1984 though, I think most baseball fans would have been. The big cocaine scandal, in which Mex would be caught up along with many others, was still just over the horizon. Pete Rose's gambling-related troubles were a few years off. The steroids investigations were twenty years in the future. Baseball fans were still enjoying the twilight of innocence in 1984.

Greenies were already well-established in all the clubhouses of the league by the time I reached the majors. We kept candy jars full of them in our lockers. Not right out in the open where the coaches and reporters could see them, but close at hand. Not that it was a secret, at least not with the coaches or trainers. The reporters didn't know yet, or the team doctors. But everybody else did.

I think the trainers knew what we were doing, and it worried them. It was their job to help us keep fit and deal with injuries and such. But it was not their job to police our behavior. We were adults. Young, stupid adults, but adults. Trainers couldn't make us stop.

We players passed the greenies around among ourselves. It wasn't like we had drug dealers hanging out in the clubhouses selling them to us. (Although it would get to that stage, with coke dealers.) We tried to keep it on the down-low. You'd be on the road, pull into town, and ask a friend on the home team, "Who's got the greenies? Can you ask him to send me a few over?"

Whenever you came to the park dragging a bit, a little hungover, you reached into your jar. Pop a couple with your coffee, and you were ready to go.

"Bring it on! Nothing's gonna stop me today. I could run through a wall right now. Wanna see?"

At first, anyway, I played better when I took them. I'd pop a few beans, stand up at the plate, and when the pitcher fired that ball it looked huge. It looked like a beach ball sailing at me in slow motion. No way I could miss.

Later on it would become more of a problem. By '86, '87, or so I was a greenie freak, eating them like mints. With speed, you hit a tolerance level where you can't feel the buzz anymore, so you keep increasing your level. Pretty soon you're eating them by the handful just to keep going. It would keep me up at night after the game, pacing around my hotel room till the early morning hours with the TV jabbering. Then it's time to go play ball. Your nerves are jangling like electrical wires, your brain is buzzing in your head, your eyes vibrating in your sockets. You feel fragile, like you're made out of glass. You're awake, but you couldn't say you're alert. You're more like one of the walking dead.

Not a good condition for playing major league ball. It makes you nasty and irritable, too. Slightest little thing can set you off on a tirade. As I and several Mets demonstrated in public from '86 on. Between the speed, the coke, and the hangovers, we could be one ugly bunch.

As long as I'm at it, I might as well tell you a lot of guys in major league baseball were cigarette smokers back then, too. I still am. You have to remember that back then the world hadn't yet become so anti-smoking. It had started, but it wasn't as universal and puritanical as it is now. So a lot of us were smokers. We'd come in off the field, slip into the tunnel where the fans and TV cameras couldn't see us, and sneak one.

Oh yeah, we were the boys of summer. The drunk, speed-freak, sneaking-a-smoke boys of summer. More like the juvenile delinquents of summer.

ONE AFTERNOON IN '84 I was so hungover that I got to the park late and missed batting practice. Davey blew up and fined me. He didn't mind us blowing off steam after a game. But he expected us to recover and be able to play the next day.

Davey pulled me into his office and suggested maybe I needed a little time off to collect myself. He took me out of the lineup for a few days of forced rest. That was a humbling comeuppance. When I returned to the lineup my hitting improved a bit.

Something else that didn't hurt was when I made the National League All-Star team as the starting right fielder. My second year in the majors. Not too shabby for a guy everyone said was underachieving and in a slump.

Ever since I was in high school, the press had built me up to be a superhuman, a freak of nature. The black Ted Williams, the next Willie Mays, the new Reggie Jackson. Never mind not being allowed to have a slump. Just playing very well was never enough for them. I was supposed to amaze and stupefy every time I went to the plate.

Even when I hit more home runs, batted in more runs, stole more bases than everyone else, it wasn't enough. Somehow I was never living up to their expectations. Worse, it really rankled them that I wasn't trying to live up to their expectations. I had my own goals. I wanted to be the best ballplayer I could be and do my part to help my team dominate. It had nothing to do with what they expected of me. That was their business. They put that burden on me when I was still a kid. I didn't ask for it and I didn't want it. I just wanted to do my best. That's all that's asked of most athletes. But there are always a few, like me and Doc Gooden in our day, who are expected to do more. We couldn't just do our best. We couldn't just be great. We were supposed to be the greatest of the greatest, breaking all the records, making baseball history.

There are some athletes who thrive on that challenge. They want to be the greatest of the greatest. They're hungry for the fame, the records, the history books. It's their ambition, it's what drives them to excel. That's fine. But that wasn't me. I didn't have a lot of interest in making baseball history. Heck, I really didn't even know a lot of base-ball history, not when I was young anyway. When they compared me to Ted Williams and Willie Mays, I only had vague ideas about who those guys were. What I knew was that I loved playing baseball and loved playing it well.

Eventually I reached a point when I just said screw the media. I am what I am. Now they look back over my career and realize how good I was. I used to bring a buzz to the ballpark. I'd step up to the plate and the entire stadium, tens of thousands of people, were rooted to their seats. Nobody moved. It didn't matter if it was a home game or on the road, nobody got up and headed for the bathroom when Straw was on deck. Nobody wanted to miss me at the plate. They might be chanting, *"Dar-ryl, Dar-ryl, Dar-ryl."* Or they might be screaming, "You suck!" But they did not move. All eyes were glued on me. When I came to the plate, it was an event no one wanted to miss, whether I struck out or put the ball in orbit. Whatever it was, they wanted to be there to see it, that little moment of history, Strawberry at the plate.

You only have a few players, maybe an A-Rod today, who bring that kind of excitement to the game. Still, there's no question the media and the fans wanted me to smash a giant homer every single time. They got spoiled.

As the '84 season went into its final weeks, the whole team was feeling stress and frustration. We were playing much better than in '83, but we couldn't quite hold on to the top of the division. We could see the pennant, but we stumbled on our way to it. There was tremendous pressure in the press for me and Doc to lift the team all the way.

Late in the season, Mex got bit by the same media who'd sandbagged me in the spring. A newspaper article appeared quoting him saying, "Darryl quit on us." He came straight to me in the clubhouse and explained that what he'd said was that I'd quit on myself—which I couldn't deny—and that the team needed me to snap out of it and do my part.

I really respected Keith for coming straight to me. And I took his meaning to heart. I finished the season a whole lot stronger than I'd started out, leading the team with 26 home runs and 97 RBIs.

I wished I could have led the team all the way to the World Series, but we weren't quite ready for that yet. We had a good season. We went from last place to second that year. Under Davey, we would never finish lower than second place. But second isn't good enough. We had our sights set on the pennant and the World Series.

TOO BAD THINGS weren't going better at home with Lisa. As '84 wore on I began to feel trapped and panicky. The whole thing felt like it was out of my control.

Looking back, it's easy to see that I wasn't really ready to commit and settle down, even though that's what I thought I wanted. My timing was way off. When it came to girls, I was really only just coming out of my shell. The shy kid who'd never been real interested in girls, who'd always been focused on baseball, who'd seen girls and relationships as a hindrance to his career, was finally getting more of a taste for it. There were girls in every town who wanted to party with Darryl Strawberry, and I liked it. I mean, I was twenty-two. I had plenty of wild oats in me to sow. I didn't even have to chase girls the way most twenty-two-year-old guys do. They chased me. Can you blame me?

Yes, there was Lisa at home. I was in love with Lisa. I thought I was committed to the relationship. But when the team was on the road, and Lisa was back home, and beautiful girls threw themselves at me . . . Okay, I was weak. I gave in to temptation. Sue me.

So yes, by the end of the '84 season I was having some serious doubts. And that was when Lisa got pregnant.

Of course I wondered if she did it on purpose to lock me into marriage, but it was too late now. There was no way of turning back the clock after that. The current was carrying us right over the falls. I did not believe in abortion. We had created this baby, and we were going to have it and raise it. Even if we did fight the whole time.

We announced that we'd be married in January 1985, while she was still pregnant. Maybe to compensate for my misgivings, I wanted to do it in grand style. We invited four hundred, maybe five hundred guests. The ceremony would be at Lisa's church in Pasadena, but there'd be a big rehearsal dinner at Trader Vic's, and for the reception we booked a place in Beverly Hills. A gala blowout.

Pretty much all my friends and my teammates were like, "Straw, you sure you want to go through with this? You two are like nitro and glycerin. And you're awful young. You still got a lot of life to live. You sure you want to settle down?"

Mom was really down on it, too, for different reasons. She didn't think Lisa was right for me. She didn't think she was trustworthy enough to be my wife and have a family. My brothers and sisters didn't think too highly of her, either. They thought she was too controlling and had manipulated me into the marriage.

"The writing's on the wall, Straw," Mike said. "Don't do this. I'm not saying she's a bad person, but she's not the right one for you."

Mike thought I was too naïve and innocent, and Lisa was experienced and took advantage of me. He didn't even like the way she and I met the first time, at that Lakers game. To him, she was a Lakers groupie. She was there looking to hook up with a Laker, and she met me instead. And then she sank her hooks into me and pushed every button I had.

Yeah, pretty much everybody thought it was a mistake. But what could I do? Lisa was pregnant. Marrying her was the right thing to do. I did not want to be responsible for bringing a kid into the world who didn't have a father around to love and nurture him. Not after the way my dad treated me. I had to step up and be a man and accept my responsibilities. Didn't I?

One sign of how many doubts I had about the marriage is that I asked Duane, rather than my best friend, E.D., to be my best man. I'd met Lisa through Duane. I figured if the marriage didn't work out, it should be on him, not Eric!

As the fateful day approached, my feet weren't just cold, they were like ice.

"I can't believe I'm going through with this," I told Duane. "This is crazy. What was I thinking? We fight all the time. I want to get out of this."

"What?" he said. "You can't pull out, man. She's gonna be the mother of your kid. The invitations went out. You got to go through with it now."

Thanks, Duane.

On the day of the wedding, I climbed into a limousine with Duane and my mom. Driving out the freeway to the church in Pasadena, I felt like a man on his way to the electric chair. I know a lot of young people get that feeling on their way to the altar, but few ever had better reason than I did. I suddenly told the driver to get off the freeway and just drive around for a while.

"What are you doing?" Duane cried. "We're already gonna be late."

I couldn't help it. I knew I was just prolonging the inevitable, but I wanted a few last minutes of not being married.

Mike remembers waiting for us at the church, with the crowd getting more and more restless. "Where's Darryl? Where's your brother? What's going on?"

We got to the church an hour late. Lisa was furious, naturally. This marriage was not off to a good start.

Little Darryl Jr. was born in June. That was a pure joy. I had a son! I already had a lot of plans for him. He was going to come to the ballpark with me as soon as he was old enough. I dreamed of the first day we'd play catch. I was going to provide him with all the love, all the opportunities, all the happiness a boy could have. For his sake, I was going to make my relationship with Lisa work. My son was not going to grow up with parents who always fought or without a father in his life.

I'm sad to say that didn't all work out the way I planned. I always loved DJ, but I wasn't always there for him when he was growing up, and I have nobody to blame for that but myself.

7

AT SPRING TRAINING in 1986, when Davey Johnson first met with us, he said, "We're not just going to win this year, we're going to dominate."

We looked around at one another and said, "Well, okay!" We agreed with him 110 percent.

We had done well in '84, and in '85 we had a great season. We came within a couple of games of beating the Cardinals to take the Eastern Division. We thought we were a better ball club, but we hadn't quite put all the pieces together yet. We were still a young club—me, Doc, Ron Darling, a bunch of us were youngsters—and we showed a ton of potential, but we weren't quite there yet. Still, everyone knew we were on the verge. Our last game of the '85 season at Shea, the fans wouldn't let us go home. They stood up and cheered and applauded like they would never stop. We hadn't made it all the way yet, but we gave them a great, exciting season, and they loved us. We all came out of the dugout and stood there with the whole stadium clapping and cheering for us, and I wasn't the only guy on the team with a lump in his throat. We kept tipping our caps to the fans, and they kept cheering. Then Wally Backman took his cap off and sailed it into the stands, and the crowd roared even louder. And then Mex did it, and then we all did it, tossing our caps to the fans.

It was a genuine lovefest. Moments like that were huge for me. I felt I belonged to a giant extended family.

When we came back in the spring of 1986, we knew this was our year. We could taste it. A lot of stories have been told about what beasts the '86 Mets were. A lot of them are true. We weren't just bad asses, we were the baddest asses in baseball. We didn't just play to win. We played to dominate, crush, conquer, and humiliate every other team in the league.

And we did. In April we went to St. Louis for a four-game series with the Cards, who'd beaten us to the top of the East the year before. We swept the series. Humiliated them in their own ballpark. All our fans—and all our opposing teams, and all their fans—knew it was all over right there, at the beginning of the season. It was just that obvious that this was our year.

We won 108 games. No team would beat that record until the 1998 Yankees—and I would be on that team, too. We finished the season leading the East by an awesome 21½ games. We truly came together as a team that year—the only year we ever would, really—and were solid all around, in batting (we led the league in runs scored), pitching (the lowest ERA in the league), and fielding.

We weren't just the winningest team in baseball, we were the cockiest and most obnoxious, too. It didn't take long for us to make ourselves hated throughout the league, by every team. When we were on the road, we played in stadiums filled to the top with fans booing and heckling us. When we returned to St. Louis later in the season the fans wore T-shirts that said, "The Mets Are Pond Scum." We just shrugged. Yeah, we're the pond scum that's whupping your team's asses.

Everyone said we thought we were hot stuff—and we did. We knew we were hot stuff. They thought we had too much swagger. Well, you know, when you're winning like we were, you get to swagger.

We liked that everyone hated us. We had a huge chip on our shoulder. We were as much like a street gang as a baseball team. We were always ready for a fight. Our bottom line with every team we faced was, "Don't come to the ballpark with no attitude, 'cause we gonna throw down." And we did. We got in a lot of scuffles on the field that season. A bunch of pileups. If you hit one of us with a pitch or throw a cleat into one of us sliding into a base, we're all coming to get you. We cleared that dugout. It was one of our favorite things to do. We were a scrappy bunch. Scrappy-do. And, like everything else, when there was a rumble, we threw ourselves into it. We didn't have those kinds of chest-pounding, shouting, wrestle-around-a-little scuffles most baseball teams have on the field. We fought. It was gang warfare out there.

Our fiercest dog when it came to a fight was Kevin Mitchell—Mitch. Mitch was a thug. There's no other way to put it. He grew up in the ghetto of San Diego, where real gang warfare was an everyday thing on the streets. Mitch was shot in the back when he was a teenager, and a stepbrother was shot and killed in a gang throw-down. When he came into baseball, he was still basically a gangbanger in uniform. Where he came from, when a fight went down it was literally kill or be killed, and he brought that conditioning with him into baseball. Mitch didn't have a medium setting on his dial. When a scuffle broke out he went straight to the kill setting. He was like a human pit bull—even when he was at rest there was always the chance that something might flip his switch to that kill setting, and then he'd come at you with everything he had and anything he could put his hands on and beat you and choke you until a bunch of other guys pulled him off you.

Even those of us on the same team with him were kind of terrified of Mitch. I got into a scrap with him once in the minor leagues, when a bunch of us were shooting hoops and talking trash at each other the way guys do. He exploded into a completely berserk rage at something I said, knocked me down with fists that were like sledgehammers, then went off to grab a bat to finish the job. Me and the rest of the guys didn't wait around for him to come back. There was absolutely no doubt that he would have killed at least one of us. He toned down his act eventually and we got to be pals, but still, you were always on your guard around him.

Mitch nearly killed a few people in our scuffles with other teams. That's no exaggeration. A scuffle would break out, both benches would clear, and guys would be wrestling and throwing punches all over the infield. I'd look around and see Mitch had gotten some player from the other team in a vicious choke hold, squeezing the life out of the guy. I mean, the guy's face would be blue and his eyes and tongue bulging out. Several of us would run over and wrestle Mitch off the guy before he really did murder him right there in front of tens of thousands of witnesses.

That's how Mitch fought. That's how he played baseball, too. Every game was a gang war, us against them.

Mitch was just an extreme example of the whole team's attitude that year. It wasn't simply the Mets versus some other team out there. It was Crips versus Bloods, or Hell's Angels versus Satan's Sinners, or any other gang war you can think of. Us versus All Y'all. We weren't just going to beat you, we might also beat you up. It intimidated the other teams. They understood around the league that the Mets didn't play. Our number one goal was to kick ass.

One of our fights that year started with my boy E.D. We were playing the Reds in Cincinnati. It was the tenth inning of a really tough game, and Pete Rose put E.D. on first as a pinch runner. My boy stole second. Then he stole third. As he did, he put his elbows into our third baseman, Ray Knight.

Ray reacted the way an '86 Met usually did—he socked E.D. right on the jaw. That was it. Both benches cleared and it was an all-out donnybrook. Ray, E.D., and, of course, Mitch all got tossed from the game. We won in the fourteenth inning.

Our fans at Shea loved the way we humiliated other teams. It was payback time for a lot of years of being the laughingstock of the league. They got as much into taunting the other teams as we did. Like the infamous curtain call. Every time a Met hit a home run, the entire crowd was on its feet for a standing ovation. You'd trot around the bases real slow, thank you thank you, really hotdogging it, while the other team just stood there fuming and grinding their teeth. When you reached the dugout, the crowd stayed on its feet, still cheering, calling you back out. So you'd jump up the steps and take a curtain call. Thank you, thank you. The other teams hated it.

I'd take forever on my trots. I'd walk around the diamond. I loved yanking that crowd up on their feet. Pitchers hated me for it.

The downside of having fans who were just as bad as we were was that when they turned on you they could be vicious. New York fans are passionate, they're knowledgeable, and they will cut you no slack if they think you're underperforming. When you're producing no fans cheer you louder, but when you're struggling they boo and heckle you mercilessly.

When I went into a slump, struggling with my swing, not producing the way everyone expected me to, they booed me something fierce. My first couple of years in the majors I let them get to my mind. But by '86 I had learned how to turn it around. My attitude was, "Oh, you're gonna boo me? Okay, I'm gonna hit two home runs today."

Go up to bat, they're booing—*pow*. Hit my first one off the scoreboard. The place erupts. Now they're all up on their feet cheering. I go around the bases all nonchalant, like I don't even hear them. Get back to the dugout, and instead of coming out for the curtain call, I go down the tunnel for a smoke. You were booing me a minute ago, now you want me to come out? Nuh-uh.

Next time I go up to bat, they're like statues all around the park. They have to pee, they hold it. Everyone staring. You could hear a kernel of popcorn drop. *Boom*, I slam another out over the left field wall. The joint goes nuts. Thirty thousand fans fly up like they're all in ejector seats from a James Bond movie. The roar is deafening. You ever hear thirty thousand people screaming at the top of their lungs and banging their hands together and stomping their feet all at the same time? You might have if you were there in '86. It's an insane racket.

But I'm still playing it cool, walking the bases, la-di-da. Back to the dugout. They will not stop cheering. This game is not going to proceed until I give them what they want. I make them wait for it. Y'all want to play head games with me? Fine. Now I'll play with all of you. I'm not giving you nothing. You punished me. Now you must be punished. Eventually I'd give in, and they'd roar.

I wasn't the only Met the fans rode hard that season. Take poor Doug Sisk, the middle reliever. Doug was actually a good pitcher, but by '86 he was plagued with elbow troubles and had a lot of control problems. He threw a ton of balls and could load up the bases with walks. His best pitch was a sinker that wasn't that hard to hit, it was just nearly impossible to get up off the ground. So batters hit a lot of dribblers off him. The problem was, he'd already loaded up the bases, so even a dribbler could produce a run. Either that or a double play. You never knew.

It made the fans nuts. They came to dread it whenever Davey sent him in. When his name was announced over the PA, the whole crowd would give out this huge groan. "Oh no, not Dougie!" They heckled him all the way from the bullpen to the mound. Then his first pitch would be a ball and they were screaming at him. "Sisk, you stink!" "Sisk, you suck!"

It got to him. He got to where he dreaded hearing his name on the PA as much as they did. He threw up before games he was so worried that Davey might actually put him in. It was awful. Doug was a nice guy and a fun guy, one of the Scum Bunch. He was struggling, and the fans had no mercy for him at all.

Doug let them crawl all the way into his head and it destroyed him. If you let them inside your head, you're done. Your focus is gone, your concentration is shot, you're standing out there all nervous and self-conscious like you're back in elementary school standing in front of your classmates to give a presentation. You have to learn how to turn it back on them and use it. It takes mental strength. From growing up under my father, I had lots of practice ignoring abuse.

. . .

WHEN YOU PLAY professional sports you're under enormous pressure to perform, to excel. You've got owners, the media, and millions of fans to please. And they don't let you forget for a second what's expected of you.

When the game's over, you need some way to wind down and release the tension. Our way to wind down was going out drinking, drugging, gambling, and fornicating. We were bad enough before, but '86 was the season our lifestyle got way out of hand. We weren't hitting all those bars and clubs at home and on the road because we liked the decor. We loved hanging out and getting hammered. We loved having all the girls coming over to us and coming on to us. Most of us took full advantage.

Most of us also had wives or girlfriends sitting at home. Their job as baseball wives was the same as that of rockers' and rap stars' wives. Turn a blind eye and make believe it wasn't happening. I'm not saying that's right or proper. It's just the way it was.

Beer was the foundation of our alcoholic lifestyle. We drank beer in the clubhouse, on the plane, in the bus, when being interviewed by newspaper reporters . . . and pretty much all the rest of the time. The average fan back then would have been amazed how much beer guzzling their team did. It's not like that anymore, but in our day we hauled around more Bud than the Clydesdales. The beer was just to get the party started and maybe take the edge off the speed and coke. We also drank more and more hard liquor. We'd go into a bar and everyone there wanted to buy us shots. Okay, we did shots. And beer. And rum. And beer. And martinis. And beer. And tequila. And beer.

When we were playing at Shea, we didn't confine our drinking to the bars of Port Washington anymore, where we used to have a few rounds with the townies, then stumble to our nearby homes and beds. By '86 we were venturing much more often into "the city," Manhattan, where the partying ramped up to a whole new level. We were the kings of New York, the princes of the city, and treated like royalty at any bar or nightclub we chose to grace with our presence that night. The drinks were on the house and the hotties were hot to trot. We'd go to parties in fancy Manhattan lofts where there were mountains of cocaine on silver platters next to the hors d'oeuvres. Those of us who had wives and girlfriends in town restrained ourselves somewhat. Those who did not took up the slack.

On the road, away from the wives and girlfriends, we cut completely loose. When we came to your town, our goal was not only to whup and humiliate your ball team, but to tear up your best bars and nightclubs and take your finest women. We actually had a kind of team cheer about it. When the bus or plane was pulling in, we'd shout it out:

"What are we gonna do?"

"We're going to drink all their alcohol, screw all their women, and kick their asses on the field!"

We were hammered, we were hardcore, and we were about as far as human males could get from being clean-cut, all-American heroes. We made a lot of headlines and a lot of enemies, but we won an awful lot of ballgames. We thought all the wild behavior was our just tribute for being the best team in baseball. We blew through those towns like a rolling frat party. We rolled in a pack, like wolves. Always eight, nine, ten, fifteen of us walking into your best restaurant, then hitting the best club your town had to offer and partying down.

Our reputation preceded us in every town on the road. "Look out, the Mets are coming to town!" They braced for us like a hurricane. But for a lot of people, we were also an excuse to go wild. For them, when the Mets came to your town it was like Mardi Gras. The clubs would be packed, waiting for us to roll in. Guys wanted to get next to us and buy us drinks or take us into the men's room and lay out a few rails of coke. And there were a lot of beautiful women all across America who'd do pretty much anything to get with a professional athlete, even if it was just for a night. The only hard part for us was choosing which hottie to take back to your hotel room. Lots of times you made it easy on yourself and picked two or three. I don't want to call them groupies, because that's a nasty term. But that's pretty much how we treated them, like rock stars with their groupies. Some of them you never saw again. Some became more like regular features on the road. You come back to her town again later in the season, she's there at the park or in your hotel lobby. Some girls even followed us around to different towns. Why not? We were a traveling party. The drinks were free, the drugs were free, and they were having sex with young athletes in prime condition. It sure was a lot more fun than their normal lives.

Sometimes we didn't even wait for the game to be over before we got the party started. To protect the guilty, I won't say his name, but I remember one time we were playing at the old San Diego stadium and one of my teammates spotted this girl in the stands. They made eye contact and they both knew what they wanted. At some point in the game he disappeared from the dugout between innings. The girl met him in the clubhouse and they had a quickie. He came strolling back to the dugout with a happy, silly grin and cracked us all up.

Another time, in Chicago, this woman was sitting in the lowest stands. A pitcher, whom I also won't name, wasn't playing that game, so he figured what the heck. He took her into a little private room and had oral sex with her.

When he came back out, I asked, "Where you been?"

"Oh, just getting me a little head." He grinned.

"Dag!" I was jealous. When I saw her heading back to her seat, I gave her a sign. She smiled, turned right back around, and met me in that same little room. Only difference is I was playing in that game, so I had to be quick and run back out on the field.

Yeah, we got offered a lot of tail, and we did not hesitate to accept. The girls started coming around in spring training and kept coming around all season. In fact, at the end of spring training one year, the whole team was on the bus, getting ready to drive to the airport and fly to New York. They all looked around and said, "Where's Straw?" They're shouting, "Straw, come on, man! Where are you? We got to go!"

I was in the clubhouse, having one last quickie with this cute little Florida girl. Charlie Samuels, the equipment manager, came in and caught us. He just stood there shaking his head while I finished up.

You have to remember that professional baseball is a sport, but it is also a wing of the entertainment industry. We really were like movie stars, rock stars, rap stars. Everywhere we went people wanted to party with us and get next to us. Everything was free and open. Life was like one long buffet table laid out with vices and temptations. We were young, healthy, on top of the world and very full of ourselves. Resisting temptation and vice was the last thing on our minds. We dove in headfirst.

I know I did, and it was definitely messing me up. Basically I'd been drinking too much since I came up to the Mets in '83. I was a superstar, but I was also a baby. I'd been drinking beer and smoking pot since adolescence, but I was still just a kid thrown in among all these raging egos and wild hairs and alcoholics and drug addicts and sex addicts. I got caught up in it to fit in and act like a man around them. I wanted to be one of the gang. By '86, I liked it. I liked it a lot. I liked the drinking, and I definitely liked the women.

I worked my way into the Scum Bunch for the same reason. The Scum Bunch had started out a few years before. It was mostly pitchers who hung together and for whatever reason became like the class clowns of the team. Jesse Orosco and Doug Sisk were early members, and Doc Gooden and I jumped in. Every road trip we sat in the back of the plane or the bus and just got completely hammered. Davey called it the Ghetto. We played cards, played our music loud, stank the joint up with our cigarettes and cigars (yes, kids, you could still smoke on airplanes back then), talked a lot of trash about the rest of the guys, had food fights, the whole shebang. Even some of the other guys on our own team hated the Scum Bunch, because we'd pick on them, crack a lot of jokes about them, and we got pretty harsh sometimes.

I was one of the worst offenders that way. I was a mean drunk. I can see it now. I was one of those Jekyll and Hyde drunks. You know the type. Normally I was laid-back, quiet, polite. But when I got some beers in me I got nasty and obnoxious, and my Mr. Hyde popped out. All my anger, my frustrations with my personal life and marriage, my constant feelings of self-doubt—all the stuff I thought I was drinking to repress, it would just come out. I'd pick on other guys on the team, like if a guy was in a slump I'd ride him about it. We all talked a lot of trash at each other, the way young guys do when they're cutting loose, but I went too far. I hurt some guys' feelings and pissed them off. I know a few of them thought I was a real jerk sometimes. I probably would have thought the same if the situation was reversed.

But we all joked around and pulled pranks on one another, and we didn't let it escalate into truly bad blood among us. At least not in '86. We were too big as a team for that. We had goals and we were working together to make them happen. We didn't let a hurt feeling lie there and become a cancer to the clubhouse. We blew off steam at one another and bickered sometimes the way any family does, but like a family we patched it up and moved on.

By '86 my consumption of speed was really out of hand, too. I'm sure that had something to do with my motormouth and nastiness. I was a stone speed freak. Drinking helped put some temporary insulation back on my speed-frayed nerves and slow down my buzzing brain. A drunk speed freak is bad news. He'll say a whole lot of things he wouldn't say otherwise.

A lot of us really needed the help by that year, because we were totally exhausting ourselves with our extracurricular activities. We wouldn't have been able to stand up without a handful of speed. I remember one day I was driving to Shea on the Long Island Expressway for a day game. There was a lot of traffic. My lane was barely crawling, and the one next to it was like a bumper-to-bumper parking lot. So I'm inching along, and I see a driver in that stalled lane slumped over with his head against his window, fast asleep. It was Mitch. Asleep behind the wheel, on his way to a game. He must have had a long night. But we all had a lot of them.

People ask me all the time how our use of drugs back then compares to the way players use steroids today. I always say there is no comparison. Players use steroids to improve their physiques and get stronger and bigger. We never got stronger and bigger. We just got wired.

There is one similarity, though, between the speed and the steroids. I know that probably nine out of ten players were taking greenies when I was playing, and I bet nine out of ten have been taking steroids in recent years. Once one guy is doing it, everyone else does it, because none of them wants the other guy to have an advantage. If they thought amphetamines would give another guy an edge, they popped greenies, too. If they think steroids are going to make the other guy bigger and more powerful, they'll take the shots, too. Trust me, that's how athletes are.

All you have to do is see how much bigger and bulkier players are today to know they're on something. That's not all from pumping iron and eating their carbs. I pumped a lot of iron and ate mountains of potatoes and I never looked like some of these guys do today, like Hulk Hogan or Steve Austin squeezed into a baseball uniform. Back in my day, baseball players were not even supposed to be so pumped up. Baseball was supposed to be about speed and agility, not brute force. It was like kung fu that way.

And you can see it in how these guys get hurt today. Injuries went up something like one-third in the 1990s. Players got too bulked up, too stiff to move right. Their joints and ligaments can't support all that added muscle weight. They get these nagging injuries that just won't go away.

In the end, it doesn't matter if it's speed or steroids. You're putting something into your system that isn't supposed to be there. It's going to have an effect on your mind and body. You may start out thinking that's a positive effect, but eventually it's going to take its toll. Even if you're a celebrity and never have to pay for your drinks or drugs, someday you will have to pay the piper, just like anybody else.

Mr. Cashen and the suits in the front office were not pleased with all our cockiness and showboating and drinking and fighting. We created a new public relations mess for them pretty much on a daily basis that season. Mr. Cashen would have liked it much better if we were a team of polite, clean-cut, milk-drinking, all-American athletes. Instead he got Animal House. And Davey was still no help. Davey loved our killer instincts, our unstoppable pride and wild reputation. Davey had been pretty wild himself as a player, and he still had a few wild hairs sticking out of his neck. He was a drinking man. As long as we kept winning the way we did, he wasn't about to act like our nanny or etiquette coach.

MY DAD CALLED me a few times out of the blue that season. We had barely spoken since he left our home back in Crenshaw. I wasn't too impressed when he popped up now that I was on a team heading for greatness. I still had a lot of pain and resentment.

Our conversations were short and really awkward.

"I've been watching you guys," he'd say. "You're my team. I hope you guys win."

I didn't say much back. I just listened to his voice and thought, "Yeah? Where were you when I needed you?"

It was Mom who was there for me, just as she always had been. Solid as a rock. She never cared that I was rich and famous. Just as she had never pushed me before, now she didn't get all caught up in the hoopla. She just loved me like she loved all her children. If we were happy and doing well, she was happy. When we struggled, she was still there for us. She never let me get a big head about what I was doing. She just wanted me to enjoy my life.

You know, I see these young celebrities today, a Britney Spears or a Lindsay Lohan or whoever is being gossiped about the most the day you're reading this, and my heart goes out to them. It really does. I have total compassion for them. Because you know their out-of-control behavior stems from having parents who pushed them into the spotlight, drove them to become famous, because they want to live through them. Always wanting to be seen with them, have all those paparazzi snap their pictures with their famous daughters. You know that's a big part of what these girls are rebelling against when they start to go wild and jeopardize it all. If their parents stayed out of the picture and let them find their own way in the world, they might still make mistakes and bad decisions, because that's what young people do. It's part of growing up and figuring out the world. But I don't think they would be driven to act so out of control. I think it's actually their way of trying to get control over their own lives and talents and fate. Britney shaves her head and everybody says she's gone crazy. But maybe it was her way of saying, "I'm me. This is my body, my image, my hair. You don't own it, I do. Here, I'll show you."

It comes out all wrong and kooky because they don't know who they are. They never had the chance to find out. There's always been someone else, starting with their parents, telling them who to be and how to act. It's only gotten crazier and crazier since my time. We lived in a spotlight, but it wasn't the insanely intense glare young celebrities live in now. There weren't fifty gossip channels on TV and a million gossip blogs on the Internet dogging our every move. There weren't a hundred rabid paparazzi sneaking into our back yards and surrounding us like sharks in a feeding frenzy every second of our public lives. Believe me, the pressure was bad enough in my day. I can't even imagine what it's like for these young people today.

So of course they stumble and struggle and make stupid decisions. They're looking and looking for who they are. Is it in my hair, is it my clothes, is it the boob job? They're looking in all the wrong areas. It's really inside of them. They just need to realize, "I'm okay. I'm okay with who I am. I'm a normal person. I just need to act like one."

They don't have to be what everybody else wants them to be. They just have to learn to make their own choices. I always tell young people, "The choices you make, the good ones and the bad, have consequences behind them. That's the reality. Your life is not a reality show. Your reality is your life. Every stupid decision you make, there's a consequence behind it in the real world."

The really sick thing is the way the media not only expect these young people to screw up and do something stupid or scandalous, they push them into it. They're only really interested in them when they screw up. They don't care about whatever talent these young people have that helped them become rich and famous in the first place. It's all about rejoicing when they fall. That's when they really hammer them. I know.

I thank God my mom didn't have any expectations. She loved me as her son and that was that. My mom never ever tried to live her life through me. She wasn't always talking to the press about my son this and my son that. She didn't throw our relationship out into the world the way a lot of these young celebrities' parents do.

WHILE THE METS soared, my relationship with Lisa sank to new lows. Looking back, I don't know how it couldn't have. My drinking, drugging, and womanizing were out of control. I spent a lot more time with the Scum Bunch than I did with my family. I was far from an ideal husband or father.

I was cheating on her. But at the time I felt like I had the right because I was the one bringing the bread and butter home. I'm paying for our grand lifestyle, and that gives me the right to do whatever I want. I was making millions, and she didn't have a problem spending it, so I figured she had no right to complain or act out if I was sleeping with a few groupies on the road.

Lisa did not see it that way. She was bitter, jealous, and possessive. It felt like every time I walked in the door she was smelling the liquor on my breath, looking for the lipstick on my collar, spoiling for a fight. And since I usually had a few drinks in me, we did fight. Crazy fights. Screaming, yelling, throwing-things-around fights. Nasty, bitter, vindictive, hateful fights.

I kept thinking, "This is insane. I'm not like this. I hate to fight."

Meanwhile, money was an issue. I am the first to admit that I was never, ever good about money, except in the sense that I was good at earning it and good at spending it. I was really good at that. We had fancy cars, I bought us a big, beautiful house in the San Dimas suburbs, in the mountains northeast of downtown L.A. She had all the clothes and jewelry and shoes a young woman could possibly want. Little Darryl Jr. was provided for. No one could ever accuse me of being stingy. We were very high rollers. But I was not good at keeping accounts or balancing the checkbook or any of that. I was a ballplayer from South Central, what did I know about saving and investing and balancing the accounts? I really had no time for or interest in managing the money. I just made it and spent it. Part of what I spent it on was accountants to count it for me. And Lisa did more than her part to help spend it.

So we were both bitter and angry at each other, and we were both jealous and suspicious of each other. A lot of bad feeling built up between us. Every time I came home with a few drinks in me, she flew up in my face. Every time she came home after being out with friends, I blew up. It was crazy.

It all came to a head that October during the National League playoffs, which started in Houston. This was one trip all the wives came along on, since it was the playoffs. In retrospect that was probably a bad idea. We guys were under tremendous pressure. We were full of adrenaline and full of beans. We had crushed our division all season, and we just had to have the pennant and the World Series. It was our destiny, our right. We rolled into Houston with our fangs bared. We were going to devour the Astros in the Astrodome and tear up the town at night. Having the wives around was probably a recipe for trouble. Having my wife around was definitely a recipe for disaster.

Besides, we courted disaster in the ballpark, too. We were so cocky by this point we thought we were going to mop the field with the lowly Astros, but they turned out to be a whole lot tougher than we expected. Game one at the Astrodome was a classic pitchers' duel between Doc Gooden and Mike Scott, the league's strikeout king that year, who pitched an amazing game. He struck us out fourteen times and held us to five hits, and they beat us 1–0. We bounced back and beat them pretty smoothly in game two, winning 5–1.

Game three back in Shea was one for the history books, a titanic battle between two teams out for blood. They jumped on us with a quick four-run lead, and we spent the rest of the game battling back. I smashed a three-run homer, and then Lenny Dykstra shocked everyone, himself included, by tagging the winning homer in the ninth, giving us a really hard-fought 6–5 win.

Then it was Houston's turn to bounce back and beat us 3–1, again behind some incredible pitching by Mike Scott. We got only three hits. Never gracious losers, we were sure he was scuffing the ball. Game five was an epic twelve-inning battle royal that we won 2–1. But it was nothing compared to game six, in the Astrodome—a sixteen-inning cliffhanger, more than four and a half grueling hours of a war of attrition that we finally won, 7–6.

To say that we partied after that game would be the understatement of all time. A lot has been written about our infamous flight back to New York that night on a chartered United Airlines jet. It was like Animal House times ten on that flight. Like Animal House with real animals. We got blind drunk. We snorted cocaine in the restrooms. We groped the flight attendants. We groped our wives. We shouted and howled. We threw our dinners at one another. We broke a lot of things. We threw up. By the time the plane finally landed, we stumbled out into the lights of the news cameras looking less like conquering heroes than like a bunch of yahoos who had all, wives and flight attendants included, been in a serious bar fight.

The front office was not amused. This was really not the image Frank Cashen wanted us to project. United billed the team for the thousands of dollars of damage we caused to the inside of that poor jet. Mr. Cashen passed the bill down to Davey, with instructions that he should collect it from us. Davey's response was typical. When it came down to a dispute between the suits in the office and his guys in uniform, Davey was on our side. Sure, we had ripped that plane up like a pack of wild gorillas, but he thought we had every reason to celebrate. We were on our way to the World Series. We worked long and hard for it. We deserved to toast ourselves, even if we did go way overboard. So he called us all together in the clubhouse, halfheartedly read us the riot act—and then ripped the bill up before our eyes.

Boy, did we love Davey at moments like that. Boy, did management hate him. Like the rest of us, Davey was sowing the seeds of his own eventual destruction.

In the midst of all that struggling and striving and tension and intense emotions, Lisa and I were going through our own struggling and tension and intense emotions. One night after one of the early games in the Astrodome—I think it was game two—I came back to the hotel with a bunch of the guys and we had some drinks in the bar. When I went up to our room, I found she had the chain on the door. My mind instantly leaped to dark suspicions. I pushed the door open quietly. I could hear that she was on the phone. And that she was talking to a guy.

I was drunk, probably on speed, and way keyed up. I flew into a rage.

"Why's the chain on this door?" I yelled, punching it. "Open up!"

Lisa rushed to the door and I burst in.

"Who were you talking to?" I hollered.

Lisa was not one to back down, ever. Her defense was offense.

"Stop shouting! You're drunk!"

"Who were you on the phone with?"

And so on and so on. It wasn't much different from a hundred fights we'd had before, but in all sorts of ways this was the wrong time and place for it. I lost control. We got up in each other's face, shouting, and I exploded. I raised my hand and smacked her across the face. Hard. Lisa was no petite shrinking violet, but I'm a big guy, and I was in my prime, and I was drunk and blind with rage. I broke her nose with the heel of my hand.

We were both shocked. In all our fights I had never hit her. I put my fist through a wall or two, but I did not strike her. After growing up the way I did, I had promised myself I would never treat any wife of mine the way my father did my mom, just as I promised myself I would never use physical punishment on any child of mine.

To this day I have never spanked a child. But I hit Lisa that night hard enough to make blood gush out of her broken nose. In a split-second my rage died and I felt stone sober. Sober and filled with shame.

Not for the last time, I wondered how things had come to this. It was supposed to be a high point of my life. Instead, it felt like my life was unraveling and slipping out of my control.

THE METS ENDED the season in triumph, beating the Red Sox for the World Series. The Sox weren't pushovers, either. They'd torn up the American League the way we'd done the National League. They were hot and came down to Shea fresh and really hungry to win the Series. They whupped us good in the first two games at Shea. But we were the comeback kids all that season. It reminded me a lot of the Crenshaw team. It was almost like we didn't really shine until the odds were against us and we had our backs to the wall and we had to fight and claw our way out. That was the kind of team we were, scrappy-do. It took us seven hard games, but we beat them.

The Mets won the World Series. We'd climbed up from the cellar to the penthouse. It was the culmination of years of planning and hard work. The end of a long dry spell for the fans at Shea. And for me personally, the fulfillment of a dream I'd had since I was a kid in Crenshaw.

It felt great. But it should have felt better. And it would have if all the success on the field wasn't overshadowed by a growing feeling of failure and doom in the rest of my life. Through the deafening cheers of the crowds, I could still hear that voice in my head, that cold and bitter voice:

"You'll never amount to nothin'."

8

SURROUNDED BY REPORTERS in the Mets clubhouse right after we won game seven of the World Series, Davey Johnson summed up our '86 season best. He said, "The bad guys won." I'm sure every other team in the majors, and their millions of fans, agreed. "The bad guys won" became one of those immortal sayings of baseball legend—maybe not as familiar as "It ain't over till it's over," but good enough that when sportswriter Jeff Pearlman devoted a whole book to the '86 Mets, he used it as the title.

We were the bad guys, the Scum Bunch, the juvenile delinquents of summer, and despite our phenomenal talent, our phenomenally bad lifestyles made it pretty "amazin'" that we won. We would never repeat it. After '86, our bad habits started to catch up with us and overshadow our talents.

If you wanted a preview of how things were going to get, you didn't have to look further than the morning after game seven, when we were all supposed to gather at the foot of Manhattan for our victory parade up Broadway, the "Canyon of Heroes," from Wall Street to City Hall. The mayor would give us the key to the city, and we'd make speeches, and a crowd estimated at more than two million would roar. Most of us partied the whole night before, roaming from bar to bar, letting the fans buy us round after round. A lot of us got no sleep at all. We dragged ourselves to the parade still drunk or suffering the start of massive hangovers, unshaven, some of us unwashed and still in the rumpled clothes we partied in all night. As much of a triumph as that parade was, it was also kind of agony for a lot of us. The deafening roar of the crowd thundered in our splitting heads, the morning light was like needles in our eyes, our nerves jangled from speed and coke. We were like life-size figures carved out of glass and ready to shatter.

Doc Gooden and Kevin Mitchell didn't make it there at all. Doc didn't get to sleep until eight A.M. I hadn't gotten much sleep, either, but when my alarm went off I dragged myself up and got dressed. Doc's house was right across the street from mine. I walked over to see if he wanted to ride in with me. It was ten A.M. Doc's house was dark and quiet, with all the curtains pulled tight. This did not look good.

I rang the buzzer. I knocked on the door. When he didn't answer, I leaned on the buzzer and pounded on the door.

"Doc, come on!" I shouted. "Doc, we gotta go!"

He never answered. Years later, he told me that he woke up and peeked through the curtains at me, but he was just too hungover to move.

Fans were really crushed that Doc wasn't there that day. He was our star pitcher and hugely popular, and he didn't show. Frank Cashen was mortified.

But that was us in a nutshell. The 1986 Mets, the Hungover Heroes, missing our own parade.

AFTER THE FESTIVITIES and sleeping off our hangovers, we all went our separate ways as we always did at the end of a season. In the front office, Frank Cashen quietly began making sure that this separation was permanent. Much as he was thrilled with our World

Series victory—a personal vindication for him as much as it was for any of us—he was appalled by our behavior otherwise, tired of all the headaches we caused with our drinking, fighting, and whoring, not to mention the widespread rumors of drug abuse. When Doc and Mitch were too hungover to be at their own victory parade, Mr. Cashen took it hard. It was the final embarrassment. Time to break up the Animal House fraternity. We were bad influences on one another.

The wobbling of his two young superstars, me and Doc, was especially troubling to him. He had invested a ton of time and money and effort in us. We had repaid him by bringing the fans back to Shea in droves. There were a lot of great players on the team, but we were the stars, the celebrities, the box office magic. If we started to fail, Mr. Cashen thought, the whole merry-go-round would grind to a halt.

And so, little by little over the next few years, he traded everyone out, dismantling the team that had so dominated baseball. He started with Mitch, our gangbanger in uniform, who he figured was the main one to lead Doc astray. Then he just went on down the line. By 1990, my last season as a Met, Doc and I were among the very few World Series players left. Even Davey got the ax that year.

I've always understood Mr. Cashen's reasoning, but it didn't work. The Mets had some good years and played respectable ball during my last four seasons with them, but we never excelled again the way we did in '86. When he thought he was getting rid of the troublemakers, he was also trading away the talent that had made us the champs.

You can't put all the blame on Mr. Cashen, obviously. Our wild lifestyle was the other half of the equation. No matter how much raw talent we had, there was only so long we could burn our candles at both ends and the middle. If we had somehow magically all come to our senses when we regrouped for spring training in '87, all agreed right then and there to clean up our act and give up the booze and drugs and parties, become milk-drinking, goody-two-shoes, clean-cut, all-American athletes who went straight home after the game and got a good night's rest and woke up bright-eyed and bushy-tailed the next day ready to win, I have absolutely no doubt we could have continued to dominate major league baseball for several years.

Instead, between Mr. Cashen's trades and our own stupid behavior, it all fell apart.

That was all still over the horizon in the weeks after the victory parade. Lisa and I stayed in New York at first and struggled to Scotch tape our marriage together. We still fought a lot. We fought about my drinking, which was really getting out of hand. Even without the Scum Bunch around as drinking buddies, I had no trouble finding people in New York who were delighted to get drunk with Darryl Strawberry. And when no one was around, I drank by myself. Lisa thought we needed to separate for a while so each of us could think things through. I didn't want us to fail as a family, so we fought about that. We fought about money, which she was going through like water. We even fought about how much we were fighting.

One night in December, it escalated again. I threw a framed photograph. I was drunk. I don't think I meant to hit her with it, but I did.

She flew out to California with DJ to stay with her mother and to get away from me. But I flew out behind her. I wanted to apologize. I wanted her to come back to our home in San Dimas. She refused. I'd get drunk and drive over to her mom's and bang on the door, calling for her, begging for her to come home. What a spectacle. Her mom was humiliated.

On Super Bowl Sunday, I got totally out of hand. Got drunk and drove over to her mom's again. According to Lisa, I got into the house, roughed her up, and took money and credit cards from her purse. I don't remember much, maybe because I was very high, maybe because I repressed it. Whatever I did I regret it. I regret the fact that I ever put my hands on her, because that's not what a man's supposed to do.

Later that month, Lisa filed for a legal separation and got a restraining order against me, barring me from being near her or my son. I was devastated, and of course I drank to console myself.

MEANWHILE, DOC'S LIFE was falling apart, too. Right after the World Series, his fiancée, Carlene, got wind that he'd had a child with another woman earlier that year, and their engagement blew up. Doc went home to Tampa, where, he says in his autobiography, he soon fell into serious cocaine abuse.

One night in December he and a bunch of his pals were driving around Tampa in a caravan, the same way my posse and I drove around L.A. Tampa's mostly white police were having a lot of skirmishes with Tampa's black population at the time. Several of them turned deadly—for the black men involved. The mood was tense and ugly when a cop pulled Doc's car out of the caravan. Doc and the cop got into an argument. When Doc thought the cop was reaching for his gun, he grabbed his hand. Even at the best of times, you don't touch an arresting officer. A swarm of patrol cars arrived, and the white cops proceeded to beat, kick, and choke Doc. They threw him in jail, charged with assaulting a police officer and resisting arrest. In January he pleaded no contest and was given three years' probation.

That same January, Doc flew up to New York, and Carlene went to LaGuardia Airport to meet him. Supposedly she wanted to try for a reconciliation. But as she was going through a metal detector at the terminal, the security people found a loaded .38 derringer in her purse. Turned out it had been reported stolen years earlier. Who knows what she had in mind, but reconciliation might not have been first and foremost.

When we showed up for spring training that February, I saw that Doc's locker was right next to mine.

"Hey look at us," I said. "It's Assault and Battery!"

That March, the press got their hands on the separation papers Lisa filed, and had a field day portraying me as a despicable wife-beating drunk. Now they were literally asking me, "Mr. Strawberry, when did you stop beating your wife?"

But their attention shifted away from me a week before opening day, when Doc tested positive for cocaine. It created a huge, sorry scandal. More even than me, Doc had always been the golden boy of New York baseball, a sweet, innocent kid who just happened to have a fantastic arm. Like they did with me, the fans and press put huge expectations on him, and at first he delivered. In 1984, his rookie year, when he was nineteen, he won seventeen games and was the youngest player ever in the All-Star Game, where he struck out all three batters he faced. In '85 he had the most wins, most strikeouts, and lowest ERA in the league, and was the youngest player ever to get the Cy Young Award. Oh man, New York adored him in '85. There were huge billboards of him in Manhattan, he was on the covers of all the newspapers and magazines, everyone loved him unconditionally.

When he began to struggle in '86, and got knocked around by the Red Sox in the World Series, the fans and the press didn't turn on him the way they did me when I struggled. Even when he couldn't drag himself out of bed for the victory parade, people bought the official line that he was overcome with fatigue.

The fans didn't know what I did that season. Trying to keep up with his hard-partying older teammates was beginning to affect Doc's game. Doc was still just a kid, just twenty-one, and until coming to the Mets he had never sowed one wild oat. He grew up in Florida a good, quiet boy, focused entirely on baseball. He never drank or went wild or pulled any of the knucklehead stunts teenagers do. Then at nineteen he found himself in the major leagues, in the midst of the baddest bunch of rowdies in sports. Like me, he drank and drugged to be one of the boys. Like me, he didn't handle it too well. By '86, the lifestyle was eroding his play.

But the fans knew none of that until a week before opening day, when he confessed to being a drug addict. The news sent a huge shock wave through the public.

To get out of being suspended from baseball, Doc voluntarily signed up for a month of detox and rehab at the Smithers Institute in Manhattan. I guess that should have been a wake-up call for me and all of us, but we didn't hear it. It was easy for me to ignore the signs of my own growing substance abuse because I was at the peak of my career. I hit a three-run homer that opening day. I hit 39 home runs and stole 36 bases that season. On opening day in Montreal in '88 I hit two stratospheric homers, a couple of the longest home runs anyone had ever seen. I led the league that season in home runs and had 101 RBIs. I was elected to the All-Stars every year, regular as clockwork. So it wasn't hard for me to tell myself I was not an alcoholic, even though I was drinking all the time, or a speed freak. The one thing I could truthfully say at that point was that I wasn't a cokehead. I dibbed and dabbled at it, but my real cokehead days were yet to come.

Besides, we sure weren't the only team in major league baseball taking drugs. It had been a big scandal in 1985 when a bunch of Pirates and others got caught in an FBI sting of a major coke dealer in Pittsburgh. Stories emerged from grand jury investigations describing how dealers were regular visitors to the clubhouse. There were tales of players snorting a few rails between innings or sneaking off during games to make a buy. Even the guy in the Pirates' mascot costume, the Pirate Parrot, was snorting! One player testified that he'd gotten his first greenies from Willie Mays and Willie Stargell. Willie Mays and Willie Stargell! Mex got dragged into it and had to testify before the grand jury that he'd done coke for three years. None of this was news inside the game, but the public was stunned and saddened. It was the biggest scandal in baseball since the days of Happy Felsch and Shoeless Joe. And the scandals just kept coming after that, with me and Doc doing more than our part.

IN A WAY, you could say that nothing really changed for me over the years 1987–89, it mostly just got worse. My drinking and drugging got worse, my woman chasing got worse, and the best you could say about my marriage through much of that period was that it was on hold. Lisa got her separation all right: We spent a lot of '87 with her and little DJ in California while I was in New York. She had a whole continent separating us. I missed DJ terribly, and the guilt of not being there to help him grow up weighed heavily on me. I was becoming my father and I hated it.

Through '88 and '89 I would periodically convince Lisa to get back together, then the fighting would start again, and we would separate again. Then she'd come back and we'd go through the whole cycle yet again. It was like another kind of addiction. We were addicted to each other, addicted to the fighting, addicted to our failed relationship. I knew in my heart it was insane to try to keep it together, but if it meant putting me and Lisa through hell to keep at least the semblance of a family, I thought it was the right thing to do.

Given that we started the season with Doc in rehab and me in the news as a wife beater, it's no big surprise that '87 was kind of a dysfunctional one for the Mets family, too. We were the reigning World Champions. It was supposed to be the start of a Mets dynasty. Everyone expected us to be great again this year. We expected it of ourselves. And every other team in the league, all those enemies we made in '86, were gunning for us.

We were still in exhibition play when Red Sox pitcher Al Nipper fired one straight into my ribs. I'd hit a big home run off him in the World Series, and then took my sweet, sweet time waltzing around the bases while he stood on the mound grinding his teeth. A bullet to the rib cage was his little way of saying he had not forgotten that moment of humiliation. It was the opening shot in a new round of gang warfare, except this year all the other gangs ganged up on us.

But we couldn't blame the other teams for our own problems. Doc wasn't the only one whose bad behavior caught up with him.

I remember one night David Cone and I decided to go into Manhattan and do some partying. We went to this club we knew, and we started drinking and partying—the usual. Now, Coney's a pitcher, and he isn't pitching the next day, so he can party all he wants. I'm an everyday player. I've got a game the next day. But we're pals and we're rolling together, so I hang in there with him, drink for drink.

Finally we're both done. We walk out the door, and *bam*. The sunlight smashes our eyes. We throw our hands in front of our faces like vampires. Aaaargh! The sun? How could the sun be up?

I groan, "Damn, Coney! What time is it?"

Coney squints at his watch. "Holy cow. It's eight o'clock."

"In the morning? We got to be at the park at ten!"

He shrugs. "What can I tell you, D? The night got away from us."

We go to his place in the city and stretch out for maybe two minutes. Then we drag ourselves up and out to Shea. I'm drunk. I mean, we'd been drinking all night. Coney doesn't have to play, but I do. I go to my locker, grab a handful of beanies, down five of them with a cup of coffee. I start to pull myself together, go through the usual pregame routine. Coney's watching me, shaking his head in disbelief.

The game starts. I'm still pretty hammered, but the speed has kicked in and now I'm pretty wired, too. I'm ready to go. I can walk through walls.

My first at-bat I hit a bullet in the gap. I round second and they're waving me on to third. The throw comes into third and I slide. I make it safe, but oh my head. I stand up and dust myself off and my head is pounding like it's a big gong and somebody's banging it with a ball-peen hammer. Ba-*dang* ba-*dang* ba-*dang*. I look over in the dugout and Coney's slumped down low on the bench with his cap over his face, trying not to let anyone see him laughing.

When I get back to the dugout he's still chuckling.

"I don't know how you do it," he says. "I just don't."

"Lord," I groan, "just let me make it through this game today. Let me make it through this game, and then I need to go home, get some sleep."

We were young, and we were healthy. We bounced back. But you can't keep on like that forever, no matter how young and strong you are. It starts to grind you down. Looking back, I can see it in how much bickering and carping we did at one another that year, not only in private but through the press. Same old Mets, hanging all our dirty laundry out in public, and I hung as much on that line as any of them—more than a lot of them, truthfully. I was not a happy person. I was deep into the drinking by then. It was my only escape, getting drunk and getting away from everything. All the troubles at home, all the bills, the constant pressure to be a superstar on the field, thrilling the fans, pleasing the press, and carrying the rest of the team with my bat. I did the best I could. I was playing the best ball of my career. But my personal life was a shambles, and having to go from that chaos to the park, where the fans and the press expected me to crush a home run every time I went to the plate and booed me every time I didn't . . . it wears on you. I was pretty tough mentally, but it still gets to you. I drank to forget it all for a while. And naturally the drinking just made all the problems worse, both at home and on the field. I was depressed, lonely, and frustrated at home, and brought that baggage with me to the park.

When I got there everyone, including my teammates, seemed to expect me to pick up the entire Mets club and carry them all on my back to victory. I got pretty bitter about that. I understood that as one of the stars of the team I was expected to do more than some of the other players. But in '86 we'd become World Champions because we played as a team, everyone doing his part, everyone excelling in his own way. Now it felt a lot more like, "When Darryl's hot, we're hot. When he's not, we're not." That was just what I didn't need, extra pressure from my own teammates. I carped at some of my teammates for slacking off. They, including my friend and mentor Mex, barked back that I was the one slacking off. The sad truth was we were all slacking off, because we were all doing too much drinking and drugging.

The only way to put it is that we fought like a bunch of drug addicts. You ever been around a bunch of drug addicts? It's nasty. Drug addicts are very unhappy people. It's why they get high. And when they're not high, all they can think about is when are they going to get high again. The drug addict always thinks everyone else is getting between him and his next high. Drug addicts are a lethal combination of self-destructiveness and supreme, infantile narcissism. The drug addict's life is all about me me *me*. Life gets really petty and paranoid and vindictive and just plain bitchy. It's awful.

And that's how we got. The Mets of '86 had done our share of squabbling and bitching at one another, but it was mostly like sibling rivalry in a family of rowdies. We'd spit and spat, then we'd go out and win another ballgame together, then we'd go party together. And God forbid if anyone outside the family keyed on any one of us, verbally or otherwise. Then we came at you as one family, and we tore your head off. We could talk trash about one another, but no outsider talked trash about any of us brothers and got away with it.

The family spirit sure eroded for the Mets of '87. We didn't fight like siblings anymore. We fought like a bunch of crackheads in an alley. It was a pretty ugly spectacle, and of course the media ate it up.

When Mex or one of the others complained that I was slacking off, truth is, I was coming to the ballpark late a lot of days. Sometimes it was because I'd been drinking all the night before, but it was also my stupid way of locking horns with Davey Johnson. I'd started feuding with him during the World Series, when I felt he didn't play me right, and I carried it over into the new season. The more he fined me for lateness, the more I came in late. It was sad, because I still loved and had enormous respect for him. I think if I hadn't been so unhappy in general I would have worked things out with him sooner.

Definitely the most ridiculous "controversy" that year was the flap over "Chocolate Strawberry," a rap record featuring the Kangol Kid, Richie Rich, and . . . me. It was my sister Michelle's idea. She got the Kangol Kid, a Brooklyn rapper and fan of mine, to write the thing, and I would go to a studio and rap part of it. I didn't think it was a big deal. The Mets were always being asked to do goofy things like that, and we were generally goofy enough to say yes.

So, one day when I was feeling too sick to play ball I went out to a studio in Queens and recorded my part for "Chocolate Strawberry," which was one verse of me bragging and fronting like a rapper.

Boy, did I hear from the rest of the team about it. Not to my face. As usual, they vented at me through reporters. "Oh, he's too sick to play, but not too sick to make a rap record?" Wally Backman said to a reporter, "Nobody gets sick twenty-five times a year."

And when I read that, I said to another reporter, "I'll punch that little redneck in the face." Ugly ugly ugly.

· · · ·

ONE SOURCE OF pure baseball joy for me that season was watching how well my boy E.D. was doing with the Reds. Like always, he and I had worked out together that winter, and he went roaring into the season and just started eating up the league. He hit two, sometimes three home runs a game. By May he was leading the National League in home runs, RBIs, stolen bases, all sorts of ways. He was so fierce the sportswriters called him Eric the Red.

A *New York Times* reporter asked me about E.D. that May, and I gushed so much the reporter wrote that I sounded like "his press agent or an admiring brother." That's because E.D. and I were like brothers. "We're not competing against each other," I told the reporter. "Our goal is to win Most Valuable Player this year. I wish we could both win it."

Neither of us made MVP that year, but my boy won a Gold Glove award, and we played together on the National League All-Star team.

EARLY IN 1988 I agreed to sit for a long *Esquire* interview with the New York sportswriter Mike Lupica. This was the same Mike Lupica who'd written some trash about me and Lisa the year before, when they all got hold of her filing for separation from me. He was one of those sportswriters who loved to dig into me, because they knew I was going to have something to say back to them and give them material for yet another article. But he went too far this time, and when I saw him in the clubhouse, I went over to him and said, "You don't know me. Next time you write about my personal life that way, I will beat the shit out of you. You want trash? I will pick your little ass up and shove you in a trash can. You'll get all the trash you want."

He cringed and turned the color of typewriter paper. We both knew I could and would do it. Like a lot of sportswriters, he was, let's say, a petite fellow. To me he looked about three feet tall. He avoided close contact with me for the rest of the '87 season.

But I'm a forgiving man, so I agreed to sit with him for an interview the following season. Partly it was my way of telling him, "Do you really understand who I am and what I can do, not only physically to you, but as a player? I'm going to let someone three feet tall think he exists in my head? You can't even rent space in my head."

That was the bottom line with Mike or any other reporter who walked through that door. Regardless of any of their opinions about me and my personal life and my wife and all the things I was going through, I never let it stop me from performing. You can talk all the trash about a guy you want, but you cannot take the champion out of his heart, and that's something I've always had. I'm a champion. From day one in high school, my coaches taught me about winning. I wasn't a loser, and I wasn't going to accept being on a losing team, not if I had something to do with it.

Besides, I was in one of my periods of feeling pretty decent and hopeful about life. I'd convinced Lisa to get back together with me. She and DJ and I were together now. Lisa was pregnant again. Soon I'd buy us a nice, big house in Encino. I thought we had patched things up for good this time. I thought that every time we patched things up. Wishful thinking, I know, but it was what I wished for, more than anything else—a happy, stable, normal, loving family life. You know, just like the one I never had growing up. The problem was, of course, that neither Lisa nor I had a clue about how to make that happen. That didn't stop me from wanting it desperately, and that's why I could keep convincing us both, against all the evidence, that when we got back together this time it was going to work.

So my personal life was on an upswing, my real family was back together, and I wanted to bring that to my professional life and my surrogate family. After the nasty year the Mets had in '87, I wanted to clear the air, begin the new season with a clean slate, set a positive, upbeat tone for me and the team. I wanted us to regain the magic of '86, and I thought it was my role to step up, have a great season, and inspire the rest of the guys.

Well, that was the plan, anyway. Like my plans for my family, things didn't work out that way. The way Lupica wrote it up, I was a beer-swilling blowhard, lolling around the clubhouse taking shots at all my teammates. I know I shouldn't have had that beer in front of him. I didn't even give it a second thought at the time. Drinking a beer was just a normal part of our clubhouse routine and had been since I joined the Mets. Lupica knew that, but in the article he kept coming back to that can of beer. He made it sound like I chugged a couple of six-packs during the interview.

What I was trying to say was that we had gotten slack in '87, hadn't been focused and given it our all, and we came in second. But I was going to give it 110 percent this season, and I hoped the rest of the guys would, too. I intended to lead through example, and keep my mouth shut around the press.

What I said in the article was that Mex had slacked off, and Wally Backman and Lenny Dykstra and Gary Carter had slacked off, and Davey had made some terrible decisions, and we would have done better with a manager like Whitey Herzog. "But if my bat's good, we're going to do well."

Here's how Lupica ended the article:

> "This year," Darryl Strawberry said as he left the Mets clubhouse, "you won't see me making headlines with any more bull."
> Bull.

Thanks, Mike. I wonder how he would have written it up if I really had beaten him the year before.

The article came out during spring training. The knives came out in the clubhouse right away. "Who does Strawberry think he is, saying he's going to carry us all with his bat?" But you know, the reality was that when I hit well, it sparked everyone else to do well. I brought the buzz to the ballpark. It wasn't just the fans I excited.

It was nothing batting coach Bill Robinson hadn't said a thousand times. "I don't care what nobody else says around here or what the media says. When you're hot, we win. You're the only player I've seen in a long time who can put a team on his back and carry it. You put it in your mind that you're gonna carry us, and everybody else is gonna jump on your back."

And you know what? It was true. I launched those two home runs into orbit in Montreal our first game of the season, and we jumped off to a great start. We were in first place in the beginning of June.

On the night of June 27, after a game against the Pirates in Pittsburgh, I hopped on a jet for New York, where Diamond Nicole was born the next morning. We named her Diamond for the baseball diamond. Then I hopped into another jet, flew back to Pittsburgh, and hit a home run that day to celebrate. I loved being a dad again. I loved having a daughter now. I felt like things were really rolling the right way. I was acting like a loving husband, a responsible dad, and a team player. I was twenty-six, and feeling like I was finally learning how to act like the man I wanted to be. I had always wanted to have a great career and a great family life. I still believed I was capable of being successful in both sides of my life.

My problem was I was still trying to figure out the manhood thing on my own. Because playing baseball doesn't teach you how to be a man. Baseball isn't life. It's a game. Whenever I hear baseball compared to life I have to scratch my head. Baseball is easy compared to life. There are clear teams and rules and regulations and stats. It has obvious winners and losers. The paths and lines are all straight and well-marked. Life isn't like that at all. Life is chaos and confusion. It's much harder to figure out.

But I was so excited when Diamond Nicole was born. I was always excited when any of my kids was born. Because I always realized they were what was really important. I was bringing them into this world, and I wanted them to see a better world and have a better time than I had growing up. Even with all my struggles I was able to give that to my kids. My kids never had to hear, "You're never going to be nothin'.'" Watching them grow, helping them do it—those were the true gifts, you know? Even in my craziest times I never forgot that.

THE METS HAD a good season. We won the Eastern Division and flew out to L.A. to play the Dodgers for the National League championship. It was a bit like Houston in '86. We were the odds-on favorite. The championship was ours to lose.

And we did. The difference this time was that the Dodgers were the scrappier ball club. They had more fire in their bellies. And, who knows, maybe less beer.

The series was reminiscent of '86 in another way. Both Coney and I made statements to the press that upset a lot of people. Dave offhandedly dissed Dodger pitcher Orel Hershiser, comparing him unfavorably to Doc. I believe what he said was that Doc won his games through skill, while Hershiser just got lucky. It made the entire Dodger organization and all their fans mad at us. Probably stoked that fire in their belly.

Then I told a Los Angeles reporter that as a homeboy I'd always had this fantasy of playing for the Dodgers with my best friend Eric Davis. The New York sportswriters jumped all over me for that. "Oh, Strawberry wants to go play for the Dodgers? After all the Mets have done for him? The ingrate. Well, why doesn't he go? We won't miss him. Good riddance." Blah blah blah. Man, those guys should have been paying me 25 percent of their salaries. I made their jobs so easy.

It wasn't that I didn't love the Mets. It was that I was starting to get the feeling that the Mets didn't love me back. I had a new agent, Eric Goldschmidt. I had ended my long relationship with Richie Bry to go with Eric. Not, as it turned out, one of my wiser decisions. I adored Richie. My family loved him. Richie was the one who was there at the start of my career. But a friend of mine introduced me to his agent, Eric, and I became convinced that Eric would be better for me at this stage of my career. He was from California, like me. I felt he was in a better position than Richie to negotiate for me with both the

Dodgers and the Mets, get me the best deal. Probably more wishful thinking on my part.

At the end of that '88 season Eric wanted to start talks with the management about extending my contract. My contract would end at the end of 1989, after which I'd be a free agent. I didn't want to go through that. I really did want to stay with the Mets. But I wanted them to give me a new contract, with both sides making a long-term commitment to stick together. And I wanted a raise, which, considering how well I'd played in '88, and how many fans I still drew to the ballpark, and how much money I was making for the organization as a consequence, didn't seem all that outrageous to me.

Management dithered. Management stalled. Management made it pretty clear that they weren't so sure I was either good for a long-term commitment or worth a raise. Despite my success on the field, I think Mr. Cashen looked at my rocky personal life and wondered if I was still a wise investment.

That hurt, and it angered me. I think it went straight to my old need to feel like I was part of a family that loved me, to hear that I was valued. Mr. Cashen was saying, more or less, that he had doubts about my value. He might just as well have said, "You'll never amount to nothin'."

Spring training '89 started, and I admit I wasn't the cheeriest guy in the clubhouse. Of course, the media heard that I was asking for a raise, and of course they put their two cents in, calling me an ingrate, wondering if I was really worth it, all that. And of course they asked my teammates their opinion, and of course some of them mouthed off. It was the Mets. It's what we did. Mex and Gary Carter were the harshest, calling me a crybaby.

Right after their comments appeared, we all gathered for a team photo. The team photographer wanted me to sit next to Mex.

"I'm not sitting next to no backstabber," I grumbled.

The photographer got us all arranged and started doing his thing, while a large crowd of newspaper reporters and TV cameramen stood behind him. I was still steaming. I walked over to Keith and told him straight up, "I don't appreciate you talking to reporters about my personal business. I don't talk to them about your contract or your pay." Truly, it just wasn't done. It was one of the golden unwritten rules. Players did not talk to the press about other players' contract negotiations. Keith was supposed to be my friend. I thought he of all people should have kept his mouth shut.

What did he reply? "We're all tired of this baby stuff." He said it right there in front of all the guys, and all the media.

And that's when I swung at him. I just lost it. In front of a whole crowd of TV and newspaper cameramen. The other guys quickly pulled us apart, but I was still steaming. I walked off the field. With all those cameramen grinning and all their cameras tracking my every step.

Not one of the high points of my career. Very embarrassing. But you know what? That was us. We were a team of big personalities, big characters, big egos, and we made big scenes. We sometimes clashed. We sometimes showed our asses. We almost always made up later when we cooled down.

The next day, at an exhibition game, Mex and I actually kissed and made up. When the game started, some fans booed me. I thought the heck with this, we can't start the season this way. So I swallowed my pride and anger. I trotted over to Keith at first base and gave him a big kiss on the cheek. Now the fans cheered. I apologized to Keith and we were fine. We played another exhibition game the next day and I slammed a monstrous home run.

By the time the season began, we'd put it behind us. On April 3, for the home opener at Shea, we beat the Cardinals 8–3.

On April 7, Lisa Clayton came calling.

9

LISA CLAYTON WAS just a girl in St. Louis who was a big fan of mine. We spent one night together in 1988. It wasn't an affair or even a fling. She had been after me for years. I came back to the hotel one night drunk during one of our road trips and there she was. We went up to my room, and nature took its course. Next morning we went our separate ways and I didn't see or hear from her again.

Until April 1989, when she hit me with a paternity suit.

I agreed right away to do the blood test. I didn't want to hesitate about it. If the child was mine I thought it best to find out right away and then go from there. And when the test proved positive, I agreed to pay child support and put money away in a trust for the kid. I figured I had helped bring this child into the world. It was my responsibility.

I didn't say anything to my wife, Lisa, at first. Considering our extremely fragile marriage at that point, I hoped to keep the whole thing on the down-low. That was very wishful thinking. Of course the paternity suit made the news. Everything I did made the news.

Lisa Strawberry first heard about Lisa Clayton when she read about her in a newspaper. She went through the roof, and filed for divorce in May.

I still didn't want it to be over. It was stupid, but I still wanted to save the marriage, not for us two so much as for the kids. I didn't want to be away from my kids. I wanted to be a part of their lives. It was extremely important to me, because I knew what it was like not having my own father involved in my life. I wanted to try to provide stability for my children.

Meanwhile, I still had a job to do. The Mets did not have our best year. I played well, despite injuring my shoulder, which caused me to miss my first All-Star Game. Other injuries dogged us, and we were still drinking and partying, which couldn't have helped. We finished second in our division.

My contract negotiations twisted in the wind all season. The longer the front office hemmed and hawed, the more I resented it. In the last week of the season, I vented about it to reporters. Maybe I needed a change of scenery, I said. Maybe I'd like to play on the West Coast, where I could spend more time with my family. Maybe it'd be nice to play where the fans didn't boo you every time you didn't hit a home run.

When the season ended, I convinced Lisa that we should all try living together in the house I'd bought for us in Encino. Her mother could come stay and be with the kids as much as she liked.

But it just wasn't going to work, and I should have known it. Lisa and I had way too much bad blood and ill-will between us by then. Too much jealousy and suspicion, too much insanity and rage, too much cheating. From the start it was like we rode a nightmare tread-mill of fighting, breaking up, making up, fighting again, breaking up again, making up again . . . and then fighting some more.

On the night of January 26, 1990, I came home from one of my usual drinking sprees—and Lisa was still out. I was enraged. When she finally came in around three A.M., I went nuclear. And Lisa, well, she did not ever once back down from a fight. If you nuked her she nuked you right back. Mutual assured destruction, like they used to say back in the Cold War.

Pretty soon we're screaming at the top of our lungs again, like we'd done so many times before. Flapping our arms around, both of us crazy, me drunk. We're right up in each other's face, shouting loud enough to wake up the whole neighborhood, our necks bulging, our eyes red with rage. Finally something exploded in me—my rage at her and at myself, my shame, my frustration, all of it boiling up like lava. I swung my fist and punched her in the head.

She flew backward and hit the carpet.

This was not the first time I had hit her, but, like Ronnie and I had many years before, I guess she decided it was the last.

When she rolled to her feet she had grabbed some kind of metal rod. A curtain rod, a fireplace poker, I didn't know. I just knew she was swinging it at me like . . . yeah, like a bat. She hit me a good shot in the ribs and one on my wrist. It hurt.

I ran to a closet where I kept a .25 pistol. A friend had given it to me, to protect the house. Lots of people in California had them. I hadn't bothered to register it, but lots of people didn't.

As Lisa charged me, swinging that rod, I turned, raised my arm, and pointed that pistol right at the bridge of her nose.

She froze. We both did. Her mother chose that moment to emerge from her room. Her hands flew to her mouth, and she stood there frozen with shock and fear, too.

It was one of those moments in your life that seem to go on forever. Everything got very still and very quiet. One of those moments when you feel like your mind has floated out of your body and you're watching the scene like it's in a movie. There was me, standing there with my arm stretched out, and that little pistol at the end of it. There was Lisa, staring right down the barrel of it. There was her mom, a look of horror frozen on her face.

And then time sped up to normal again, and we played out the rest of the sad, shameful scene.

"Get out of my face," I growled.

I never intended to fire. The safety was on. I just pointed it at her to get her to stop swinging that rod and back away.

Just like my dad probably never really intended to use his shotgun on us years earlier.

Many, many times since that night I've thanked God that Lisa, for once in her life, backed down. I would never have fired at her intentionally. But isn't that always the excuse when a domestic dispute gets ugly and there's a firearm in the house? "It just went off. I didn't mean to do it."

Lisa's mom ran out of the room and called 911. In a few minutes the LAPD were pounding on the front door. They arrested me for possession of an unlicensed handgun. Put me in the back of a squad car and drove me to the station.

I was sitting in the holding cell when it hit me that Lisa and I had just re-created a certain other night of my life, in a tiny house in Crenshaw, when I was thirteen. Things had come full circle. Now I was the big, violent, raging drunk who'd threatened his wife with a gun.

It was the first time in my life I'd been arrested. How had I come to this? Darryl Strawberry, major league ballplayer, in jail.

I knew—not that this was a stroke of genius—that this really was the end for me and Lisa. It had to stop now, before someone actually got hurt or killed.

THE NEXT MORNING I got out on $12,000 bail. It was all over the news, of course. Another humiliating Darryl Strawberry field day for the press. Luckily, Lisa decided not to press an assault charge, and the city of Los Angeles eventually decided not to prosecute me on the misdemeanor gun charge.

Back in New York, Mr. Cashen and the management decided it was time for an intervention. Right away they sent Dr. Allan Lans, the team psychiatrist, to come sit and talk with me. He said it was obvious my drinking was out of control. He suggested I fly back to New York and enter the Smithers rehab facility, where he also worked, to let my head dry out.

I spoke to my mom before I flew to New York. I was really depressed, naturally, and she was a rock as always.

"You don't have a problem with alcohol," she said to me. "You have a behavior problem. You need to get that straightened out. Your problem is women. You'll have to go through what you're going to have to go through, and I just hope and pray that you come out on the other side of it okay."

I was at Smithers for eight weeks. A great institution, with a very kind, knowledgeable staff. They dried me out, but I was still in denial about the extent of my substance abuse. I admitted the drinking to the counselors—it would have been pretty hard to deny—but I didn't tell them I was also doing too much speed during the season, as well as dabbling with coke. I told myself that was okay because all the guys did speed, and as for the coke, I was just a recreational user. Nothing heavy, and never during the course of a season. I realized that I was having problems with substance abuse, but it took me much longer to figure out why I was having problems with substance abuse. I wasn't anywhere near ready to confront my real issues at that point.

Doc had treated his time at Smithers the same way. It was something we had to do to please management, to demonstrate that we were serious about getting straight. But we weren't all that serious about it.

So I just dealt with the symptoms. For eight weeks I didn't have a drink or pop a bean. My head did get much clearer, my mood improved. As I walked out of Smithers, I told myself I was clean and sober now.

It wasn't the last time I'd tell myself that, and it did not last very long. As my mom said, my problem wasn't substance abuse, it was my behavior. Until I began to deal honestly with the emotional and psychological causes of the abuse, there was no way I could stay clean and sober. Drinking, drugs, and carrying on were how I dealt with my problems. When I stepped out of Smithers, those problems hadn't magically disappeared. They were standing right out on the street waiting to greet me. Hey pal, where ya been? Remember us?

The divorce took another three long years to finalize. Basically it was just a matter of the lawyers spending a long time going back and forth over carving up all my assets and income, and cutting off huge slices of fat for themselves in the process. Lisa demanded a tremendous amount of money for herself and for child support for DJ and Diamond Nicole. I guess as far as she was concerned it was payback time, and I was gonna pay and pay and pay.

We have not kept in touch. I'm really not concerned with what she does. My concern is and always has been for the children I had with her, DJ and Diamond Nicole. I'm overjoyed that they are still a big part of my life and always will be.

So you see, young people, when I tell you the decisions you make in your youth can have huge and lasting consequences, and you need to think long and hard about them, not get caught up in the moment and let yourself be pushed or dragged into stupid choices, I know what I'm talking about. Oh, do I know. Marrying Lisa wasn't the only stupid decision I made in my youth that haunted me for years after, but it's Exhibit A.

I GOT OUT of Smithers in time to start the 1990 season with the Mets. It was my free agent year, and Mr. Cashen still had not decided on a new contract. That really hurt, though in retrospect I guess I can see his reasoning. I was still bringing fans to the park and performing very well there. In fact I had a great year in '90, hit 37 home runs and batted in 108 runs. But I guess Mr. Cashen looked at all my personal troubles, all the negative press, and wondered how long I was going to be able to keep it up. By '90 he had weeded out pretty much all the rest of the old Mets. Mitch was long gone, Lenny Dykstra was gone, Gary Carter was gone, even Mex was gone now. He'd struggled a lot with injuries in '89, and Mr. Cashen chose not to renew his contract. He signed with the Indians, but only managed to make it to the middle of the '90 season before his injuries benched him for good. I missed him. For all our squabbling and spats, we loved each other like brothers. There were a lot of great guys and great players on the

'90 Mets—my buddy Coney, Sid Fernandez, Howard Johnson, Bobby Ojeda—but it wasn't the same.

Still, it was my team, my surrogate family, the place where I grew up and shone as a player. I wanted to stay. I just wanted a commitment and a raise. It was my way of saying I wanted to know that my surrogate family loved me back. I really needed some family to love me that year.

I didn't hear a lot of love from the front office. In fact, in the middle of the season, Mr. Cashen came right out and told the press he didn't think I was worth what I was asking for. It was the first time he actually said it, and in typical Mets fashion, he didn't say it to my face, he said it to the press. It really hurt and angered me. And then of course the press came running to me to ask me how I felt about what he'd said. How did they think I felt? But I sucked it up and hit home runs. Lots of home runs. My 108 RBIs were the most I ever drove in for the Mets, and would turn out to be a career high. At the end of the season I came in third in the sportswriters' Most Valuable Player voting, behind Barry Bonds and Bobby Bonilla, a couple of pretty impressive players. If I didn't prove my worth to Mr. Cashen that year, I never would.

Did I start drinking again? Yes I did. Between the end of my marriage and what was looking more and more like the end of my time with the Mets, I was very sad and lonely. Everything going on in my life played my doubts about myself and my worth like kettle drums in my mind. Maybe I really was no good. No good as a husband. No good as a father. No good as a ballplayer. No good as a man. I coped the way I'd learned to—by drinking, partying, fornicating.

Somewhere in there I reached out to the one person I wanted to tell me I was okay. The one person I'd wanted to hear that from for a long time.

I called my father.

When he picked up the phone he sounded as shocked to hear my voice as I was to be calling him. It was really stiff and awkward. We mumbled a little small talk at each other, with uncomfortable silences in between. "How's the team? I hear you might be coming to the Dodgers." Things like that. And then we hung up.

I called a few more times in there. We never did much more than the shy mumbling. No grand reconciliation. We never really got to any of the enormous issues between us. I tried in my heart. But we never had a personal relationship where the man could give me any guidance. I know it was probably painful for him to see me go through so much. But I was not in his life. I'd like to think he felt bad about not being there and giving me fatherly advice to help me overcome so many different things.

What do you do without a father? What do you do as a kid? What do you do when you grow up and become a man, live through your own struggles and your own issues, and you never have a father's love or advice? Every young man needs that in his life. I see all these boys in America growing up without fathers and it breaks my heart, because I know the confusion and damage that can cause. I'm sure some kids adjust and weather it better than others. But I see a lot of young men who remind me of myself, struggling terribly to figure out by themselves who they are and how to be a man because no one is there to guide or advise them. Some of them turn to the only role models they see around them—gangbangers, drug dealers, criminals, pimps, and macks. They think that's what it means to be a man. That's tragic. The following year, 1991, I would become a Big Brother in California— in fact, I was honored to be named California's Big Brother of the Year that year—because, even in the middle of struggling to figure out my own manhood, I felt this great need to try to help at least a few young men avoid some of the pain and confusion I went through.

Meanwhile, my talks with the Mets were in about the same sorry state as my frustrated efforts to reach out to my dad. I kept saying, "I'm having a great year. I am a valuable asset to this team. If you don't see that, other teams will. I'm walking." And they kept replying, "Well, okay, if that's how you feel. We're not really going to pursue you. If you want to go, go."

Way late in the season, they came back to my agent, Eric, with an offer. It wasn't what we asked for, and it was offered with a tone of, "We're not going to haggle over this. This is our final offer, take it or leave it, we don't care."

That stung. After all I'd done to make the Mets World Champions, to put butts in the seats and put wads of dough in the owners' pockets?

So at the end of that 1990 season I said, okay, I'm outta here. My decade with the Mets was over. The Dodgers had made it very clear they wanted me. I'd go play where I was wanted. Sayonara, New York. Rotsa ruck, Mets.

It was another of the dumbest moves I've ever made.

10

REMEMBER THE DAY I cleared out my Mets locker for the last time. Doc was there, looking really sad. Not surprised, because this day had been coming all season. But not happy.

"So you're leaving, too," he said.

"This is it, Doc," I said. "I'm outta here."

He and I had been through so much since 1984. So many triumphs, so many mistakes. But I had made up my mind, and so had the Mets, and there was no turning back.

I should have turned back. I wish there was someone there to wave their arms in my face and shout, "Go back, it's a trap!"

I never should have gone to Los Angeles. I should have taken the Mets offer and stayed in New York. I think Eric mishandled his negotiations with the Mets and turned my head with bad advice. But I hired him, and I took his advice. More bad decisions I can't blame on anyone but myself.

On the professional level, playing in L.A. was a huge letdown after a decade in New York. The sports atmosphere in New York was insane and intense and that was what I was used to. Lunatic fans screaming at you when you lost and tearing the joint up when you won. In Dodger Stadium the fans were much more, you know, Californian. Laid back. Drifted into the park late, filtered out early. They had no fire, no passion. When you got a hit, they gave you a smattering of polite applause. When you struck out, they were like, "Oh, bummer, man. Better luck next time."

It was, to be honest, boring. I never would have thought I could miss those insane New York fans booing me, but I did.

On a personal level, moving back to L.A. was absolutely jumping out of the frying pan into the fire. I was still a hometown hero in L.A. Everyone was happy to see me back. I couldn't set foot anywhere in L.A. without people offering me drinks, drugs, themselves. I knew everybody, including all the bad, bad influences. I knew every backstreet and where all the best parties were happening. I knew just where to go looking for trouble.

It was in L.A. in 1991 that I was introduced to smoking crack. A girl I was hanging with turned me on to it. One night she was like, "Try this." And as usual, I said, "Sure, okay." I smoked it that one time, and just like they say in the antidrug commercials, that was all it took. I was hooked right away. It was such an intense high. You float right out of your body, and your mind. I think LSD, which I never tried, has some of the same effect. It was an instant and complete escape from my life and my troubles and my pains. With somebody like me, with my addictive tendencies, it had no trouble sliding its hook in deep.

I know this is something many people could never figure out about me. I was Darryl Strawberry. I'd been a star since high school. I was one of the greats. I was a millionaire. I was a celebrity. Everyone adored me. I was a hero.

And I was a drunk and, now, a crackhead.

How could this possibly be? I had the world on a string. I had been gifted with an enormous talent. I might have been the greatest ballplayer in history. What more did I want? And why did I think I would find it in the bottle and the crack pipe?

All I can tell you is that I was in great pain, and the drinking and drugs brought me some temporary relief. I'll say it again: All the fame, all the success, all the money in the world don't add up to a thing if you're hurting in your soul. It does no good to have millions of people and all that press telling you who you are, when you haven't figured that out yet for yourself. And I still hadn't. I'm at the height of my career, I've just signed a huge contract with the Dodgers, more than $20 million over five years, I've come back home and everyone is overjoyed to see me—but who am I as a person?

I didn't know.

ONE OF LISA'S uncles saw what spiritual pain and confusion I was in, and suggested I go to a Morris Cerullo convention in Anaheim. Cerullo was a Pentecostal evangelist and healer well-known in California. Thousands and thousands of people went to hear him preach and have him lay his hands on them.

My brother Michael had already been saved—born again. He and his girlfriend were saved together, when he was in his early twenties. He brought it into the family. When he first brought it to my mom she was like, "Get away from me." She had always been a good Christian, a Baptist. But at first she wasn't into this born-again thing. Then eventually she saw the light. When she got saved she became totally dedicated to the church, very involved in the work of the church, very helpful to the pastor.

Mike got a little preachy about it with the rest of us. We used to joke, "Here come Michael. Here come the reverend. Put your beer away." Because he was on fire with it. He really got on me and Ronnie. "Man, you have got to get your lives together."

But he wasn't just talking the talk. He walked the walk, and we could all see the difference it made in him, the peace it brought him. He didn't curse anymore. He'd never been a big curser anyway, but now he never said a curse word at all. He had joy. He wasn't rich, he wasn't famous, but he was happy.

I could sure use some happiness. Not the fake happiness that comes from drinking or drugs or fame or sex. True happiness in my soul, the happiness that comes from being at peace with yourself.

So I went to Anaheim. It was a three-day weekend. There were thousands of people in the auditorium, but when Morris Cerullo spoke it felt like he was speaking directly to me. All the confusion, all the things I was going through.

"You're searching," he said, "and God has called you here for a reason. You're here for a purpose." That really struck me, because my mom always said the same thing. "You got a call on your life," she told me over and over.

He said, "Sunday we're gonna have an impartation. I'm gonna lay hands on everybody in this convention. I'm gonna walk through the lines and I'm gonna lay hands on you and pray over and deliver you."

Through the weekend there were lots of classes, where we were taught about how to avoid the evil forces and recognize the destructive impulses in our lives. It gave me plenty to think about. Evil forces and destructive impulses were the only kinds I seemed to be attracted to.

On Sunday I joined the long line of people going up to Morris Cerullo to be saved. Standing in that line, I was crying, crying, crying, crying. All the anger and pain and frustration and self-loathing were just pouring through me, and I let them all out.

I finally get up in front of him and he looks into my eyes. He's speaking. But he isn't speaking to me. He's speaking to an evil spirit inside me.

"Oh no, demon, you gotta come out of here," he says.

It was a real fight. He had me standing there for a long while, telling this demon, "You're coming out of him." And that demon hung on tight.

Finally, he laid his hands on me.

Boom! The power of God hit me like a lightning bolt, and I fell right down on the floor.

I don't know if you've ever had that experience. Maybe you've seen evangelists on TV lay their hands on people, and when those people fall to the floor you think, "It's fake. Those people are acting. They've been coached."

Well, all I can tell you is that nobody coached me, and I wasn't faking a thing. What I felt was absolutely real, a physical force, and it truly knocked me to the floor. The best way I can describe the feeling is that it was like a roaring river pouring through me. Even after I stood back up I could feel it flowing through me. I was holding my stomach, where the feeling was strongest. People around me were like, "What is it? Are you all right?"

"Something's wrong with my stomach," I said.

"Son," an older man said to me, "your life will never be the same."

And boy, he wasn't lying. It was never the same after that.

But it didn't change the way you might expect. That's something else a lot of people don't understand about being saved. I sure didn't understand it for a long time. It's that accepting God into your life, feeling that power rush through you, isn't the end. Your life doesn't suddenly become all peace and light.

In fact, it's just the beginning. You're born again—now what are you going to do with this new life? It's really just the opening salvo of a spiritual battle. You have to follow up, study, meditate on what it means and what God wants of you. And the devil, the Enemy, doesn't make that easy. In fact, he sends all sorts of tests your way.

And let me tell you, all hell broke out in my life from that point on. I had no idea at the time of what was to come. I didn't have the knowledge of the biblical way of living. My attitude was, "All right, I got touched and delivered, thank you very much. Now I'll just go along my own way."

Oh no. Morris Cerullo warned me. He said, "A full attack is going to come on your life from the Enemy because of what has happened to you today."

I had no idea what he meant, because I hadn't studied at that time.

I really didn't take this new spiritual life seriously. In a sense, I treated it the same way I had my time at Smithers. I'm saved? Okay, thanks. Bye now.

That's why when the attacks came I was completely unprepared.

The first thing the Enemy did was to try to take baseball away from me when my first season with the Dodgers had barely begun. We were playing the Expos on May 15. I was in right field in my brand-new Dodger uniform when Marquis Grissom hit a screamer that rocketed toward the right-field wall. I ran all the way back to grab it, and banged my left shoulder into the wall. A sharp pain shot down my arm, but I held on to the ball and played out the inning.

But I didn't play the next one. I had dislocated my shoulder. I missed twelve games while we worked on it. I tried to get back in and play in June, but I couldn't, and went on the disabled list. It just hurt too much. I couldn't swing, I couldn't throw. It was my first season with the Dodgers, my home team, the team that was paying me all those millions to come home and be a star, and I went straight to the disabled list.

Talk about a test of faith. Here I was struggling to get right. I had been saved. I was back in the ballpark, doing what I loved and excelled at. And boom, I hurt myself a month into the season.

That's when the doubts started creeping into my mind and my soul. I didn't realize that I was being tested. I just thought, "Oh man, what's the point? Maybe I need to go back to my old ways." And I did.

And guess what? When I got back on the field in the second half of the season, after the All-Star break, I started playing great again. I pounded 28 homers and knocked 99 RBIs. If I hadn't injured myself, it might have been my best season ever. The Dodgers were happy, the fans were happy, even the sportswriters had to say nice things about how powerfully I came back.

Is the Enemy clever or what? I thought the old ways were working for me, so I should stick with them. If I had to be bad off the field to be good on the field, well okay then. Sorry, God.

I know that sounds like a weak justification. But that's just what substance abusers do. Any justification to keep using.

It wasn't that I didn't love God. In my heart, I loved God very much. But I didn't know what true love is and how to live love. And I refused to find out.

See, we think our purpose in life is what we do in our careers. We think it's all about our jobs and making money and buying and having things. But that's just what we do and have. It's not who we are.

That's what I learned, but only after going through hell. I mean, when I look back over it all, I think, "Wow, I went through a lot of stuff and God kept me here. He kept me standing. There was always a purpose."

Every minister I ran across, different ones from different countries, always pulled me out of a crowd and said, "God's called you for a great purpose, and he's gonna get all the drugs and alcohol out of your life."

Yeah, God came calling. But I pretended I wasn't home when he called. I hid, like Doc had done on the morning of the parade.

The truth is, the call was so great that I was scared to answer. Terrified. I used to argue with God about it.

"I can't do it," I told him. "I am not qualified to do what you have called me to do. I am a wreck."

Writing this book and going back over these years in my mind has not been easy for me. It fills me with shame to remember my addictive behaviors and all my failures as a husband and a father and a man. I'm telling it all to you in the hope that you won't reach the lows I did before I made things right.

I caused a lot of deep harm to others. Bad childhood and self-hatred notwithstanding, I was still responsible for what I did. I was faced with the choice to get help and change or to go on destroying myself and hurting others. Every bad choice I made had consequences that I have continued to live with to this day.

Instead of facing my responsibilities and making the tough decisions, I ran. I ran from my responsibilities. I ran from God. I ran from myself.

BUT GOD MUST not have wanted me to face the Enemy all alone, because he sent me a helper that year. I was at E.D.'s twenty-ninth birthday party in Beverly Hills that May when I saw this stunningly beautiful woman across the room. I was not the only guy in the place gawking at her, not by a long shot. She was a real head-turner. There were plenty of other women there, and plenty of them wanted to talk to Darryl Strawberry. But she was the prettiest woman there, and the only one who acted like she couldn't care less that I was in the room. I was really intrigued, on both counts.

My days of being shy around women were way behind me by then. I walked over as she was dancing and tapped her on the shoulder. I just cut right in on the other guy.

Her name was Charisse Simon. She lived down in Orange County and came to the party with friends. She didn't know Eric. And when I laid my famous name on her, she didn't seem to know who I was, either. It had been a long time since I met anyone who didn't know who Darryl Strawberry was. I liked it. I liked that she wasn't falling all over me the way most women I met did. She was polite, and proper. Kind of old-fashioned. When I asked for her number, she wouldn't give it to me. She gave me a friend's number instead.

I couldn't stop thinking about her after the party. She was so pretty, and so different from most of the women a guy in my position encountered. I kept calling her friend.

"Charisse doesn't want to talk to you," she'd say.

"Tell her I want to ask her out on a date," I'd say.

"She doesn't want to go on a date with you," her friend would say. "But you can ask me on a date."

"Okay, well, just tell Charisse if she ever wants to talk to me she should give me a call."

She wasn't gaming me or playing hard to get. She was just different. She was quiet, serious, wasn't interested in any nonsense.

At some point she noticed that one of her brothers had a poster of me and Doc on his wall.

"Hey, I met that guy," she told him, pointing at me.

His jaw dropped.

"You met Darryl Strawberry?"

"Yeah," she said with a shrug, "at a party. He tried to talk to me."

"And you wouldn't talk to him? Are you nuts?"

She told her mother that I kept dogging her girlfriend. Her mother said, "Well, go out with him once. He just wants to go out on a date, take you out to dinner or something. Maybe you'll like him."

We finally got together for a date, and right away I could see that my first impressions of her were correct. There was nothing phony or flirty about her. She was a nice, sweet girl with her head on straight. She really didn't seem to care that I was some kind of celebrity. She was either going to like me or not for who I really was, not what other people said or thought about me. That was so refreshing, and also a little intimidating. She really put me on my best behavior. I could see I was going to have to court her if I wanted her. It had been a while since I was the one doing the courting. I really liked it. It was sweet and romantic.

I fell for her right away. When the Dodgers were on the road I called her every night. We talked about everything—our families, how we grew up. I didn't hide any of my past from her. I told her all about me and Lisa, including the night with the pistol. I told her about going into Smithers. I didn't want to hide anything from her. I wanted her to know what she might be getting into with me. I mean, it wasn't like she couldn't find it all out easily enough. Everything I'd gone through over the past decade had been all over the news. But between my experience with Morris Cerullo and meeting Charisse, I really hoped that I was on the right path now. I was going to clean up and get right.

THAT TURNED OUT to be easier thought than done. You can't get right because you love God, or because you love any other person, if you still don't love yourself. I was still a long way from loving myself, or knowing how to love anyone else. Because of that, I would put Charisse through hell many times during our years together.

Even though I was falling in love with Charisse, and wanting desperately to be good for her, I was still drinking, drugging, and getting involved with other women. She knew. She was nobody's fool. But she loved me. Before 1991 was out, we both had this very strong sense that God had brought us together for a reason. I'm sure it was much easier for me to see why God had brought her into my life than for her. She was a blessing to me. A lot of times I was more like a curse to her. But her love, her will, and her faith were very strong. Charisse loved me a lot more than I loved myself. That was our relationship in a nutshell. She loved me from the day she committed to me, and I was never fully committed to anybody, because I wasn't totally committed to myself. I was hating life.

By '92 my behavior was completely out of control. Even after Charisse and I moved in together, every night was a party. I was a full-blown alcoholic and using crack. It was ugly. And, not surprisingly, it became impossible for me to keep my terrible behavior off the field from affecting my playing with the Dodgers. One night we were playing the Phillies in Philadelphia. It was a cold, wet night. I scored on a base hit, and as I was rounding third to head for home I felt a twinge of pain in my lower back. I sat down in the dugout, and when it was time to go back out to right field, I couldn't stand. I could not get to my feet.

"No no no," I thought. "This can't be happening."

But it was. I had ruptured a disk in my lower spine. Just twisted the wrong way coming around the base. I knew it was all the wear and tear on my body from the constant partying, drinking, and drugging, then going to the ballpark and playing full-tilt, trying to excel despite the abuse I was putting myself through. It finally caught up with me.

I didn't go to surgery right away. I did not want to be laid up the rest of the season, no way. I went to a bunch of physical therapy sessions first. I was so frustrated. The therapy seemed to help some, so I tried to make some adjustments so I could play again, like switching from right field to left. In a lot of ways left field is harder than right. In right the ball tends to come straight off the bat toward you. When hit to left, it can slice off the bat at unpredictable angles and with odd spins. But left was shallower than right, and we figured the shorter throws would be easier on my arm and back.

It didn't help. I still felt really uncomfortable. I got to the point where I just said, "Forget it. I have to have the surgery."

I avoided it as long as I could, because I knew what it was going to be like afterward. And it was as bad as I expected. I was on my back for a couple of weeks. And then when I could get up, I could only hobble along with a cane. Me, a lifelong athlete, shuffling along like an old man. Humiliating. I wanted to play. I wanted to show everybody that I could play. The Dodgers were paying me a lot of money to play, not to lean on a cane and watch the rest of the guys play.

In my frustration, I tried to bounce back too early. It didn't work. Every time I swung the bat it burned. I tried altering my stance, my swing, and it only made things worse. I only managed to play forty-three games that '92 season.

It didn't go away the following year. In fact, it got worse. It grew into one of those nagging long-term ailments that just won't heal and begins to steadily erode your physical and mental strength. I played a paltry thirty-two games in 1993, and batted a pathetic .140.

The media were really on my case by then. They wondered if my back was as bad as I was making out. Maybe I was just malingering and pulling a scam on the Dodgers. They wondered if the Dodgers had bought a pig in a poke. They hinted that the team was considering canceling my contract. I hated them for it, but looking back, who could blame them?

All through '92, '93, I was one bitter, foul soul. Full of rage and hate, incredibly frustrated, and forced to be idle. Terrible combination.

I coped the way I always did, slipping deeper and deeper into the alcoholism and drug addiction. Looking for the next party, the next one-night stand, anything to distract me from myself and my self-inflicted problems.

Charisse stuck with me through it, but she wasn't a patsy. We fought. Not about the insane nonsense Lisa and I used to fight over. Charisse and I fought over the very real pain I was inflicting on us both, the very real damage I was doing to myself, my career, and our relationship. She was concerned about what my outrageous behavior was doing to my kids DJ and Diamond Nicole as well. Charisse fought with me because she could see the good man and loving father underneath all the rage and self-loathing.

Meanwhile, just to brighten my mood, the lawyers finally squeezed the last drops of juice out of negotiating the divorce with Lisa, and I found myself sitting with a pen over the final documents and a pile of checks. Just at a time when my ability to play baseball and earn a salary were in serious question. I imagine that's one reason the lawyers finally wrapped it all up. They wanted to make sure they got their pound of flesh while there was still some meat on my bones. When I signed the whopping checks to Lisa's lawyers and to mine, I gripped that pen so tight in my fist it's amazing it didn't explode into a million pieces.

I'll tell you what though, even more painful than the financial consequences of my failure with Lisa was the feeling that I'd failed DJ and Diamond. Failed them miserably. Because now they would grow up like I did, without a father in the house. The very thing I'd sworn to myself I would never do to my children. It infuriated me that I was following in my father's footsteps that way.

In moments of clarity, I had to ask myself what kind of father I'd be to them even if I was home with them. How could I have taught DJ how to be a man, when I was still struggling to figure it out myself? What kind of example would I set, when I was still out of control myself? I always loved my kids. I loved everything about being with them, playing with them, feeding them when they were babies. No kidding, I even loved changing their diapers. But I was failing them anyway. No, I never beat them. I always tried to provide for them financially. But my behavior would cause them pain and humiliation for years to come. You can't take that back.

As all that was going on, Charisse told me she was pregnant that June. There was no question of an abortion. We both wanted this child. We both wanted to get married as soon as my divorce was settled. But I didn't let that stop me from drinking, drugging, and partying. Pretty much nothing could stop me at that point.

That September, Charisse and I had our biggest fight ever. Here she was, pregnant with my child, and I was out doing who knew what with who knew who. She was terribly hurt and outraged, as she had every right to be. But I flew into a rage.

I hit her. My pregnant girlfriend. The woman I loved.

She called 911. The police came, and for the second but not the last time in my life, I was under arrest.

Once again I was filled with shame, remorse, and self-loathing. Charisse, don't ask me why, forgave me and refused to press charges.

In October my divorce was final. In December, Charisse and I were married. This time it was an intimate ceremony, just family and closest friends. We did it at her church in Orange County.

I was so happy that day. I prayed in my heart, "Thank you, God. Thank you for bringing this angel into my life, and the other little angel she's got inside her. Thank you for giving me this amazing opportunity to straighten up and get right. Next year is going to be completely different, I just know it. The start of a whole new phase in my life."

I was right. My life went into a whole new phase in 1994. It just wasn't the sort of phase I expected.

11

PICTURE A MAN falling down a long, long flight of steps. Bang. Crash. Boom. Bang. He falls and falls, head over heels. Sometimes he throws out his hands, grabs the railing, slows his fall for an instant. But momentum, gravity, and his own weight are against him. He keeps crashing down those steps, down and down and down. Until finally he lands at the very bottom. Cut, bruised, broken, his head swimming, he lies there flat on his back.

It's only then, after he's crashed down the whole flight of stairs and hit bottom, that he can begin to rise up again. Get himself back on his feet. Stand there looking up that long, long flight of stairs and think, "How did I survive that?"

That's me, from 1994 into the 2000s. Falling, falling, falling, and finally bottoming out.

It wasn't pretty. There were a few bright moments, but they came like brief rest periods among a lot of sad, tragic, and sordid ones. I came close to losing my life, losing my mind, and at times losing my faith. I did lose my career, lose another marriage and other things.

But I survived. And that's the point of dragging you through the next bunch of pages with me. If you've heard or read anything about me, the sad and tragic parts may be all you know. They're certainly all other people seemed to want to write about me. But I'm here to tell you now I got through all that trouble and sorrow. God had a purpose for me, and he never let go of me.

ON MARCH 3, 1994, the IRS announced that it was investigating me for tax fraud. It stemmed from a bunch of appearances I'd done in the 1980s at baseball memorabilia shows, signing autographs, meeting the fans and collectors. Nothing unusual for a star player on a winning ball team. Doc did them with me, some of the others. You'd collect $10,000, $15,000 an appearance. Can you imagine? Sometimes, riding in the limo afterward, Doc and I would roll down the windows and toss $100 bills out, just to see them fly away. It was free money, what did we care? It was insane, but those were wild and crazy years. And then, of course, when we got back to the hotel with those big wads of bills, it was time to par-tay. All that cash bought an awful lot of par-tay.

None of us, and I mean none of us, gave a second's thought to filing that income with the IRS. That wasn't our concern. We had promoters who set up the gigs, we had tax accountants who kept our books. We paid all these people a lot of money to take care of all that stuff, the business end of our lives. We were too busy being celebrity baseball players. It honestly never occurred to me that my people weren't properly reporting the income or taking out taxes from it or whatever else they were supposed to be doing. All I knew was I showed up at a baseball card collectors' convention, signed hundreds of autographs, got my picture taken with hundreds of fans, got my money, and went back to my hotel.

That's all I knew until 1994, when it turned out that the promoter hadn't been filing the proper tax forms, and the IRS had come after him, and he turned me over. And now they were accusing me of tax fraud to the tune of more than $300,000! Exactly what I needed to hear, a few months after signing my life and income away to finalize my divorce.

I went and talked to the IRS. They asked me about other players I knew who'd been involved in these events, and I didn't say anything. They said, in effect, "If you give us some other players, we can work out a deal on this thing. If not, you're going to take a very big hit."

I didn't give them any names, and when all was said (or not) and done, a year later, I took a very big hit indeed.

And rightfully so. As a celebrity athlete, I'd been living like a big child all those years. Playing games, living the high life, and paying others to take care of all the dull business of being a responsible adult. That dream life was beginning to turn into a nightmare. I was starting to learn that in the end, when the real bills come due, no one pays them but you. No matter how many helpers and hangers-on you surround yourself with, it's your life, and you face the consequences.

Two weeks into all this, on March 17, my son Jordan was born. That was a joyous day. I didn't have many that year. I was in a bad, bad state, angry at the world, angry at myself. And doing what I always did to find some relief.

Meanwhile, I was still a Dodger, but just barely. I was drinking and drugging so heavily at night that I could barely drag myself to the park the next day. I showed up late for several preseason games. And then, on April 3, I failed to show up at all for an exhibition game against the Angels at Anaheim Stadium. I was out partying all the night before. That next day I could not even get up off my back, let alone go play baseball. Nobody even knew where I was.

My sister Regina later said that she and the rest of my family were startled. I had done a good job of hiding my pain and my struggles from them. To them I was a success, a champion, a star. Sure, they knew my relationship with Lisa had been a fiasco. They knew I drank and partied some. But they had no idea of the extent of my substance abuse until this incident.

Everybody decided it was time for another intervention. Charisse, the Dodgers, they all thought it was rehab time for old Darryl. Even

I thought it. I was ashamed of myself, disgusted with my behavior, humiliated, exhausted.

On April 8, I was admitted for a month of rehab at the Betty Ford Center in Rancho Mirage, California, just outside Palm Springs. A very, very nice place. High-class and swanky. All your better class of substance abusers went there. Movie stars, sports stars, the very wealthy. I wouldn't say they went easy on you, though. They gave you a very high level of treatment and counseling, and they were very strict. They tried to get you to understand your addiction and how powerful it was, get you to realize the mood-altering effects the substances have on you. They wanted you to see that your substance abuse was an attempt to escape from the painful things going on in your life, that getting high was a way to avoid dealing with them.

Part of the program was a family day, when members of your family come and you have a big group talk, with everyone sharing how they feel, because substance abuse is a family issue in so many ways. My mom came, my sisters, my brother Mike—and my dad. I guess since I had reached out to him a couple of years earlier he was trying to show some support and make some kind of amends. It was the first time I ever came out and told him to his face how I felt about him and what he'd done to us all. How I felt he never was in my life, never there to give me any direction in my life, so I had to learn everything on my own.

He sat there with his head hung and listened. He didn't have a lot to say back. In fact, he kept muttering, "I don't know what to say. I don't know what to say. I wish I could have done better." I think he did wish that. I think he was sorry, but he also didn't know what else he could've done. Seeing him that day didn't do a lot for me at the time, but later I realized that he had been damaged by his own childhood, and, like me, maybe he just didn't know any other way to act. After all, alcoholism and abuse are genetic. They're passed down, generation to generation. His father had been an abusive, raging alcoholic. He became an abusive, raging alcoholic. Two of his sons, Ronnie and I, became raging, abusive alcoholics and drug addicts. I know there are people who argue against that genetic theory, but all I can say is my family—and a lot of other families—are living proof.

At Betty Ford they dried you out, and then they taught you the basic steps to follow once you got back out to the world, to help you keep clean and sober and avoid falling back into your same old addictive patterns. Go to your AA meetings. Don't pick up any dope. When you need help, talk to someone else in recovery who's been around and done this a long time.

But, you know, I noticed that just about everyone who went through this recovery process would relapse. And they would continue to struggle until they realized that they couldn't really address their addictive behavior until they dealt with the bottom-line personal issues that caused that behavior in the first place. If you don't deal with your personal issues first, you're never going to get straight.

Like me. I was blaming everyone and everything in the world for my terrible behavior. It was my father's fault, my ex-wife's fault, the paternity suit, the IRS, my back injury, blah blah blah. I was nowhere near admitting yet that I was the problem, that I was bringing all this chaos and sorrow into my life, and that I had a lot of work to do on myself before I was ever going to get right. You can go to all the programs in the world, go to meetings every day and every night, but if you're not dealing with the real issues and the real problems, you're never going to see the other side of your struggles.

But I didn't get it yet, and I came out of Betty Ford truly believing I was a new man, clean and sober, finally right with the world. We moved down to Rancho Mirage. The idea was to get me away from all my bad influences in L.A., and to put us near Charisse's family and church, which were very positive influences. It was very nice out there in the desert. Palm Springs, Desert Hot Springs, Joshua Tree National Park. All the houses are big and nice, there's a golf course or country club everywhere you turn. It's not like I couldn't get into trouble out there. I had a car, and if you go looking for trouble you can find it anywhere, anytime, especially if you have a lot of experience in it like I had by that time. But I wasn't looking for trouble, not just then anyway. I was clean and sober and turning over a new leaf.

I wasn't even that upset when the Dodgers dropped me that May. It wasn't a surprise. After my dismal couple of seasons with them, going into rehab was the last straw, you might say. Or the last of Straw. Manager Tommy Lasorda and some of the Dodgers blasted me in the media. They were over me, and I couldn't really blame them.

For me, the Dodgers were my past now anyway. I was looking clear and bright-eyed to the future. When the Dodgers dropped me, the San Francisco Giants picked me up. We held a press conference up there at Candlestick Park that July. Charisse and my brother Mike were with me. He had quit his job with the LAPD to come act as my assistant and, to be honest, my chaperone. Back when he'd played for the Dodgers, he and Dusty Baker had gotten really close. Dusty was now the manager of the Giants. When the Giants signed me, Dusty wanted Mike to come on board, too. Officially he was a batting practice pitcher, but his real job was to keep an eye on me. But he had a locker, a uniform, everything, and he was really excited about it. He was back to his first love after a decade on the police force.

That press conference was a very emotional thirty minutes. I choked up. I told the reporters I was completely clean and sober and grateful to be alive and sitting there before them. I don't remember now, but I don't think I mentioned that part of my deal with the Giants was to volunteer for regular urine tests, so they could make sure I remained clean and sober.

Dusty Baker said, "Whatever happened in Darryl's life, he's beyond that now."

For that brief moment, we all believed that was true.

I STARTED PLAYING with the Giants that July. And right away we started winning ballgames. We won ten of the first eleven I played in. Management was delighted, the fans loved it, even the sportswriters were impressed, and Dusty Baker felt his faith in me—and in Mike— was justified.

I loved having Mike with me. We did everything together. On the road, we slept in adjacent rooms, and prayed together before we went to bed. We talked a lot. He was a powerful influence, helping me keep myself together. He was more than my big brother. He was more like a guardian angel.

But even he couldn't guard me against myself and my own worst instincts.

In August, the major league baseball players went on strike. Right on time for my brand-new start. Timing is everything. I played fewer than thirty games before the whole season was shut down. No more games, no World Series, nothing.

So I was idle again, deeply disappointed, and really frustrated. Not a good state for me to be in.

The other big Strawberry family news that year hit me like a tsunami. My mom was diagnosed with breast cancer. She was only fifty-five. She kept it from us at first, but eventually we found out, and we were all devastated. We loved our mom so much. She was all we ever had. She was our guidance, our rock. Guiding us to the right road of life, even through our trials. It was Mom who always said, "You will come out of this on the other end."

Her doctors suggested radiation treatments, but she refused. She put her faith in God. Mom's faith was powerful. She was very active in her church. If she didn't want the radiation, we weren't going to be able to talk her into it. She said that her fate was in God's hands and that was the end of it.

Besides, through '94 she seemed to be doing well. The rest of us kept an eye on her, but we also went about our own lives.

In December, I was formally indicted on those tax charges. In talking it over with my attorneys, it was apparent that the best thing I could do was to plead guilty and take my licks. Sure, bring it on. Bring it all on.

My new leaf had shriveled and died by then. With everything else going on, I had slipped back into drinking and drugging. I was falling back down that long flight of stairs. I just couldn't face my issues head-on, accept them, and deal with them. Instead, I ran and hid from them. Ran to the crack pipe, hid in the bottle.

In January 1995, in one of those routine drug tests I was taking for the Giants, cocaine showed up in my urine. I don't know how I failed it. I had been beating drug tests for a while by then. All ballplayers knew the tricks for beating them. My preferred method was not to do any drugs for a few days, then pee in a bottle and save it. When I went in for a test, I snuck that bottle in with me and used that clean sample. Usually there'd be a guy standing somewhere behind you, but I got really clever about making the switch.

But this time I got caught. The commissioner of baseball suspended me from playing for sixty days. Not surprisingly, the Giants let me go.

With me out, Mike had to leave the Giants, too. He was crushed. His dream of returning to baseball was ruined because of me. He couldn't go back full-time with the LAPD, either, so he was really screwed. By me. We didn't talk about it much at the time. I was too caught up in my own struggle to acknowledge how much trouble I'd brought on him, too. Or the rest of the family. It's part of the package of substance abuse. You isolate yourself from your loved ones and refuse to face the suffering you're causing them. You leave them out in the cold, because the relationship that matters most to you is your relationship to the substances. The pain you bring on your family and loved ones is just one more issue for you to avoid, until you're finally ready to start dealing with all your issues.

"It didn't just affect you," Mike told me later. "You didn't realize how much it affected all the rest of us. Like, when you did something that made the news, when you failed a drug test or got arrested or something, you were always able to go hide afterward. Darryl on his island. We didn't have anywhere to hide. We still had to go to work and school and face people. We had to deal with people looking at us funny and asking us, 'What's up with your brother, man?' My fellow police officers would ask me that, and I had to say, 'What are you asking me for? Worry about your own business.' Everything you experienced trickled down to us. Don't think I wasn't ashamed sometimes to go to work, having to deal with my superiors looking at me sideways, thinking, 'What about you? Are you doing drugs?' And it was everywhere. 'What's up with your brother, man? What's wrong with him, man? He's had it all. Why did he do that?' You even made Ronnie embarrassed to be your brother."

That February, I was in court pleading guilty to felony tax evasion. I would soon be sentenced to six months of probation and home confinement, and fined $350,000. So I wasn't just forbidden to play baseball. I couldn't even leave the house without my probation officer's express permission.

Was I hating life?

BUT GOD SENT me a flock of other angels that year to help out. One was a new agent, Bill Goodstein. Through all the difficult times in that period, whenever it looked like everything was over, Bill was there for me. Bill was the angel who resurrected my career.

Bill brought another angel into my life, George Steinbrenner. I had never met George before. I had admired him from afar for years. In the midst of all this bad news about me—I'm washed up, I'm a drug addict, I'm suspended, I'm fired—Bill talked to George and said, "You need to get this guy back to New York."

And George, God bless him, agreed. George Steinbrenner picked me up when everybody in the world was saying, "No no no, he's too much trouble, he's through." George didn't care what anyone said. He thought I deserved a chance to bounce back. And, I'm sure, he thought it would be exciting for Yankee fans to see me play.

We signed the contract in June. "The once unfathomable notion that Strawberry could return to play baseball in New York, or return to play at all, was obliterated because the principal owner of the Yankees, George Steinbrenner, vigorously pursued the former Met with the questionable past," the *New York Times* observed.

Not everybody in the Yankee clubhouse was happy about it. Buck

Showalter, the manager, didn't want me. "I'm concerned about him as a player and a person," is what he said. I guess he thought I would be more trouble than I was worth. He didn't know me. I never played for him. But he figured I couldn't play.

Maybe also he resented that George and Don Mattingly, who was captain of the Yankees, wanted me.

"I'm glad he's here," Donnie said. "Put the welcome mat out."

Donnie's always had high hopes and a lot of respect for me, just like I've always had for him. Back in the eighties, when I was with the Mets and he was with the Yankees, there was always this buzz about which one of us was the best baseball player in New York. We never got into the hype. We had great respect for each other.

But Buck didn't want me. I wasn't one of his boys. "The boss brang you here, but I'm not gonna play you. I'll play you when I want to play you."

So Buck didn't play me much. I joined the team early in August—we had to wait out my six months' house arrest, which of course the media loved joking about—and I spent a lot of the rest of that season on the bench. Which was his loss. I didn't resent it. I did not say one word of complaint to the media about it. For once I kept my mouth shut. My feeling was Buck was losing a good opportunity to have me play and help him win. He didn't play me, and he didn't win. We finished second in the American League East, seven games behind Boston. And Buck was fired at the end of the season.

Derek Jeter came up to the majors that same year, '95, and Buck didn't play him much either. We sat on the bench together a while before Derek got sent back down to the minors.

"Don't worry," I told him. "You'll own this town someday. First of all you're good-looking. You can play. And you're not afraid. But the most important thing I want to tell you is don't make mistakes. Do the right things. Make the right decisions and live right. I wish I had to do it all over again. I wish somebody told me what I'm telling you now. You're going to be great in this town. They're gonna love you in this town. But don't allow this town to eat you up."

Next season, Derek was the starting shortstop, and never looked back after that.

It was Bill Goodstein who hooked me up with the Yankees, and I so loved him for it. Bill wasn't in it for money. Bill was in it for nothing. He didn't want anything except Darryl Strawberry back in New York. I went on to help the Yankees win three championships because of Bill. I dedicated everything that I did playing for the Yankees to him.

I can hardly describe how excited I was to be back playing in New York. As far as baseball went, New York was my true home. I felt like that—like I was coming home. I'd run away, and found nothing but sadness and trouble, and now I was back, and everything was going to be all right.

Charisse and I rented a little house in Fort Lee, New Jersey, right across the Hudson. Just a typical suburban house on a quiet little street. She'd bring little Jordan with her to games. Woulda been nice if Buck let them see me play more, but still it was great having them there. And the Yankee fans were fantastic to me. They were so excited to see me in pinstripes. They didn't care what all the experts said. They were glad to have me on the team.

I was so grateful to be given this chance to prove myself again. I was determined to make it work. There was always a champion inside me, ready to rise to the challenge if only I would let him. So I cleaned up my act. New York City was still Party Central, but I did not participate. After the games I went straight home to our quiet little street in Fort Lee, to my family, which that year had grown by one more soul: my daughter Jade, another angel, born that May.

At the end of the season, the Yankees asked me to fly to Puerto Rico and play some winter ball there. I think it was because I hadn't really played enough during the season to show them what I could do. I wasn't keen on it—it seemed to me they should know what I could do by that point—but I said okay. I was in my new humble, quiet, obedient Darryl mode. The family and I flew down there in November. I played maybe a dozen games and smashed the ball all around and out of the park. I think I hit a dozen homers in those dozen games. I batted near .500. And then I said, "Enough. They've seen what I can do. Let's go home."

So I'm not drinking anymore, I'm not doing drugs anymore, I'm clean and sober, I'm back on the right track, I'm doing everything the Yankees ask of me, and I'm keeping my mouth shut. Model behavior, and I felt good about it.

And yet . . . I wasn't 100 percent convinced the bad old days were over. In the back of my mind, I still had doubts, and in my soul there was still turmoil. I still had never fully explored what I was so unhappy about and why I didn't like myself. I was keeping it together that summer and fall, but it was fragile. It was like the cracks were still there, I had just taped over them.

And the next series of shocks was still to come.

THROUGH MOST OF '95, my mom was quiet about the breast cancer. She didn't want her children to fuss and worry. But that fall she finally agreed to let them operate on her. It was after that surgery that her doctors let us know her cancer was terminal.

And we were like, "What do you mean, terminal?" We knew what the word meant, but they weren't being very clear about the timing.

They said she had five months, give or take, to live.

Five months!

Charisse and I spent as much time as we could with her during those last months, in the house I'd bought her in San Dimas. It was the main reason I was antsy to get back from Puerto Rico. We all gathered around her. It was painful for all five of us kids. We all were going through various ordeals in our own lives, and now Mom was dying. We're thinking, what the heck are we gonna do with Mom gone? She held us together.

Her condition continued to deteriorate, pretty much on schedule. We had hospice nurses come in to take care of her, and Regina moved in with her. When I couldn't be there Regina would call me and tell me how bad it was getting. She had to change the dressing on my mother's chest, and she'd cry telling me how bad it looked, all open and eaten up by the cancer. When Regina told me that, I knew it wouldn't be long, and I started coming to stay in my mom's house three, four days at a time, as much as we could.

We were all there a lot those last few months. Even Ronnie was back and forth. He was still not doing well. Ronnie was on his own journey. But he loved Mom as much as we all did. I spent a lot of time there, along with Michael and the girls. We just wanted to be around her as much as we could in the time remaining. It was a very, very difficult time.

And in the midst of it, while we were all steeling ourselves for Mom's final days, Charisse and I got a terrible shock out of the blue. Bill Goodstein, my angel, died of a heart attack that January 1996. He was such a workaholic, in the office 24/7, and that's where he died, at his desk. He was only fifty-six, just about my mom's age.

Charisse and I cried so hard. We loved Bill so much. It was not about what he had done for us, it was just him, the way he loved us. He called us every other day just to let us know that everything was going to be all right. He was going to make sure everything was okay in our lives. He always said we were wonderful people and deserved it. And he did everything he said he was going to do. And now he was gone.

We came to New York for the funeral. I was just devastated. You have somebody who really cares for you, and you care about him, and he's suddenly gone.

Then we fly back to the West Coast, and my mom is going. We all came together at her house to be with her and be together in those last days. We never had anybody else in our lives. She was all we ever had. She raised us. All the memories came flashing through my head as she lay there.

But her spirits were good. She kept telling us it was all right, she was ready to go, ready to get out of this painful situation and move on to the other side. Her faith was unwavering. She wasn't worried. She knew where she was going.

One morning that February, just a few weeks after Bill died, her time came. We were all around her bed, holding her hands, and she was looking around at all of us, very peaceful. We could feel that it was about to happen.

She looked me in the eyes, and I said, "Mom, it's okay. You can let go. I'll take care of the girls."

I felt that was her last concern, for the girls. And when I said it, she let go. That was it. I watched her pass away. She died with all our arms around her.

It was the hardest thing ever, for all of us. We all just cried, cried, cried our hearts out. It tore me up. We had to get prepared for the viewing, the funeral, and burying her. When we went to view the body, I just couldn't take it. I just totally lost it. I didn't know what to think. I just couldn't understand, and even at the funeral, I still couldn't understand it. I yelled at God, "Why Mom? Why not me?"

My father and his wife came to visit us at Mom's house before the funeral. That's the day I really cut the cords with him. We're sitting around and he just said, "I don't know what to say to you guys." True to form. No words of comfort or love. Just, "I don't know what to say to you guys." That hurt us all. I haven't seen him and have had very little to say to him since that day. We talk on the telephone every now and again, but that's it.

It's so sad. Months go by, and then he'll call, and we'll have one of our forced conversations. Like when Darryl Jr. was playing basketball for the University of Maryland, my father would call once in a while and say how he was watching his grandson on television. The shame is he doesn't even know his grandson. He just watched him on TV, like any other sports fan. He's got a bunch of grandchildren he doesn't know. That's just tragic to me.

AFTER MY MOM'S funeral I crawled into bed and didn't get up for a couple of weeks. Charisse was worried to death about me. I couldn't do it, I couldn't get up. I had nothing left. I wanted to die so bad.

My mom had been the one person in the world I could always turn to. She was the only one I truly felt I could trust unconditionally. Now she was gone. And then there was my feeling that I had let her down. I'd been living my life as though my father was a much bigger influence on me than she was. I knew that must have disappointed her.

Looking back, I wish so much that she'd lived long enough to see me as I am today. She always knew I'd pull through, but she didn't get to see it. I know she's with me in spirit. I know she's looking down on me now and smiling. I just wish I could see that smile. I still cry sometimes, I miss her so.

Just to make sure my will to live was at its lowest after my mom died, the Yankees decided not to bring me back in '96. I was crushed. I thought I'd played well in 1995, the few times Buck let me. The Yankee fans adored me. I'd gone to Puerto Rico like they asked and done great there. I couldn't understand why they didn't sign me up again. Now I'd lost my mom, a dear friend, and my job in a matter of weeks. I felt as low as I'd ever felt in my life. "Oh whatever. When is my time? What else is there?"

Eventually, it was Mom who got me up. I could hear her saying, "Get up and go." She had told me before her passing that God was going to get out of me what he had called me to do.

"You can run, you can hide, but he's gonna get it out of you," she said. "You're gonna have to do what he has called you to do."

It took a while for it all to sink in. I didn't want to go on. I had no job and no plans. I didn't eat. Didn't want to be bothered with life.

But I couldn't just lie there forever. I had children to provide for.

The obvious question was, how? That's when God sent me another angel. Bill Goodstein's son-in-law Eric Grossman took over as my agent. He came into my life when I really needed him, and he's still in my life today. He worked for nothing.

When the Yankees said they weren't renewing my contract, Eric set out immediately to find me another team. One day he said to me, "D, I've got an offer I think you should consider."

DARRYL'S graduation, 1980, with sister-in-law Bridgette Strawberry

DARRYL and his mother, Ruby Strawberry

DARRYL and his father, Henry Strawberry

RUBY Strawberry and her mother, Gene Hill

DARRYL with sisters
Michelle and Regina
Strawberry

BEST friend Eric Davis and Darryl at Eric's wedding

DARRYL at bat for the Mets

DARRYL playing for the Mets

CHILDHOOD friends Darryl, Eric Davis, and Chris Brown

DARRYL'S mother, Ruby Strawberry

BROTHERS Michael, Ronnie, and Darryl Strawberry

DARRYL, Regina (sister), Ruby (mother), Michelle (sister), and Michael (brother) with Darryl's nieces and nephews

DARRYL and Eric Davis

DARRYL at bat for the
Yankees

DARRYL playing for
the Yankees

DARRYL with Yankees manager Joe Torre

DARRYL with Derek Jeter

DARRYL with former wife Lisa and their son, Darryl Jr. (DJ)

DARRYL'S daughter Diamond and son DJ

JOE NAMATH celebrity golf tournament to raise money for the March of Dimes, 2008: Julius Erving, Jim McMahon, Darryl, Howard Johnson, and Bobby Ojeda

DARRYL, Yogi Berra, and Tracy Strawberry

DARRYL and Tracy on their wedding day, 2006

DARRYL and Tracy on their honeymoon

DARRYL and Tracy receiving an award for their autism work

FOUNDATION work: Darryl, Tracy, Tracy's sister Angie Moynihan, friend Amy Buie, and Amy's parents

CHRISTMAS, 2008: Daughter Jade, Darryl, daughter Jewel, Tracy, and son Jordan

DARRYL and Tracy Strawberry

TOP: Jade Strawberry, Evan Olivares, Omar Olivares, Jordan Strawberry, Austin Olivares; *bottom:* Darryl, Jewel Strawberry, Tracy

"Great!" I said. My heart beat a little faster. "That's great news. Who is it?"

He hesitated before answering, "The St. Paul Saints, in the Northern League."

My heart dropped.

"The St. Paul who? The what league?"

I had never heard of either.

The Northern League was one of several independent leagues that played in smaller cities and towns around the country. They're similar to the minor leagues, but separate, not affiliated with the major league franchises the way the minors are. And where the minors are mostly kids on their way up, this was mostly veteran players who'd fallen out of the system for whatever reason and were trying to revive their careers by showing that they could still play.

This league played in the Upper Midwest and Canada—St. Paul, Duluth, Sioux City, Winnipeg, Thunder Bay. Nowhere I'd ever been or dreamed of going or even heard of. I pictured a bunch of has-beens stumbling around potholed cow pastures, and endless bus rides to rinky-dink ballparks with no lights and no crowds in the rickety stands and outfields smaller than the sandlots I played on as a kid.

It sounded depressing and humiliating. How could I say yes to it? I wasn't a prima donna, but I was Darryl Strawberry. A World Champion. An All-Star. How could I go from Shea, Yankee Stadium, Dodger Stadium to . . . Thunder Bay, wherever that was?

"No way, Eric," I said. "Thank you, but no. I'd rather quit baseball altogether than go back to that."

But I needed to get back into life. I needed a job—even one that paid a pathetic $2,000 a month. And I needed to play baseball. I loved baseball. I was still good at it. And, let's be frank, I didn't know how to do anything else. Baseball was the only job I ever had.

And there was something else. One of the co-owners of the St. Paul team (along with comedian Bill Murray) was also a limited partner in the Yankees. Maybe, Eric said, if I went to St. Paul and showed them I still had it, the Yankees would ask me back . . .

That May, Charisse and I packed up Jordan and Jade and we all flew from the hot, dry Palm Springs desert to chilly, damp St. Paul, Minnesota. No crowds waited for us at the airport. I rented us a mini-van and drove us to a motel, just a normal Holiday Inn or Days Inn or whatever. From St. Paul there were, in fact, long drives to places like Duluth, and we really did pass lots of pastures with lots of cows standing in them along the way. The term "culture shock" does not even apply.

But you know what? Once I put on the uniform and started to play, I found I liked it. Sure, the stadiums were terrible and the crowds were one-tenth the size I was used to and the clubhouses were tiny and dim, but it was a competitive league. There were a lot of former or struggling major league players there. Jack Morris, who pitched with the Detroit Tigers, was on my team. We were both putting our time in and hoping to be rediscovered. There were a lot of guys like us playing.

And what I rediscovered was the pure fun of playing baseball. Not playing in front of hundreds of reporters and cameras, not playing in front of fifty thousand people booing me, not having every single thing I did or said blown up into major headlines every day . . . was really nice. I relaxed. The pressure was low. All I had to do was play baseball and do it well. That's all I had ever wanted to do, from day one. Just let me play baseball and take all that other baggage and gar-bage away. Then I'll show you what I can do.

And I did. I played well, and within a month scouts from the ma-jors were dropping by to watch. A couple of teams expressed interest, but I just kept playing well and having fun doing it while Eric held out for the one we really wanted to hear from.

In July '96 we did. I had a good time playing for the Saints. A nice organization and a good bunch of guys. And the fans were great—really warm and polite. But I didn't hesitate a second when Eric called me and said, "The Yankees want you back."

12

CYNICS LIKE TO say there are no second chances in life. Cynics say a lot of things that sound true because they appeal to the defeatist inside us. We all know the world is hard and cruel, and it hands us no end of good excuses for quitting, giving up on ourselves, not even trying to overcome our weaknesses or come back from our mistakes.

But if you ever wanted proof that the cynics are wrong, just look at me. God had a purpose for me, and he gave me lots of second chances. Third chances, fourth chances, fifth chances . . . He also tested me every step of the way, and I failed those tests over and over and over again. Failed them miserably, many times. But God didn't give up on me. I truly believe he doesn't give up on any of us. We just give up on ourselves.

WHAT A GREAT Yankees team I joined that '96 season. My friends David Cone and Doc were both pitching. Derek Jeter was back. Andy Pettitte, Tino Martinez, Bernie Williams, Wade Boggs, John Wetteland, a great team all down the line. And Joe Torre was managing now. I had huge respect for Joe, and he respected me back. He was another players' manager, a former All-Star who understood the game from the grass up. And he was a really down-to-earth guy, a Brooklyn boy. The whole atmosphere in the clubhouse under Joe was the opposite from the year before under Showalter.

And then there was Mr. Steinbrenner. Over the next few years George became another father figure to me. He supported and encouraged me, even when everyone else was down on me. When you became a Yankee you became one of George's guys. If you stumbled and struggled, he defended you and gave you the chance to prove yourself again. He did it for me, he did it for Doc, he did it when Steve Howe struggled with his own addictions. And many other players who had personal problems. George was there for them. He lifted them out of whatever slump they were in, brought them into the Yankee family, and made everybody see them and believe in them as Yankees. He took care of all of our families and tried to make sure things went well for us. It was a much more personal relationship than I'd had with the owners of any other ball club.

I know that's not the image of George that's portrayed in the media, but, you know, don't get me started about how images are portrayed in the media. Sportswriters didn't know George any better than they knew me. They get a simple image of someone—crazy George Steinbrenner, lazy Darryl Strawberry—and they stick with it no matter what you do. They might as well be drawing cartoons. In years to come, when all the dust has settled, other writers are going to look back at George's career, like they've begun to look back at mine, and recognize what he really achieved and accomplished.

I was so grateful to him for giving me another chance, and I was proud and happy to help the team take the American League pennant and then go on to beat the heavily favored Atlanta Braves in the World Series.

We headed back to Rancho Mirage with me feeling, once again, like my life was on the right path. I wasn't acting out in any way.

In Rancho Mirage, I was surrounded by good influences, including two more angels: "the godparents," Paul and Margery Leonard. Or Ma and Pa, as we called them. Two of the most wonderful, kind, loving, accepting people I have ever met. In '95, I had started attending church with them and Charisse—St. Stephen Baptist Church, in La Puente. I fell back in love with God, and it kept me alive. I was still messed up. I still hadn't dealt with my real issues. But at least I was committed to being back in church, going to church every Sunday with Charisse and the Leonards. Oh, you talk about a blessing. They are strong Christians, and they have been nothing but a tremendous blessing in my life. They did everything with us. Traveled with us, came out to Rancho Mirage to spend time with us. I still go out to California and spend time with them to this day.

St. Stephen was a big congregation and an active ministry. It wasn't just about going to church on Sunday. It was about applying Christian values to your whole life, and getting out and doing good in the community. I became close with Josh Johnson, who ran what they called a spiritual twelve-step program there. Josh was a former substance abuser himself, so he knew the score, and he knew that getting clear of drugs and alcohol took more than just changing your bad behavior. You have to get to the root causes of the behavior. You can't solve your physical addictions if you're not right in your spirit. So his program was modeled on the typical Alcoholics Anonymous and Narcotics Anonymous steps, but with a strong component of biblical study. I really liked that. My mother had raised us on the Bible, but I'd gotten away from it. Getting back into reading and studying the Bible was like going home. It was the part I hadn't really followed up on when I should have after being saved by Morris Cerullo.

Through Josh, I also got involved in the church's program of collecting and giving away food to the homeless in downtown L.A. We loaded up vans with food and drove up from La Puente one night a week. Drove straight to skid row and distributed these meals and hot coffee and tea to the folks living on the streets. They'd rush out of the darkness and surround the vans. It was probably their one hot meal a week. Some of them would recognize me. "Hey, it's Darryl Straw-berry! Mr. Strawberry, it's so great to see you out here helping us, bringing food to us." Others had no idea who I was. Just somebody in the church group handing out food and coffee.

It was heartbreaking to see all these folks who had lost hold on their lives through alcohol or drugs or whatever it was. A sober les-son to those of us who were struggling with our own addictions. It wasn't like, "Oh, look at these poor crackheads, all strung out and sleeping on the streets, eating out of garbage cans. I'm grateful I'm not one of them." Because I was one of them. I was lucky enough not to be homeless, but otherwise, the way I was living and acting out, I was right down there with them. No difference. We're all people, and we all struggle.

I made that food run whenever I could for a couple of years. You didn't read about that in the news. I mean, I never tried to get any press for it. I didn't want the press for this anymore than I wanted the press for anything else I did. Still, it was kind of funny that they never found out about it and followed me to skid row with their cam-eras. They were only interested in showing me slipping and failing. Me doing something good and positive wasn't news to them.

I WORKED HARD on staying in shape all that winter, hoping that Mr. Steinbrenner would bring me back to the Yankees for the '97 sea-son. I was in the gym six days a week. I wasn't a young pup anymore. I was going on thirty-five, which is kind of ancient in baseball-player years. I had more than a decade of wear and tear to contend with, not to mention all the extra strain I'd put on my body with my extracur-ricular activities. There were a lot of young and hungry ballplayers out there. I knew I needed to get in top form to compete.

Just as important as my physical shape, I thought I had my mind right. I felt at peace with myself. I stayed clean and sober all that win-ter, participated in the church, studied the Bible. I surrounded myself with my family and all those good people, and it had done my attitude a world of good. I set a goal for myself to have not just a good year in '97, but a great one.

George did sign me up again. I went to spring training in a great mood. The Yankees were going to win the World Series again, and I was going to help power them to the top. Doc was there. He wasn't a baby anymore, either, and he'd been struggling with his own personal problems as much as I had. But I said to him, "Doc, we're going to have a great year. I can feel it. Let's show these young men how it's done."

There wasn't a doubt in my mind. I told Joe Torre, "Bring it on. Play me. I want to play 150 games this season." I had full confidence in my abilities. Joe's attitude was like, all right, take it easy there, champ, you're not as young as you used to be. Let's not wear it out. Let's see if you can go nine innings and get back out there for nine more the next day. He appreciated my eagerness. I was an athlete. Athletes are champions in their hearts. Champions rise to the occasion. He knew that.

I charged full-tilt into the preseason schedule. I went at it hard—too hard. Almost right away, I banged up my left knee sliding into second base in an intrasquad game. It swelled up a little. I ignored it. I figured I'd just play through it. That's what you do as an athlete. Then Bernie Williams and I ran into each other chasing a fly ball in an exhibition game and I went down on that knee, hard. It really swelled up this time, filled with fluid. Joe and I were both concerned, but when the regular season came around, he decided to start me in left field anyway. That felt great, his having that much confidence in me.

But it wasn't happening. The knee wouldn't heal. I couldn't run right in the field, and I couldn't swing right at the plate, the knee just couldn't pivot correctly and support the weight. The doctors drained fluid from it to reduce the swelling. They talked about surgery. Behind the kneecap the cartilage was basically ground down to nothing from all the years of wear and tear. It was bone on bone in there.

I played five games and went 0 for 14 at the plate. Joe put me on the disabled list.

It was only April. My 150-game season was already sliding away from me. Doc hurt himself, too, pulled his groin, and joined me on the DL. So much for showing the youngsters how it's done.

In May, we both got sent down to the minors, the Yankees AA team, to see if we could rehabilitate our injuries. I limped around left field, tried to get my swing back at the plate, all the time nursing the knee. Doc pitched a few games and did well enough to be brought back up to the Yankees and hit the road with them. His groin was healing, but he was in mental pain. His disappointment and frustration got to him. While the Yankees were in Texas, he got into an altercation with a cabdriver. I don't remember what they fought over. It didn't really matter. I think it was Doc's pure frustration uncorking itself. Mr. Steinbrenner let his own frustration show. He yelled at Doc, yelled at Joe for bringing Doc back up to the team too soon—and didn't want to hear it from me when I told him I was ready to come back myself. I used all my persuasive charms on him, but it didn't work.

"Don't rush yourself. Look what happened to Doc," he said.

"I'm not Doc," I said. "Doc is Doc. I'm me."

I kept trying to play, putting off surgery, but it wasn't happening. I got to where I could hit the ball all right, but otherwise my movement was too restricted. By late June, we all—Joe, George, and I—faced the facts. I had to have knee surgery. My '97 season, my great 150-game season, was over before it really ever started. All my work, all my good intentions and optimism, were for nothing. It was devastating for me, and I know Joe and George felt terrible for me. They'd wanted me to have a good year as much as I did.

I coped in my usual fashion. Just figured that once again all my Bible study and clean living and getting right with God had led to nothing. What was the point? All it did was lead to disappointment and defeat. Might as well look for a little happiness where I could count on it.

YOU KNOW WHO kept faith in me, even when I lost it for myself that year? George Steinbrenner. In January '98, despite my disastrously disappointing '97 season, he re-signed me. My surgery had gone well, the knee had pretty much healed—slowly and frustratingly, but it healed—and he decided I deserved yet another chance.

We packed up the kids again and moved back to Fort Lee. The Yankees were smokin' that year. The whole team had a disappointing '97 season, coming in second in the Eastern Division behind the Orioles, where E.D. was now playing. This year the Yankees were loaded for bear. I was really, really happy to be back on board. Joe didn't expect me to be in the outfield. He wanted me in the lineup as the designated hitter. He was convinced I could still hit the long ball and drive guys home.

I hit well. In '98 I had something like the comeback season '97 was supposed to be. By the end of the season I would rack up 24 home runs and 57 RBIs. Not bad for an old guy with a bum knee.

But something was wrong with me physically. I felt it all summer long. I just didn't feel right. Something was wrong with my stomach. It was like nothing I ever felt before, and it wasn't preventing me from hitting, so I didn't say a word to anyone, not even Charisse—not even when some odd symptoms began to show.

I was always a big eater, but that summer my appetite disappeared. It was like my stomach was empty and growling, but my brain was not interested in food. My brain was telling me something was wrong with my body. I couldn't eat a normal meal. I'd dip and dabble at it, then get up from the table and go lie down to watch television or something.

"Why am I bothering to cook if you're not going to eat?" Charisse complained. I didn't tell her that something was wrong. Over the course of the season I dropped from 220 to 210 pounds. Ten pounds may not sound like a lot, but when you're an athlete in the peak of the season, it's not normal.

Then the stomach cramps came. Late at night, they would jolt me awake. It felt like a demon was twisting a glowing hot poker in my guts. I remembered how I had felt when the spirit entered me at the Morris Cerullo convention—how the sensation of a river running through me had centered on my stomach. Strange, huh? And now here I was doubled up on the bed with these terrible stomach cramps, completely soaked in sweat.

I never told anybody outside the house. I used to come to the ball-park every day and drink Maalox, hoping it would make me feel better. I wanted to play. I had a lot to prove, and I felt I owed it to Mr. Steinbrenner and Joe Torre for sticking with me.

The cramps were manageable for the few hours of a game. It wasn't a sharp pain. Nothing specific where I could say it hurt when I did this or that. It was more like a constant stomachache. I'd gulp down the Maalox, go out and swing. Later that night the really bad cramps would twist me in knots.

Athletes live with injury and pain. It's not just the contact sports like football that bang you up. Baseball players experience lots of joint and muscle problems—even before the use of steroids made some guys particularly fragile and susceptible. Major league pitchers spend much of their careers battling the pain and stress to their arms and shoulders. Like I said before, we may make it look easy out there, but it's not.

This wasn't like any of the injuries I had sustained before—the ruptured disk in my spine, the time I banged up my shoulder, the knee. This was a pain deep inside. And that made it easier to hide. After '97, I didn't want to go to the doctors and have them find something that might keep me from playing. I wanted to finish the season. The Yankees were having a blazing season, on their way to a record-breaking 114 wins and only 48 losses. We would finish an amazing 22 games ahead of the second-place Red Sox. And I was contributing. I was happy to repay Mr. Steinbrenner's and Joe's continuing faith in me.

And then there were the other expectations. After my bitterly disappointing '97 season, a lot of people thought Mr. Steinbrenner was nuts for bringing me back into the Yankees once again. Every time I went to the plate, it was a chance to prove them wrong. When I connected and the ball went soaring over the heads of the outfielders, screaming up into the sky like it was going into orbit, all the criticism turned to cheers. *Dar-ryl! Dar-ryl! Dar-ryl!*

Of course, it was a lot harder to hide my distress from Charisse. I did tell her late in the season that I had blood in my stool. I didn't tell her how much.

"Darryl, go get a checkup," she said.

"Nah. It's just stress on my body. Hemorrhoids or something. Once the season is over, I'll go in and get checked," I said.

The cramps kept getting worse. I was losing more weight and my energy was low. I knew in my heart that something more serious than a stomachache was going on. But I kept telling myself it'd be all right. I'd go get checked out right after the last game of the season. They'd figure out what was wrong and fix me up, and I'd be in the playoffs.

In mid-September we went to Baltimore to play the Orioles. That was great, because I got to see E.D. He had gone through a much more frightening year in '97 than I had. I had only banged up my knee. He had been diagnosed with colon cancer that spring.

The really frightening thing about it was that he had shown absolutely no symptoms. No pain, nothing. Then he slid into third base on a sacrifice fly and was hit with an excruciating burst of pain inside him. He hobbled back to the bench and sat down, and the pain was so intense he couldn't stand back up for a while. Because he's a champion, he went right back and played the next day. In his hotel room afterward he was in such agony that he really couldn't move now. They packed him on a train back to Baltimore, where an ambulance was waiting to take him straight to the hospital. He was in the hospital for a week taking tests before they determined it was colorectal cancer. Two days later he was in surgery. He was still taking chemo when he made it back into the ballpark that fall and crushed a game-winning home run in the American League Championship Series. What a comeback. That's my boy.

After our game in Baltimore, I told Eric how I was feeling.

"Don't fool around," he said. "Go get it checked out right away."

I knew he was right. I put it off until we played our last game of the season. Then, at the end of September, the day before our first postseason game against the Rangers, I spoke to the team doctor, Stuart Hershon.

He took me straight to Columbia Presbyterian Hospital, in the Washington Heights neighborhood of Manhattan. They ran some tests.

They said they thought what I had was diverticulitis, a condition where painful bulges form in the colon. Mild cases can be treated with diet and medicine. In more extreme cases the surgeons go in and cut away the affected portion of the colon.

That didn't sound so awful. They said they wanted me to come back for more tests. I figured sure—let me play out the postseason and I'll run right back to you.

Next night I sat in the dugout at Yankee Stadium while we beat the Rangers in game one of the Eastern Division Series. Joe Torre had scheduled me to sit that one out and play in game two the following night.

First, though, I had to go back to Columbia Presbyterian the next morning for a CAT scan. The procedure went smoothly, and I headed home still thinking this would all turn out to be no big deal.

The doctors were on the phone as Charisse and I walked in the door back home in Fort Lee. The CAT scan had revealed a growth on my colon, and they wanted me back the next morning for a colonoscopy.

So no game two for Darryl Strawberry. I watched on TV at home as we beat the Rangers again.

I went back to the hospital the next morning. They doped me up and performed the colonoscopy. Afterward, I woke up on my back in a hospital bed, still drowsy and dopey, and saw Charisse and my doctor standing there. The look of worry on Charisse's face should have told me all I needed to know, but I was still thinking positively.

"So," I asked sleepily, "what's the story?"

The doctor said, "You have a tumor in your colon the size of a walnut. It's inflamed. It's big enough that it's blocking your colon, which is why you've been in such pain. And . . ."

"And?"

"And it may be malignant."

"Malignant?"

I knew what that meant. I guess I just needed to hear him say the word. And he did:

"Cancer."

13

CANCER. MY HEART plunged. Just hearing the word said in general conversation is enough to put fear and dread in anyone. Hearing it applied to you—being told, "You have cancer"—freezes your whole body and your mind.

"You have got to be kidding me," I groaned.

It wasn't a total surprise, of course. My talk with Eric had put the idea in my head. I mean how weird is that, that we both got colon cancer, within one year of each other? As he put it, maybe there was something in the water back in L.A.

Still, after I spoke with Eric I had shoved the thought of cancer way back into a tiny corner of my mind. I was focused on positive thoughts. It wasn't going to be cancer. It was going to be no big deal. The docs were going to fix me up in a week or two and I'd be back in uniform for the World Series.

How could I have cancer? I was thirty-six years old. I had just put my life back together. Things were just going well. I was living clean and sober and quietly.

And now this? After everything else I'd been through? What else could possibly go wrong? Was I going to die?

I thought back to what Morris Cerullo said about the full-on battle I was in with the Enemy. I thought of all the pain and trouble of the last few years—the deaths of my mom and Bill Goodstein, my own injuries, the divorce from Lisa, the money troubles, my addictive behavior and stupid decisions, the public humiliation . . . And now cancer.

I was only half listening as the doctor explained that they wanted to operate right away, cut the tumor out and have it biopsied. If it was malignant, which they were pretty sure it was, they would want me to take chemotherapy. He talked about survival rates, the chances of the cancer coming back despite the operation, cheery things like that.

I felt like I was at a crossroads. I could just give up, give in, let nature take its course. Tell God, "Go look for someone else. I'm done."

Or I could follow my mom's example. I remembered how strong she'd been through her cancer, how firm in her faith. I didn't feel anywhere near as strong or firm as she was. She'd always been a rock. That tiny woman was one of the strongest people I ever knew. I felt her watching me, telling me that this was just one more trial I had to go through.

I thought, "All right, Mom. I'll try. If this is what it is, let's get it over with."

SO THE YANKEES flew off to Texas for game three against the Rangers, and I stayed home in Fort Lee to get ready for surgery. That afternoon in the locker room in Texas, Joe Torre told my teammates I'd been diagnosed with cancer. I heard that a lot of them broke down and cried when they heard that. That really touched me. My friend Coney took it especially hard.

When Charisse and I woke the morning I was supposed to head back to the hospital, we saw that the media had descended on Cedar Street, our little suburban lane. Vans with satellite dishes were parked all up and down the block. Camera crews and TV and newspaper reporters were standing all over the front lawn. Meanwhile, the phone was ringing nonstop. It was madness. Everyone wanted to know what was going on, how I was doing. Friends called to give their support and let us know they were praying for us. Media wanted interviews. It was like the whole world was right outside the door, wanting to be let in, wanting to talk to me.

Charisse kept Jordan and Jade home from preschool that day. At four and three, they were too little to know anything really serious was going on. Charisse told them Daddy had a boo-boo and the doctors were going to take it away.

Thank God Eric Grossman was with us. He was another rock for us, as always. We let two TV crews, ESPN and NBC, into the house to do on-air interviews. NBC interviewed me with E.D., who was back home in California now that the season was over for the Orioles. As a cancer survivor, Eric had become a big proponent of early detection. NBC also let me send a message to my teammates in Texas. I think basically I told them to win the series for the Gipper.

Then I had to walk out the door and face the mob on the front lawn. Charisse went out with me. Facing all those cameras and microphones, that's when it all came crashing down on me. I choked up and tears welled up in my eyes. I mumbled some words. I don't remember what I said, really. Charisse had to take over. She thanked everyone for their concern and asked them to pray for me. That's when the tears just poured down my cheeks. I just stood there crying. No, I was not nearly as strong as my mom.

We rode into Manhattan and checked me back into Columbia Presbyterian. I spent the night in a hospital bed, because surgery was scheduled for the next morning. The hospital could not have treated me better. All the nurses were kind and professional, and my team of doctors was the finest you could ever wish for. There must have been a dozen of them—surgeon, cancer specialist, colon specialist, heart specialist, anesthesiologist, and I don't remember what all else. I don't think the president of the United States would get better care.

That night the staff wheeled an extra bed into my room so Charisse could stay with me. When everyone left us alone, we were quiet and subdued. I knew Charisse was worried to death. But now that the time for the operation was almost here, I felt a new confidence. Somehow I knew this was not going to be the end of my time on earth. I still believed I had a purpose here, and I had not yet even begun to fulfill it. This was another trial, another test. I knew somehow that I would go through it and get to the other side.

"Everything's going to be okay," Charisse and I kept saying to each other. I'm not sure she believed it, but I did.

Early the next morning they gave me a sedative and wheeled me into the operating room. There, they put me on the operating table, and the anesthesiologist put my lights out. The surgery lasted four hours. A couple of Charisse's girlfriends came to stay with her in the waiting room. And one special friend came and sat with her, too: George Steinbrenner. His team was in Texas, competing in the playoffs, but he elected to stay in New York to be with us. He was with her the whole four hours of surgery.

I came to that evening in intensive care. The surgery had gone beautifully, and the prognosis was good. Yes, the biopsy showed the tumor was malignant, as expected. But over the next few days the doctors would report that they'd removed some tissue and lymph nodes from the area around the tumor and their tests showed the cancer had barely spread. They said it was because I'd been in such great physical shape. My good muscle tone and six-pack abs had kept the tumor in one place. If I had jostled it in some way—running for a ball, sliding to a base, swinging the bat—it could have ruptured and spread cancerous cells everywhere. As it was, I'd have to take chemotherapy for six months, but my chances of a full recovery were about as good as they get.

I spent the next two weeks in the hospital, hooked up to an IV, weak and helpless as a baby at first. That was frustrating, and I was anxious to get up and out. Still, I knew I was one of the lucky ones. My cancer had been discovered early, the operation had gone smoothly, and I was already on the way to recovery. There were patients all around me on the ward who were in much worse shape. There was one whole section just for children with cancer. Some of them wrote me letters. That broke my heart, thinking about those kids who'd been struck by this disease when their lives were just starting. Their letters cured me of any temptation to feel sorry for myself. These little kids were so brave and strong. I'd be ashamed of myself to whine about my condition with these kids right down the hall.

I got letters and cards, in fact, from well-wishers all over the country. Hundreds a day. It was amazing. Some of them made a point of telling me they were not Yankee fans, no way—but they were Darryl Strawberry fans.

A few days after my surgery, the Yankees faced the Indians in the first game of the American League Championship Series. Mr. Steinbrenner invited Charisse to come to Yankee Stadium and throw the first pitch. She was terrified, but I told her that if that was what the boss wanted, she should go. She very reluctantly agreed.

Yankee Stadium was packed that day, and when Charisse walked out toward the mound, the stadium exploded with cheers and applause. Watching it on the TV in my hospital room, I felt tears in my eyes. There's nobody like New York fans. I was so sorry I couldn't be there and light the place up with a home run or two to thank them.

I really don't know what it is about me that has made fans so kind to me over the years. I know there were times when I didn't live up to their expectations or acted in ways that disappointed them. Yet they always stuck with me. Maybe it's because despite my being a "celebrity" and a superstar athlete, my troubles and mistakes made it clear—sometimes painfully obvious—that I'm just a human being. I had a great gift for playing baseball, but that didn't shield me from going through a lot of the same troubles and struggles many of them have—addiction, divorce, money worries, and now cancer. I stumbled and fell, but I picked myself up and survived. Somehow I think that has brought me closer to a lot of fans than if I were Mr. Perfect, a sports god who never faltered or doubted himself or showed his human side.

People sometimes ask me how I can be so patient and accommodating with fans. I've always been one to sign autographs until my hand is about to fall off and get my picture taken hugging fans until I was blind from the flashes. When people ask me how I can be so good to my fans, I tell them they've got it backward. It's the fans who have been so good to me.

THOSE TWO WEEKS in the hospital felt like an eternity. I grew increasingly bored, restless, and irritable. Every time I took a stroll around the halls, wheeling my IV around with me, I was tempted just to keep going out the doors, grab a taxi, and get the heck outta there. I was also starving, and I'll be the first to admit that hunger has always made me cranky. They fed me nothing but Jell-O and soup for two weeks, and my body was screaming for real food. So was I. I even dreamed about food. Charisse told a reporter that I was dreaming about cheesecake, and suddenly dozens of cheesecakes came to our house in Fort Lee, sent by bakeries all over New York. See what I mean about New York fans? Only problem was I didn't get to eat one bite. Charisse, her grandma, and Ma Leonard ate as much as they could, fed some to the reporters who were still camped out there, and brought a lot in for the nurses. Toward the end of my stay I was getting really bad-tempered about it. "Give me *food! Real food!*" The nurses ignored me. That left Charisse to bear the brunt. I don't know how she put up with me.

Finally, the docs okayed me to leave. We got home to Fort Lee just in time to watch the Yankees on TV beating the Padres in the first game of the World Series. Man, it was hard to sit there watching them do that. I wanted so badly to be there.

The Yankees went on to win the second and third games. The media and fans, meanwhile, were clamoring to see me up and about. The docs said it was okay for me to make a brief public appearance, as long as I was careful. So on the day of game four, we drove into Manhattan and went to the Modell's sporting goods shop on Forty-second

Street, where they were selling a Darryl Strawberry towel, with a dollar from every sale going to cancer research. I don't think the store manager and staff knew what they were in for. I'm sure they expected a crowd, but this was a mob scene. When I showed up, creaking my way along slowly, feeling the staples in my gut with every step, the crowd went berserk. Yelling my name, cheering, photographers elbowing one another to get closer to me, their flashes going off like fireworks. It probably really wasn't all that safe for me to be there in my condition, but I loved every second.

Katie Couric showed up with a crew and interviewed me for the *Today* show. She wanted to speak to me about colon cancer and how I was feeling, because it had taken her husband's life. I could see in her face the pain of what she had experienced losing him. She wanted to talk to me about the process of surviving it, because her husband had not.

The Yankees won game four at Yankee Stadium that night, sweeping the Series in four straight. In the locker room celebration afterward, my teammates lifted bottles of champagne and toasted, "This is for the Straw Man!" I felt like they really had won it for the Gipper. Then the phone rang. It was Derek Jeter, calling from the locker room. In all the pandemonium it was hard to hear what he was trying to say, but I didn't have to. I knew.

A couple of days later, I got to join the other Yankees in their victory parade up Broadway from Wall Street to City Hall. George wanted me there, my teammates wanted me there, and my doctors said they'd allow it as long as I went home the instant I felt fatigued.

We met up at Yankee Stadium, and my teammates all hugged me. A couple of them joked around with me. "Man, you look so thin! Look at you!" That's how athletes tell you they've been concerned about you and are relieved to see you up and around.

The parade itself was awesome. I had done it before, in '86 and '96, but it's always an amazing event to take part in. It was a bright, crisp October day in Manhattan. An enormous crowd choked the sidewalks for blocks, and tens of thousands more cheered and tossed a snowstorm of confetti from all the windows of the tall office buildings that line the Canyon of Heroes, where so many historic parades have been held. The team stood on a parade float in their uniforms and rolled slowly up the street as fans cheered and chanted their names. I wasn't healthy enough for that. I was still really tender and weak. Charisse and I sat in the back of an open car and I waved, carefully, to the crowd. It was all a little bittersweet for me, of course, but I was thanking God that he kept me around for it.

I was proud to be there and really happy to have done my part that season. But it did tire me out, and I ducked out before the ceremony with the mayor in front of City Hall.

A FEW DAYS later we had the Fort Lee house packed up and were flying back out to Rancho Mirage, where I would start the chemo and start getting myself back into playing shape. I was absolutely determined on getting myself healthy again to play the '99 season. I still had a year left on my contract with the Yankees and I made up my mind I was going to fulfill it.

Maybe that was crazy of me. It was November. Spring training in Florida would begin in February. That gave me a little more than three months. And I'd still be in the middle of my six months of chemo.

I knew it was going to be a battle, on two fronts. First, there was the chemo itself. Eric had told me about how that could knock me out, mentally as well as physically. At the same time, I had to rehabilitate my body. I had dropped from 220 pounds to around 185. At six-six that's really skinny. I'd look at my gaunt and bony reflection in the mirror sometimes and think, "Oh man, why don't I just waste away and die?" Plus what muscles I had left lost their tone from all the lying around. I not only had to bulk up, I had to spend a lot of time working out to put the bulk on in the right places.

I repressed the doubt and worries and said, "If that's what I got to do, let's do it." I went at it full swing, 24/7. Put my game face on and got down to it.

First, I went to an oncologist in Palm Springs and started the chemo. Once a week, they hooked me up to an IV and poured the poison in my veins. There's no better word for the antineoplastic (anticancer) chemicals they shoot into you. It's fiercely strong poison that goes after malignant cells, but it kills normal cells, too. Most patients have very strong negative reactions to chemo. Eric had warned me about vomiting, diarrhea, weakness, and fatigue.

But I surprised everyone. I experienced no side effects. I'd watch TV with the IV needle in my arm pumping the poison into my veins, then thank the nurses and head home. Take a little nap, hit the gym. No big deal.

I worked out every day. All the time I spent in the gym worried my doctors. I promised I wouldn't do anything to strain or stretch my abdomen, but who was I kidding? When you're working out and lifting weights, your midsection is your center of gravity and strength. It doesn't matter if you're working your legs or your shoulders, you're also working your abdomen. I had a lot of work to do to get back in playing shape by February, and I wasn't going to let those staples in my gut stop me. Besides, the docs were pleased with how quickly and cleanly it healed. That was exactly because I'd always had those strong six-pack abs. I had to get that muscle tone back, for my whole body.

I progressed well through December and the Christmas holidays. I was confident that I could meet my goal. I even felt well enough that Charisse and I celebrated our fifth wedding anniversary with a romantic weekend alone at the beach.

Then one night in January the Enemy came creeping into the bedroom. He stood over me in the dark and said, "What, you think you're winning this war? You think your mom's death and Bill's death and your cancer were all I had left to throw into the battle? You think it's over? Why you want to insult me that way?"

And he reached into my gut with both hands and twisted my bowels into knots. The next morning I could not get out of bed. Charisse tried to get me up and I wouldn't budge.

"Darryl, what is it?" she asked.

"I don't know. Maybe it's a stomach virus or something."

I didn't fool either of us, and as the day went on, the cramps got worse. My guts felt like a big ball of rubber bands, all twisted and knotted.

It wasn't any virus. Scar tissue had formed over the surgery site, twisting and blocking my intestine.

The doctors decided the only recourse was to open me up again and remove that area of my intestine.

Aaaaarrrggghhh! Now? More surgery now? A month from spring training?

"All right." I sighed. "Do it now. Get it over with."

So they did. And there I was again, on my back in a hospital bed, weak and sore. Right back where I started in November. To say that I was angry, frustrated, and depressed would be the understatement of the century.

But I was also determined. I had to overcome this. I had to play again. I felt a little like I did back when the Mets were on the road and all the hometown fans booed and taunted me when I walked up to the plate. "Oh, you're booing me? Here, let me give you something to really boo me about." *Pow.* The ball flies out of the park, and the entire stadium falls silent as tens of thousands of people who jeered me a second ago sit there staring with their mouths open as I trot around the bases. Thank you for the lift. Boo me anytime.

I thought about E.D., and what we always told each other about how we were survivors and winners. Look at where we came from, the obstacles we overcame, everything we'd achieved. A couple of black kids from South Central, tearing it up in the big show. He beat cancer. I beat cancer. I could beat this, too. I was going to play the opening day game. Play, heck. I was going to hit a grand slam.

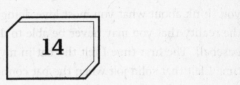

14

I WENT HOME AND got back on my program instantly. I ate lots and lots and lots of potatoes to put some weight back on my bones as quickly as possible. I ate the state of Idaho clean out of potatoes. Pretty soon I wasn't just back up to my normal playing weight, but twenty pounds over.

I hit the gym so soon Charisse blew up at me and appealed to my docs, who told me to take it slow and easy for a couple of weeks, let things heal.

A couple of weeks? I didn't have a couple of weeks. I had weights to lift, sacks of potatoes and mounds of broccoli to eat.

In mid-February we packed the kids up and flew to Tampa. I had made a lot of progress. I wasn't anywhere near 100 percent, but if I kept going the way I was I'd be fully back in plenty of time for that opening day game. I still had three months left of chemo to take, and we arranged for that to continue in Tampa. No big deal. Chemo and batting practice. I can handle it.

Spring training began at Legends Field (now, appropriately, George M. Steinbrenner Field) the third week of February. What a great feeling it was to see the guys and start training with them. And what a warm reception they gave me. I know a lot of them doubted they'd ever see me alive again, let alone back in uniform and swinging a bat.

I swung pretty well, too, which was a relief for everyone. Joe Torre and the team trainers told me to take it slow and easy. They didn't want me to overdo it and possibly reinjure myself. But batting practice was a pure joy. One thing about cancer is that it really makes you think about what you most love doing, because you have to face the reality that you may never be able to do that thing again. I loved baseball. The first time I felt the bat in my hands, and then the first time I felt that solid jolt when the bat connected and shot a ball soaring up into the blue Florida sky . . . well, the joy that rushed up in me almost cracked my heart it felt so good.

By the first batch of preseason exhibition games I felt really confident that I was almost back. I did fine out in left field, running with no sense of trouble or pain inside, not even my knee bothering me anymore. I did well at the plate, too. One week in March, I took chemo one day, and hit a three-run homer the next. Chemo and home runs. No big deal. I didn't let anyone know that the chemo was sometimes making me sick as a dog now. I'd go home afterward and fall into bed, sleep like a dead man for hours, then wake up with a terrible headache, a real skull-cracker banging like a fire gong in my head with every heartbeat. It made me dizzy and sick to my stomach, and nothing helped but to sleep some more until it receded.

Yeah, the side effects had finally kicked in, big-time, but I tried to keep that a secret from Joe.

Still, Joe and George didn't seem quite as confident about my return as I felt. Joe kept telling me to take it easy, not overtax my body. And George kept hesitating over whether to re-sign my contract for the year. I couldn't get a straight answer from them about whether I was going to be with the team when they headed off to start the season. I knew Joe was thinking of both me and the team. I knew George had good cause to hesitate and wonder if I could play. But I'd worked so hard to come back, and here I was, hitting home runs. How much more did I have to do to prove I was strong enough? Pick the whole stadium up on my back and carry it around? I kept repeating my mantra: "One day at a time. One day at a time." It had gotten me this far.

But as each of those days brought the regular season closer and my future remained in doubt, I grew more tense and worried. And I pushed myself harder, hoping to convince them. I was an athlete. I was driven to succeed. You play through. You even play through cancer and chemo. I just had to convince everyone else I could do it.

Around the end of March I told Charisse, "You and the kids go up to New Jersey. Get settled in. I'll be up there soon."

The truth was I was so nervous and anxious I figured it was best if they weren't around. I didn't want to snap on them. My frustration gave way to flashes of anger sometimes, fits of sullen moodiness others. The more preoccupied I was, the more quiet and withdrawn I got, with my family as well as my teammates. I figured if I was alone I could focus better and keep my attitude up.

Ultimately, I pushed too hard. I overextended myself in every way—physically, mentally, emotionally. I think that's why I reacted the way I did when the word came down in early April: The rest of the Yankees would go start the season, but I'd stay in Tampa on extended spring training. "Let him finish up his chemo. Then we'll see."

Joe agreed. He'd just been diagnosed with prostate cancer himself. "You've been a champ," he said. "Finish up the chemo, then come join us. I want you completely healthy. That's the most important thing."

IF I HADN'T pushed myself so hard and built my hopes up so high, maybe I would have dealt with it better. Instead, I crashed. I plunged off those high hopes and dove headfirst into a pit of despair. When everybody went off, I didn't feel merely left behind, I felt abandoned. All my hard work and hopes were for nothing. Why even try?

I guess that sounds pretty immature of me. It was immature. All I can say is that I wasn't as strong as I tried to be. I don't just mean physically, but emotionally and mentally, too. I'd been so battered that I was weak in my mind and my heart as well as my body. I felt I had put up with so much, tried so hard, and now this. Another disappointment.

I tried to rally. I really did. The first couple weeks of April, while my teammates were off playing ball, I went to the ballpark every day, worked out, knocked some balls around. But it was beginning to seem futile.

I made myself go to chemo on schedule, even though it had been making me sicker and sicker. I had come to dread every week's session so much that now I was throwing up before they even stuck the IV in me. Not from the poison itself, but just from the anxiety and expectation.

Chemo doesn't just take a vicious toll on your body. It weakens your mind and your spirit as well. If you've been through it you know what I'm talking about. All that poison sloshing around in your system gnaws away at your thoughts and your emotions as well as your body. You're so weak and sick you begin to think some really dark thoughts. You start to wonder if all the misery is worth it. Maybe you'd be better off if you just gave up and let the cancer kill you.

My doctors had always warned me that this moment might come. Most everybody going through chemo gets to a point where they just don't think they can keep it up any longer. I didn't believe them. But now I was there.

Where was my faith? I had lost it. Maybe if I had gone back to California I could have borrowed some from Ma and Pa Leonard. Their faith was so strong there was always plenty to go around. But I was alone in Florida.

I was sick and miserable and losing the will to fight it anymore. All the old self-doubts and feelings of worthlessness crept back into my mind. Maybe I really was washed up. Maybe I was a has-been. Maybe I wasn't the superhuman I was trying so hard to be. Maybe I should just give up.

I did. The second week of April, I went and had chemo one morning, same as always. When I came home, feeling miserable again, an old, old thought slipped into my mind. It was the notion that there was only one way in the world to ease my pain, one way to quiet the voice of doubt and despair in my head.

I got in the SUV and drove straight to a bar and had my first drink in four years. As every alcoholic knows, you can't have just one. It's no twelve-step cliché. If you're addicted, it doesn't matter if you haven't touched a drop in four years or forty. That first drink throws open all the alcoholic switches in your body and your brain, and instantly you're drinking again like you never missed a day.

I picked a little hole-in-the-wall dive to have my relapse in, figuring nobody would see or recognize me there. I guess that shows it was a conscious decision on my part. I can't play the innocent victim and say I was pushed off the wagon. I jumped.

I had another drink, and another, and another, drinking through the day and into the night. Somewhere in there I must have decided that I didn't just want to drink again, I wanted some cocaine. I was too drunk to remember now how I bought it, but hey, it was a bar in Florida. In a lot of those places, cocaine was as easy to buy as a beer.

So now it's night, and I'm drunk and high, and I'm ready to partay. I'm as crazy out of control as I ever was back in my highest-rolling days. It's like those days never ended, and the last four years of sobriety were just a dream I had about somebody else. It really is amazing how instantly you can drop right back into old habits. It's like you never stopped.

I still knew plenty of people on the wrong side of town. I got back into the SUV and headed out on Kennedy Boulevard. I hit a pretty desolate stretch where a lot of prostitutes walked, and pulled over.

A girl strolled over and leaned on my door.

"I'm looking for the good stuff," I said.

"I am the good stuff," she replied.

"Where can I get some good stuff to party with?" I asked.

"Anywhere around here."

"You want to go out and party?"

"What do you mean by party?"

"I want it all."

This is where it comes down to her word against mine. She later said that she offered me sex and we agreed on a price of $50. I say that did not happen. I did not offer her money for sex. I just asked if she wanted to go party. She stayed there on the street and I began to roll on.

Anyway, she was an undercover cop. It was a sting operation set up to curb prostitution in the area by busting johns. As I pulled away, she signaled a nearby squad car, and they quickly pulled me over.

An officer walked over to my side of the SUV, and as I watched him I thought, "Here comes the end of my career." Whatever I was about to be busted for, I knew it would mean a huge scandal. The Yankees had not re-signed my contract and now, I thought, they never would. What a sad end to my career, I thought. Busted on Kennedy Boulevard.

When the officer saw my face his jaw practically hit the road. It turned out he grew up in New York City and was a huge fan of mine from my Mets days on. It was an embarrassing situation for us both.

"Mr. Strawberry, you've been pulled over for solicitation," he said.

I said, "Solicitation? I didn't offer her any money. I just asked if she wanted to go out and party."

He asked me to step out of the vehicle. I didn't resist. We were strangely polite with each other, like we were both ashamed to be involved in this moment. I sure know I was.

They searched me and the vehicle and found 0.3 grams of cocaine in my wallet. If I hadn't been carrying that coke we might have worked the situation out right there. I had not solicited sex from that girl. They probably would have let me roll. But while they pulled me up for solicitation, they now busted me for possession.

What a mortifying scene. As the officer put handcuffs on me, he said he'd been following my recovery from cancer.

"I know you've been doing great," he said. "I guess this is going to hurt your career?"

"Oh yeah," I said, "it's gonna hurt."

. . .

I SPENT THE rest of the night in a Tampa holding cell. In the early morning hours they allowed me to call Charisse. No phone call was ever harder to make. She was devastated. Eric Grossman had called her earlier to let her know what happened. She'd been ducking media all night since then. I was all over the news, of course.

She asked me if I was all right and I told her I was miserable. I also told her I was sorry, knowing that it didn't mean much. I could tell she was rocked to the core, but she was being brave. She said she'd come right down to Florida and we'd work it out.

When my attorney got me released that morning we stepped out into a media zoo. They had descended like locusts. There was even a news helicopter circling overhead. The newspapers' sportswriters and editorials went into righteous overdrive, calling for Mr. Steinbrenner to fire me, demanding I go to jail, condemning and ridiculing me. The closest any of them came to a little sympathy was to shake their heads rhetorically over what a huge disappointment I was to them.

I didn't care so much about disappointing the media. They'd been building me up and knocking me down for so long I was used to it.

What I was ashamed about was what I'd done to Charisse and the kids. I'd been so inconsiderate to them, so careless about their feelings and how my actions affected them. I'd thought only about myself and taken out my miserable feelings on them.

But Charisse stuck with me. She was terribly shaken and hurt, but she stuck by me.

And so did George. When everybody in the country was howling at him to fire me, he said, "I'm not getting rid of him. He's got a wife and those little kids to support. Okay, he made a mistake. But you know what, he's been clean until now. He hasn't slipped up from the time I brought him here. He probably was an emotional wreck from the chemo. He thought he was going to be ready for the season, and he wasn't. Cut him some slack."

15

WHEN THE TRIAL for possession of cocaine came up, I
pleaded no contest. I was guilty. I didn't want to fight it.
I just wanted to get it over with and get out. I was still
with the Yankees, and I had to face the music with the
organization. Couldn't get around it, couldn't hide from it—and I
sure couldn't say it wasn't me. I was sentenced to eighteen months of
probation.

The commissioner of baseball, Bud Selig, suspended me for 120
days that May. I felt horrible. I was so looking forward to getting
back to playing that year, after having the cancer surgery, and fighting through chemo, and coming to spring training, then sitting back
and not playing because they wanted me to finish up the chemo. And
then to fall back again and get suspended on top of it. I knew it was
a just punishment. He could have suspended me for the entire year.
I believe he went easy on me because he knew everything I'd been
going through. But still, it was crushing.

I stayed on my best behavior those four months I was suspended.
They regularly tested my urine for drugs and found I was clean. I went

to the Tampa ballpark every day and worked out. Hitting, running, lifting weights. Trying to keep in shape, trying to keep my spirits up, counting down the days until I could play again.

Charisse stuck with me through it. She had nothing but love and compassion for me.

August finally came around and my suspension ended. I rejoined the team in time to help them wind up another fantastic season. I can't say I was feeling 100 percent, but I was feeling much better than I had. It was a real struggle to get back to feeling almost normal. I had my regular checkups, and they said things were going well. But at times I just didn't feel right.

The New York fans were great. I'll never forget the first time I stepped onto the field in Yankee Stadium and the fans gave me a standing ovation. It was the first time they saw me in uniform since before my cancer diagnosis, and the first time since my bust in Tampa. Yankee fans were always so gracious to me. They had compassion for me, they knew I was in a struggle, they knew I was fighting and trying to get back.

It was the opposite on the road. When I walked onto the field in other cities, the locals booed, yelled that I was a scumbag, whatever. But I was used to it. I loved it. "Oh yeah? I'm a scumbag? Watch this." *Pow.* Ball's in orbit, I'm trotting around the bases, thank you thank you.

I finished my very short season with a respectable .327 batting average. In fifteen at-bats during postseason play, I got five hits, including two homers, and four RBIs. The Yankees won the Division Series against the Texas Rangers, then went on to beat our archrivals the Red Sox in the League Championship Series, then beat the Braves in the World Series that October, our second in a row.

I was so pleased and grateful to be there to help out. There was another victory parade up the Canyon of Heroes, and this time I felt well enough to be there for the whole thing, including the ceremony on the steps of City Hall. In fact, they asked me to say a few words. I walked up to the microphone and looked out at the sea of cheering Yankee fans. I thanked Joe Torre for standing behind me during one of the most trying years of my life, and as I did I felt this surge of gratitude and joy and sadness inside me all at once, and I choked up. Joe jumped up to the lectern and hugged me, and the crowd chanted *"Dar-ryl! Dar-ryl!"* And that's when I stopped even trying to hold back the tears.

I was thirty-seven years old. That's pretty old for a baseball player. I knew I was coming to the end of a long haul. Mr. Steinbrenner signed me up for another year. I didn't know how many more I'd have after that.

CHARISSE AND I had moved to Florida. We just wanted a change from California. We were tired of Palm Springs. And Florida was where the Yankees were, so I figured I might as well stay there. We moved to a place called Lutz, a very nice gated community outside Tampa. Big houses, everything landscaped, pools, a golf course. I wasn't yet playing golf at that time. Too bad. If I had a hobby to keep me occupied I might not have been tempted by the women and drugs. Or maybe that's wishful thinking.

Moving to the Tampa area turned out to be another one of my really stupid decisions. In Rancho Mirage I'd been surrounded by good influences—the Leonards, the church. In Tampa I was surrounded by temptation. Tampa was Sin City. Party Central. The Wild West. Loose women, fast cars, nightclubs, drinking, drugs. Maybe I put myself in temptation's way on purpose. I'm honestly not sure now, but maybe I was thinking I'd tried to be good, I'd tried the straight and narrow path, and all I got for it was cancer and degradation. Maybe, as I'd done before in my life, I thought, "The heck with it. Being good didn't work. I'll go back to being bad."

So there I was back in Tampa, Darryl Strawberry, and there were lots and lots of pretty women who wanted to hook up and party with me. And I did not resist. I convinced myself I just couldn't stop. I was addicted to alcohol, addicted to cocaine, addicted to women, too. And like a lot of guys, I still thought that having bunches of women is part of what makes you a man. That macho attitude was very big in Florida, and I rolled with it. Sure, I knew in my heart what nonsense it was. When you're a married man, and you have a loving wife and two (soon to be three) kids at home, all that running around with other women does is create havoc in your life and destroy everything around you.

That January the inevitable happened: I failed a mandatory drug test. They found cocaine in my system.

Charisse was crushed. Again. I was filled with shame and remorse. Again. And Commissioner Selig was put in the position of having to consider suspending me. Again.

I was really scared about that. This would be my third suspension in five years. I knew he had to consider throwing the book at me and suspending me for the entire year. If he did that, I knew in my heart it would be my last suspension. If I didn't get to play at least some of the 2000 season, I knew my chances of coming back the following year were somewhere around zero. The '99 World Series would turn out to have been my last hurrah.

The thought of not having baseball in my life anymore scared the heck out of me. Baseball had always been my refuge and my escape. The ballpark was the one area of my life where I had focus and discipline. Even when I was making a huge mess of the rest of my life, I excelled at the park. Baseball came a lot easier to me than anything else. That's why I beat injuries and surgeries to play. I beat cancer to play.

How was I going to get by without baseball? Without baseball, I'd have to face my life. I'd have to really start searching for who I am and what I am. I knew that day was coming soon, but I didn't feel ready for it yet.

I spoke to Mr. Selig. I told him how sorry I was (again), and begged him not to suspend me for the full year.

He announced his decision in February: suspension for a full year.

I wasn't shocked. I knew he had to make a strong statement against drugs, make me an example. I didn't think it was an unfair decision. I didn't hate him for it. I just felt empty. Hollow. I knew it meant I would never play major league baseball again. The 1999 World Series really had been my last curtain call.

OF COURSE THE press had another field day. I sometimes wonder what all those sportswriters would have found to write about if I hadn't been around. The usual suspects, the ones who had dogged me pretty much my entire career, howled for my head. I was a loser, an ingrate, a joke, a terrible role model for the kids. Selig had to make an example of me. But a lot of the press was kinder about it. They'd seen me beat cancer and come back to play well. They sounded sad and worried for me. They wrote, correctly, that what I needed to do now was forget about baseball and concentrate on beating my addictions.

Mr. Steinbrenner told the press, "My hopes and prayers are that he can do the things he needs to do to get his life in order." Davey Cone told them, "He's got to get his life back on track. He's got to get his addictions under control. Beyond that, he's got a lot of life to live." I knew they were both speaking to me through the press.

When I look back now, I realize it probably was the best thing to happen to me, because it was at that point that I began my final spiraling down to hit rock bottom in my life. And it was only when I bottomed out that I was able to look up and see change.

So there I was. February 2000, I'm no longer a major league ballplayer. I'm an ex-ballplayer. Even though I knew the day would come, I wasn't really prepared for it. I didn't feel immediate money worries. We had some money in the bank, even though both Charisse and I could go through it like water. It was just the scary feeling of "What am I going to do now?" I hadn't made any plans. I didn't have a second career lined up. You know, the way some ballplayers as they're aging start to get into real estate or buy a chain of car washes or whatever, some business they can slide into when their playing days are over. I'd always avoided thinking about that, frankly. It just seemed like a whole other set of headaches and problems and dealing with business partners who may or may not be trustworthy—just an extra load of worries to add to the ones I already struggled with. I was a baseball player, not a businessman. Besides, if you're a star athlete and you get involved in a business, most of what you seem to do is party with clients and investors, and I sure didn't need extra partying and temptations in my life right then. Even now, it seems like I can't go anywhere without some business guy handing me his card, inviting me to party or play golf with him, telling me about this or that business I could get involved with. Happens all the time.

Some small teams outside the major league system made me offers to come play for them. The pay would be a fraction of what I made in the major leagues, but at least I'd be in a uniform—some uniform, somewhere—and playing ball.

But I couldn't do that. If major league baseball was over for me, I decided, baseball was over for me.

Anyway, the first thing I had to do was try to get off the drugs again. I went into rehab for the third time. Third time's the charm, right? I went into Hazelden, a top-notch facility in West Palm Beach. They dried me out, but I think they knew as well as I did that if I got back out on the street, any little thing that disturbed me would send me right back to the bottle and the pipe. After three and a half months there I went stir-crazy and said, "Thank you very much for your help, but I'm outta here. I got a family to support." They said, "We don't really think you're ready."

But I just couldn't stay cooped up like that any longer. I left, and they were right. I got into the using, really heavily. I just wanted to die and not come back. Just escape from everything. The ex-wife, the IRS, paternity suit, bills bills bills bills bills. I was like, "Why am I making all this money just to hand it all over to them? I'd rather spend it partying and kill myself. If I'm gone, they don't get nothin'."

16

IN JULY, GOD decided to test whether I was really serious about that. I went in for a routine CAT scan, just part of the postsurgery checking up they do when you've had cancer. I didn't think anything of it.

Until they dropped the bomb on me that the test had revealed the cancer was back, and spreading.

I couldn't believe it. I really could not believe it. Why me, God? Why do you keep torturing me this way? What's next? Will the house cave in on me? I'll be flying somewhere and the plane will explode?

I mean, I never kidded myself that the cancer couldn't come back. Every cancer patient knows the stats. My doctors had always been cautiously optimistic. I'd impressed them with my quick recovery, and they were happy about what they saw that second time they cut me open in January 2000. But they never told me that the cancer couldn't return, just that they liked my odds.

It's one thing to know it might happen someday, and an entirely different feeling when you actually hear them say that it has. Charisse and I were not surprised, but we were both in a state of shock. This was the last thing we needed to hear right then, in the midst of everything else. Another operation, another six months of chemo, the whole thing.

"There's no way I can go through this again," I told her.

"Darryl, you have to," she said.

"I'd rather just die," I told her, and I meant it. I just didn't feel that I had it in me to go through the whole process again.

"You can't die and leave me and the kids," she said. "It's not fair. I won't let you."

"The kids" by then included our third baby, little Jewel, who was born that year. I called her the Jewel of my life. She was a fun baby and added a lot of excitement to the household. Jade loved having a little sister to take care of. And Jewel turned out to be the smarty of the bunch, smarter than any of us. By the time she was seven she'd be texting me all the time on her own cell phone. She'd ask me where I was and I'd text back that I was in New York. Then she'd tickle me by texting, "Cool! What hotel are you staying in?" At seven. My baby. My smarty-pants 2000 baby.

But all three of them, Jordan, Jade, and Jewel, are special. I'm so grateful that they were still babies when I was going through my crazy struggles. They don't remember any of that. I'm just Dad. They get a kick out of being with me in public, seeing how fans still react to me, watching me sign autographs. That's the me they know, not the crazy man I was when they were little. Jewel cracked me up once when I saw her practicing signing her autograph. I guess she was thinking she'd go out and sign autographs with me.

So, because of them, I agreed to the surgery. Not for me. I really didn't care much about me at that stage. I did it for Charisse and the kids.

In August we flew up to New York and I went back into Columbia Presbyterian. They wasted no time getting me onto the operating table. Cut me open and took out the affected area, including my left kidney.

I'd love to tell you that I was a brave soldier about it all as I lay around with tubes in my arms and staples in my belly in the days after the operation. I wish I could say my faith in God was my rock and my foundation through this time of trouble and pain.

But my faith was not strong enough. Other people around me had plenty of faith.

"You need to hold on to your faith now," Ma and Pa Leonard told me and Charisse. "Get back to your faith and believe, and God will see you through it."

I knew it was a great blessing having them in my life, but right then I just couldn't feel it. I was as depressed and demoralized as I'd ever been in my life. I had no rock or foundation. I was sinking to the bottom.

When I was able to, we flew back to Florida. I was in a lot of pain. My whole midsection was extremely tender and sore. I couldn't move without pain. I had a lot of trouble sleeping. My weight dropped back down to around 190.

My doctors prescribed Ambien to help me sleep, and Percodan and Vicodin for the pain. And I took them. I mean I really took them. Soon I was popping them like candy. I substituted prescribed medications for alcohol and cocaine, but it was the same addictive behavior, and for the same reason: escape. After all, I had a lot to escape from at that point.

Charisse could see I was abusing these drugs the same as I'd abused the others. She was coming to the end of her rope. I'd been to rehab after rehab, cleaned up my act several times, but I always slid back to the old ways, because I never really faced the root causes of my behavior. She thought I needed to do some serious time in a lockdown treatment center. It was time to break the cycle once and for all.

To me, it sounded like Charisse just wanted to put me away to get me out of her life. She wanted to lock me up like a criminal.

"I'm not a criminal," I argued. I wasn't out robbing convenience stores to score dope on the street. These were prescription medications for the pain. "I'm in a lot of pain here," I said.

"Darryl, drug abuse is drug abuse," she said. "It doesn't matter whether you buy the drugs on the street or at the drugstore. You've got to get control of this. You're killing yourself. And you're tearing our family apart. I don't think I can take much more of this."

In my heart I probably knew she was right, but to an addict there's a huge difference between hearing the truth and accepting it. I just got hurt and angry and suspicious. I remember the way Ronnie reacted that time Mike and I went to drag him out of that crack house. My response to Charisse wasn't all that different.

When she couldn't convince me, Charisse called my probation officer. She knew my probation period was coming to an end, and she wanted to get my probation officer's help before that. My probation officer asked me to come see her one morning that September.

I know this may sound like a handy excuse, but what happened that morning is mostly a blank to me. Full of Ambien, Percodan, and Vicodin, I got in the Ford Expedition to drive into Tampa. I don't remember doing that. Then I must have blacked out behind the wheel. I'm told I was swerving on the road. I swiped a pole and tore up the front of the Expedition, then kept driving like nothing happened. At a stoplight a police officer saw the condition of the vehicle and pulled me over. When he came up to my window I was talking out of my head. He pulled me out and called for backup. I must have told him I had to get to my probation officer, because he called for her, too.

I'm telling you what they told me, because I don't remember any of it. All I remember is finding myself in the back of a police car with my probation officer.

"Darryl, are you okay?"

"I don't know," I remember saying. "I don't know what's going on. I don't know what just happened."

They took me to jail. They ran a drug test, which showed no illegal substances in my system, but a lot of those meds.

The upshot of that weird morning was that they decided I'd violated my probation again, and they extended it another eighteen months.

Charisse was beside herself. She started distancing herself from me at this point. I had put her through so much, and she had stuck with me and stuck with me, but I think now she was beginning to wonder if I was ever really going to pull myself together again. She wanted me out of the house, away from the kids. She was convinced I needed serious intervention, serious substance abuse treatment, and my probation officer agreed.

I went to a place called HealthCare Connection. It was a recovery facility in a little apartment complex with maybe two dozen guys in it, two to an apartment. (Women had a separate setup across town.) They were all different kinds of guys—doctors, lawyers, businessmen, young guys, older guys. What they all had in common was that they were lunatic drug users like me.

I went in there for what I was told would just be an evaluation. I told the counselors I wasn't using illegal drugs. It wasn't like I was out on the streets buying crack. I was using prescription pain pills. I just didn't want to feel the pain anymore.

And they said, "Well, we think you're in serious trouble with your addictions. We need to keep you a few days."

It wasn't what I expected, but I said okay. I'll stay a few days.

That few days turned into five months. Five months under house arrest at HealthCare Connection, still on probation, with an ankle bracelet on to keep me from running off. Five months of classes and lectures and group sessions every day.

I did everything they asked me to. I got clean and stayed clean. I went and took the chemo. It made me sick as a dog. I dreaded the chemo so much I started to get sick before they even put the IV in my arm.

My probation officer called every night to make sure I was still on the path. Of course the media called all the time, too, but the people running the program strictly limited their access to me. They said it would help me focus on my recovery work and also keep my ego in check. I didn't mind that part so much. At this point all they'd write would be about what a sad, tragic has-been I was anyway.

As the months wore on I really came to hate being at HealthCare Connection. I was angry at Charisse, angry at my probation officer, angry at the counselors. They were all controlling my life and telling me what to do. I was feeling like Ronnie when we were teens and nobody was gonna tell him what to do.

By March 2001 I was arguing with my counselors constantly that I really was clean and sober now. The chemo was still making me sick and I was still crazy out of my mind, but I was making it. I was proving it to them that I was making it.

And they were like, "Yeah, well, you're doing great, but it's only five months."

"What the hell do you guys mean it's only five months? That's five months clean, no trouble, nothing. Let me go back home and continue this outpatient."

"Your wife doesn't want you there."

"What do you mean she doesn't want me there?"

"She's got some stability going for herself and the kids. She doesn't want you coming back into the house and disrupting that."

"What are you talking about? It's my house. I paid for everything."

In my heart I knew they were right. Charisse was starting to see it was a dead-end situation with me. She'd had enough. For five months I had to twist her arm to get her to bring the kids to visit me.

"If you leave now we don't think you'll make it out there," they said.

"I don't care if I make it!" I replied. "Let me out of here. I can't stay here a year."

"You know you'll go right back to using and end up in jail again."

"So what? Who cares? That might be the best thing that could happen to me."

"You're gonna get what you're gonna get," they said.

And I said, "Well, I just have to get it then. I don't care."

One night that March I just said forget it. I was supposed to have chemo the next day and I just couldn't face it. I was lunatic stir-crazy. I had to bust out.

I called a drug user I knew and had her pick me up. We went and got high.

Yeah, that's how cured I was.

When they checked my bed that night, I was gone. Ankle bracelet and all.

MEANWHILE, NATURALLY, THE news was all over the media. They camped out on the front lawn of our house and laid in wait for Charisse to show her face. *Darryl Strawberry Escapes. Darryl Strawberry Is on the Lam. Manhunt for Darryl Strawberry.*

It wasn't much of a manhunt. To the cops I was just another drug addict who skipped on his probation. I'd turn up soon enough.

My friends looked harder. Ron Dock and Ray Negron from the Yankees organization, and Doc Gooden, who had just retired from baseball. They knew the streets, the dealers, the places I might be holed up.

After four days I turned myself in. I always turned myself in. I called Ray and asked him to come get me. He and Ron met me at a gas station. I was just sitting on the curb waiting for them. Exhausted, in more kinds of pain than I can describe, lost in more ways than I can count. I cried the whole way back to Tampa to face the music.

"You know what's the worst thing?" I told Ray. "I don't have anything left to leave to my kids."

Ron and Ray were shocked at my condition. They were really concerned I might do myself in if I had to go back to a jail cell or Health-Care Connection. So they took me to a hospital in Tampa, St. Joseph's, where I was admitted to the psychiatric ward for evaluation. They put me on suicide watch. The psychiatrists evaluated me and thought the best place for me was right there where I was.

Charisse gave a press conference that month for media from around the country. "Please understand that Darryl is not a bad person trying to be good," she said. "He is a sick person trying to get well." She pointed out that what we were going through, thousands of families in America were experiencing at the same moment. They just weren't doing it in the hot TV lights.

In May, I went in front of Judge Florence Foster of Hillsborough Circuit Court to hear what she'd decided to do with me. She was a sweet, caring person. The prosecutors wanted her to send me to prison for eighteen months for violating my probation. They went on about how I was a danger to society. Judge Foster said, "Mr. Strawberry, you may not care about yourself, but I care about you. You're not a criminal. You're not a danger to anyone but yourself. You're a sick person who needs help." She ruled that "the preponderance of evidence suggests the defendant will be better served at the present time" in another rehab facility.

So off I go again. This time to Phoenix House in Ocala, right in the middle of Florida between Tampa and Daytona Beach. Phoenix House is like boot camp for drug abusers. It was started as a self-help community by a group of heroin addicts in New York City back in the sixties. By the time I went there it was a large and thriving organization with facilities in several states. It was known for its very strict behavior-modifying rules. It wasn't just alcohol and drugs that were forbidden, but sex and cigarettes, too. They were very big on instilling discipline in your life and breaking down your ego.

For example, when I arrived they told me, "You dress too classy for this place. Strip." They took my clothes away and told me to pull some things out of a bin of used clothing. And there was a very heavy program of classes, individual sessions, group sessions, a precise program of steps you had to go through, graduating from one to the next.

I guess the strict rules made sense, because to me Phoenix House was like another Animal House. A bunch of wackos and loose cannons trying to get off drugs. Everybody there was court-ordered. Everyone was a stone addict who'd been through the mill of other programs and slid right back into their bad habits. Phoenix House was like their last, and toughest, chance. If you failed at Phoenix House, there was pretty much no place left to go but prison.

I ended up being there for ten months. I wasn't a model participant. At first I cooperated. I got clean of the drugs, I finished up the chemo,

I got healthy. By eight, nine, ten months, I was telling them, "Okay, I've done the program. I'm clean and healthy. Let me out now."

And they said no, I needed to stay at least up to eighteen months.

I flipped. I was already going stir-crazy. I didn't think I could stand being under all their rules and regulations. My life was passing me by outside while I hung around for months and months in these facilities.

I could have just walked off. There wasn't a fence around the place. But I'd be violating my probation again if I did. So I stayed, but my anger and resentment and impatience kept building. I started giving the counselors lip. I got caught smoking cigarettes. I was always getting caught doing little things like that, minor infractions of their rules.

And then I got caught with a female participant, which was a huge no-no. The counselors threw their hands up and kicked me out of the program, April 2002. Out of Phoenix House, and back to a county jail cell in Tampa, and then back in front of Judge Foster.

17

J UDGE FOSTER WAS still decent to me. She knew I wasn't a criminal. She knew I had an addiction problem. But I guess she was coming to the end of her rope with me, too.

"Well, Mr. Strawberry, what do you think I should do with you?" she asked me.

"Your Honor, I don't care what you do with me," I said.

"You know what?" she said. "You'll just go back and sit in the county jail until I've made a decision and I'm ready to see you again."

I thought that meant a couple of days. It ended up being a month. Judge Foster got sick, and they handed the case over to a new judge. Meanwhile my lawyer and the prosecutors went back and forth discussing various deals. And I laid up in a Tampa jail cell for thirty days.

The prosecutors offered my attorney a deal where I'd agree to spend a year in a lockdown treatment facility, then have five years' probation when I came out.

My heart sank when my lawyer told me that. I was looking at six more years in the system? The whole reason I was in jail was because I'd gone nuts in the system and run away from it and been bounced out of it. Six more years sounded like an eternity to me. Another year shut away in rehab, followed by five years of mandatory drug tests, of not being able to walk out the door or scratch my nose without asking my probation officer's permission. I knew there was no way I could make it through five years without violating my probation somehow. I'd proven that time and time again. I'd just end up violating it somehow, and we'd be right back here again.

"I can't do that," I told my lawyer.

"I'm afraid it's that or prison," he said.

"What's the difference?" I snapped. "If I refuse the deal and go to prison, how much time will the judge give me?"

"Eighteen months."

"And if I'm good in there, how much will I really serve?"

"I'd say eleven months."

"Then what are we talking about here?" I said. "Eleven months in prison, or six years in what might as well be prison? Tell the judge I'll take the eighteen months."

I don't think Judge Foster would have let me do it. But the new judge didn't know me and just said okay, if that's what he wants, let's do it.

So the sentencing day came. April 29, 2002, I stood in a courtroom with Charisse and a whole crowd of media behind me. The judge gave me the eighteen months, and I was led out of the courtroom.

"Okay," I said to myself. "I'm on my way. Let's get this over with."

THEY TOOK ME back to the county jail. That night they let me call Charisse. Man, that was a hard call to make.

"This is a sad day for the Strawberrys," I said. "I'm sorry I brought this on you and the kids."

I sat in the cell that night and thought about how I'd come to this place in my life. I put myself there and I was ready to deal with it, but it was still hard to believe. Darryl Strawberry, eight-time All-Star, four World Series rings, sitting in a jail cell, headed to a Florida state prison.

Judge Foster never bought the prosecutors' line about me being a menace to society. My probation officer was a decent human being toward me. I would find the corrections officials and officers a pretty cool bunch as well. But those D.A.'s . . .

The next morning they put me in the back of a squad car and drove me to Orlando, where they process new prisoners into the state correction system before they send you to the actual facility where you'll do your time. I have to say the policemen, and the prison's officials and staff, were all very polite. They all knew who I was. They knew I wasn't a criminal or a menace to society. I wasn't a menace to anyone but me and my loved ones. It saddened them to have me in their system.

"Take your time, Mr. Strawberry," the man who processed me in said. "You need to take your time and do your time, and don't ever allow this to happen again in your life. You don't deserve this. You don't belong in a place like this."

They stripped me down and handed me prison clothes. We went through all the paperwork. They led me to a cell away from the general population. I spent a week in isolation there. They do that with a high-profile inmate. They don't drop you into the midst of the real criminals.

"I'm not afraid of the other inmates," I told them.

They said, "Yeah, we understand you may have no fear. But it's our job to keep you protected while you do your time."

A week later they transferred me to the Gainesville Correctional Institution. It wasn't like a *prison* prison. There weren't high stone walls with barbed wire and guards with shotguns up in towers and all that like in a prison movie. It was a minimum- and medium-security campus with dormitories, a cafeteria, a playground, a softball field, basketball court, running track, lots of lawn. There was a fence around it all, and guards. You knew you weren't setting foot outside that fence until they let you, so it was definitely a prison, but it wasn't like *Oz* or anything.

Some of the inmates were career criminals, but low-maintenance and nonviolent. Thieves, drug dealers, guys like that, some of them serving ten- or fifteen-year sentences. The corrections system was like a revolving door for a lot of those guys. They were in and out of prison all their lives. But they weren't murderers or violent, hardened criminals, so they were in this place.

I was put in the separate drug treatment center, a 220-bed dorm and classrooms run by an outside contractor called CiviGenics. Me and two hundred–odd other substance abusers, from all walks of life. Every morning we went to classes as part of the substance abuse treatment program. There were ascending levels of classes, and you had to keep passing from one to the next or they'd ship you to a real prison. In the afternoons we had jobs. Mowing the lawn, collecting trash, folding laundry, things like that.

I was saddened to be there, but there was nothing for me to do but settle in and do my time. The other inmates were cool about having Darryl Strawberry among them. I mean let's face it, when you're in there you're all in the same boat. I was just another one of them, going to classes, working on the grounds crew, hanging out, doing my time.

The corrections officers were nice, regular guys. I'd spend time at night talking with them.

"A lot of these guys here, they come and go and come back again," I remember one of them telling me. "They'll spend their whole lives going in and out of joints like this. You're not like that. This is not a place you ever want to come back to. Just straighten up and get yourself together and fly right."

Believe me, that was my plan. The treatment program was a very good one and I took it seriously. The counselors definitely wanted to see you make progress. I felt the other guys in the program were pretty much like me—good people who had an abuse problem and made some bad decisions. There were guys in there who'd driven drunk and gotten into serious accidents in which people got killed. They were serving eight, ten years. They'd killed people, but I wouldn't call them murderers. I did well in the classes, listened to the counselors, thought about what they said. I was clean the whole time. It's not like you couldn't get drugs in there. It's the prison system. Drugs are easier to get in prison than out on the street. But I stayed clean, went to my classes in the morning, did my groundskeeping in the afternoons. After I'd been there a few months I got one of the guards to let me cut the grass outside the fence. Just to go out the gate and breathe free air. He knew I wasn't going to run off.

But still, it ain't easy being locked up. I missed my kids something terrible. I did not want them to see me in prison. They were young, but I still didn't think it would be right. I felt really bad about not being there for them that year. I told myself I'd make it up to them when I got out.

I don't think Charisse would have brought the kids to see me even if I wanted her to. She only let me talk to them a couple of times on the phone. She only came up to visit me once herself the whole time I was there. Things were not going very well with us, obviously. I felt she was putting more and more distance between us. She had her doubts that I was going to come home and everything would go smoothly from then on. I mean, she'd seen me come out of rehab clean and sober and determined to stay on the right path, only to backslide again. There were doubts in my mind, too, that we would ever get back together.

So I did my eleven months. One morning in April 2003, Charisse drove up in an SUV. I shook the guards' hands and thanked them for being so nice to me while I was there. They offered me the standard $100 inmates are handed on their way back out into the world, and I took it.

"Good-bye, thank you, and you won't ever see me again," I told them.

Reporters and cameramen were standing around the gate, but we drove on by. I did not feel like making any statement to the press. I just wanted to get away from that place as quickly as possible.

There was only one problem. I'd forgotten to collect my personal belongings on the way out. So we turned around, drove back, and a guard grinned and handed me a bag of my things.

Then we got out of there, and I did not look back.

18

THE PLAN WAS to come back now and restart my life. My baseball career was over and I didn't have another career in mind. I just wanted to settle back into life before I worried about that. I went back to church again, with Charisse and the kids. I grounded myself in church, really centered my life around faith and family and doing the right things. It was a great relief to get involved in church so deeply. Pastors at various churches asked me to come and speak to their congregations, give my testimony about what I'd been through and how God had moved in my life and helped me get through all the trials and tribulations.

"When God has a plan for your life, he's going to fulfill that plan, no matter how far he has to allow you to go down," I would tell people. "I believe God protected me from myself, because I couldn't protect myself. I was sick and crazy out of my mind, doing all kind of crazy things, so there was no way for me to protect myself. So you know what? God says, 'Well, I'll lock him up in prison and protect him from himself. Maybe that'll be the starting point to his getting his life together.' And it worked. That big change in my life forced me to change how I behaved and how I thought.

"See, I never thought very highly of myself. When you grow up with a father who beat you as a kid and told you you're never going to be nothing, you believe it. It stays with you. I don't care how successful you are as an adult, you still carry that stuff around inside you. I carried a lot of bad stuff for a very long time. I had to learn how to be a man on my own. I had to make all my choices on my own. My father wasn't there to advise me. I made some good choices, and some really bad ones.

"How do you learn to accept yourself and like yourself under those conditions? My whole problem all along was that I didn't believe in myself, I didn't love myself, I didn't even like myself. Even when I was hitting grand slams. You can hit all the grand slams in the world and still feel worthless if that idea was beaten into your head when you were a kid. The image you have of yourself, the one you carry around in your head through your life, starts forming very early. If that's not a good self-image, you can struggle with it for a very long time, like I did. But you know what? I have walked through a lot of storms, but I will finally come out on the other side. And you will, too."

I enjoyed passing that message on to others who were struggling. But I wasn't quite done struggling myself.

It soon became painfully clear that I'd done too much damage to my relationship with Charisse. I had put her through more than any wife should ever have to face, and her faith and love remained strong. But the last few years, all the time I spent away from her in all those rehab facilities and then in prison, put a gap between us that we couldn't reach across anymore. She had gone on with her own life while I was struggling through mine. Because of what she went through with me she had helped start a Florida chapter of the National Council on Alcoholism and Drug Dependence, and was very involved in being a spokesperson and raising money for them. She had made that and the kids her major focus. It was like she'd been forced to build a life for herself and the kids that didn't have much of me in it, and now that I was back around I didn't really fit.

Also, we had money worries. I was out of a job, but I still had huge bills to meet every month. I had put some money away and we could get by on that for a little while, but money still became an issue Charisse and I fought over with increasing bitterness. I thought she was spending too much, trying to maintain the old high-rolling life when we couldn't afford it anymore. And she started really getting on me about my tithing for the church.

Like a lot of Christians, I strongly believe in giving 10 percent of my earnings to the church. I've always believed in that. The Bible teaches us to do it. I was taught it by my mother. "I don't care what you do," she would say, "God has always blessed you. Whatever you make, you give 10 percent back." I do it to this day. I did it even when I was sick in my head back in the day. It's just who I am and the way I was raised. It's a biblical principle that I've always stood by, and I've always seen rewards. My rewards may not always be financial, but I've been delivered from the sickness of cancer and delivered from all the craziness and chaos that were in my life. That didn't happen overnight through me alone. That happened through a process of believing, of reading and understanding the Bible, and of committing myself to the church. So I see 10 percent of my earnings as a very wise investment. I've always made that sacrifice to God, and it has always paid off. Because of my obedience, God has healed me, he has protected me, he has covered me over and over in my life.

Sometimes people will say they don't understand why someone would give so much of his hard-earned money to the church, just to buy the pastor gold Rolexes and Cadillacs and Armani suits. My answer is I'm not concerned with how the pastor lives. What he wears and what he drives are for him to look to. My concern is about my personal relationship and spiritual covenant with God.

Charisse just couldn't see it. And now, as we faced money worries, she thought it was crazy of me. She argued that it was money I should be spending on my family. I thought that was greedy of her. She and the kids still did not want for a thing.

As we fought, my good feelings and good intentions crumbled. And I dealt the way I had a million times before.

Charisse finally couldn't handle it anymore. She filed for a separation. And by that point my feeling was, "Fine. I'm done. I'm not coming back."

Charisse and the kids stayed in Tampa, and I moved to West Palm Beach. The one bright thing I did was to move in among some friends who knew I was in recovery and wanted to help me. I had met them through a recovery program a few years earlier, back around 2000, and they had always been there for me. They loved me unconditionally when nobody else ever thought I would turn my life around. They were all in recovery themselves, knew firsthand what I was struggling with, and believed in me.

One of them was my sponsor, Will G. Yet another replacement father in my life. An older black man. He was a recovering drug addict, had done some time in jail, and now had been clean for fifteen years. Will didn't push. He was quiet and gentle. He'd tell everyone, "Don't you worry about my boy Darryl. He's going to get it one day." He knew that everyone in recovery has to go through the process in his own way and on his own time. "When he gets on his journey, you'll see what I've been telling you."

Another was my friend Kim. I had met her through recovery as well. We were really close buddies, nothing sexual. She was on the same journey I was.

Then there was June Bug. We were a lot alike. He called me Junior, so I called him June Bug. He was stable when I met him, but he had floundered, struggling with addiction and trying to get on the other side. He talked to me a lot about how crazy and reckless he had been, and what a struggle it was for him when he started to get with the program and listen to the advice of others. He was like me, always wanting to do things his own way, thinking he knew best, and having to do a lot of messing up before he would listen.

And John, who was the oldest of the bunch. We called him Grandfather. He was stern and strict with us. He'd been everywhere and seen it all, and when I met him he'd been in recovery for more than twenty-five years. He had very definite ideas about what you have to do to change your life and your habits. He watched over all of us and mentored us.

They didn't love me because I was Darryl Strawberry, the celebrity baseball player. They truly didn't care about that. I was just Junior. They loved me because I was struggling to recover and they wanted to help. They'd all been through hell themselves. They were a huge part of my life, and they still are. We still check on one another all the time, visit one another, are there to help when needed.

When people ask me about the recovery process, I always tell them how important it is to find a support group like this. When you're lost in substance abuse, you cut yourself off from others. The most important relationship in your life is the one you have with the bottle or the needle or the pipe. You'll damage or sacrifice all other relations—to your family, friends, colleagues—to keep that one going. Part of recovery is reconnecting with the rest of humanity, relearning how to build loving, trusting relationships with others. A support group of people who have been through it and know what you're experiencing can be an enormous help.

Not that I made it easy on them. Being among them helped keep me from using drugs every day, but I'd binge. I would put together thirty, forty days without using, and then something in my dealings with Charisse would trigger another binge. After we separated we started fighting about when she would file for divorce.

In my heart it was done. I would never not be there for our kids. But the relationship had taken too many hits, and she and I had grown too far apart. It was over. Better for us both to move on.

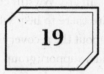

19

WILL AND I went to a Narcotics Anonymous recovery convention. It was there that I met Tracy Boulware. She had gotten straight a year earlier and was farther along in her journey than I was in mine. She'd been reluctant to go to the convention, where there can be a lot of drama she didn't feel she needed to be around, but her friends insisted.

I knew one of her friends and was sitting talking with him when Tracy decided she wanted to get out of there. Her friend was holding her keys, so she came over to us. I watched this pretty blond lady walk toward us, and something in my chest turned over.

"I'm ready to leave," she told her friend, really straightforward and businesslike.

He said, "Have you met my friend Darryl? Darryl Strawberry?"

She looked down at me and shook my hand, politely, but there was none of that "Oh my God, Darryl Strawberry!" reaction I got so often. Her attitude was just like yeah, hello, whatever, I'm outta here. She turned back to her friend and asked for her keys. I didn't want her to go.

"Leaving so soon?" I asked.

I got her to stick around awhile and we got to know each other some. Sitting in an NA convention, it wasn't like we needed to hide anything. Then and over the next few times we saw each other I heard her whole story, and she heard mine.

She wasn't originally from Florida. She grew up in St. Charles, Missouri, a suburb of St. Louis. She had a nice, stable, middle-class, Catholic upbringing. But she said she was "a small-town girl with a big-world mind." She always knew she was going to get out of the Midwest, go see the world and have a lot of experiences. She just didn't know what dark corners of the world she might see and the kinds of experiences she might have there.

When we were first getting to know each other, I said to her, "What do you think about Jesus? Because I love him. Would that be a problem for you?"

She just laughed. "Me too!"

A month earlier, she had joined a program of Bible study. Growing up Catholic, she knew something of the Bible, but had never really read it closely. Catholicism had put more emphasis on the rules of the church than on the actual words in the book. Now she completely reexamined her beliefs.

A woman she met in recovery invited her to the regular prayer meetings she and a big group of women held in their homes. When twenty women surrounded her and laid their hands on her, Tracy was skeptical at first. Then, just like me, she felt the spirit enter her. She said it felt like they were laying hot towels on her. Nothing in her Catholic background had prepared her for this kind of experience, this direct contact with the spirit. It was exciting, but also frightening. And, just like with me, when it was over, a woman said to her, "That's just the beginning. All hell is going to break loose in your life now."

When she and I met she had just begun her journey of faith. She was clean and straight, and very deeply into the church and the power of the Word.

When she left the convention I convinced her to give me her phone number. I couldn't stop thinking about her the rest of the day and night. Around one A.M. I called her. I told her I was just making sure she got home all right, or some such excuse.

I started falling in love with her right away, but I didn't see how somebody in my condition could be anything but a burden to her after the hell she had already gone through. I told her straight up, "You don't know what you'd be getting yourself into with me. A tornado's coming."

Her dad warned her to be cautious, too. He was a baseball fan, and he knew all about me and my troubles. He was willing to keep an open mind about me, but he didn't want her not to know.

She heard us both. But she didn't want to be judged for her past, and wouldn't judge me for mine.

"I know what I know," she said, "and I love who I love."

"All right," I said. "Don't say I didn't warn you."

IT WAS NOT a traditional romance. We didn't go out on dates and hold hands and act like kids. The basis of our love was compassion. We both knew we were struggling and hurting. We'd both been through hell and didn't have any starry-eyed illusions.

I really liked that she didn't care that I was Darryl Strawberry the former baseball star. She came with none of the agendas so many other people brought when they met me. She didn't care that I was famous. She didn't care about what I'd done. She impressed me early on when she said, "I don't care how many home runs you hit. That's not going to do anything for us living happily ever after. Forget the old Darryl. You have to find out who you are now."

That was so different and incredible to me. She cared about me as a person. I had nothing to offer her but me, and she opened her arms. She just wanted me to be well. Having somebody care about you like that makes all the difference in the world when you're at as low a point in your life as I was.

You meet some people in recovery who've lost all sympathy for people who are still struggling. They get clean and sober, and now they can't understand why anyone would still be struggling. They get all high-horse about it. "Why are you still drinking? Just quit." It's like they've totally forgotten how hard it was for them.

Tracy was the opposite. She understood what I was struggling with because she had walked through her own struggles in life. She loved me through the pain. Her life had been nowhere near the mess I made of mine, but it still meant she could empathize better than most.

"Our struggles weren't all that different," she would say. "It's just that yours were public."

She was different from any woman I ever met. I think a lot of it had to do with her being from the Midwest. Folks from there don't shuck and jive. They're more down-to-earth. She wasn't caught up in material things at all. She didn't want glitter and glamour. She wasn't fooled by all the things people think will make them happy.

Of course, if she'd only been into me for the money, she would've found out pretty soon that I didn't have any. I'm sure she had more money than I did when we met.

She had no problem with that.

"Let's find a simple life for us," she said. "A life where we can be happy and contented and go forward together."

And that's what we did. We went forward together. We built everything together. It wasn't like, "Go out there and earn us millions of dollars while I sit at home and do nothing. Buy us a big house. Buy me jewelry and a fancy car. Take care of me. Provide for me." Tracy wasn't into any of that. From the start, we were a team, equal partners. The two of us committed ourselves to our relationship and to our faith.

Still, as I had warned her, I did proceed to put her through hell. My life was still a mess in a lot of ways. I was broke. I was still struggling with my addictive behaviors. And I was still hugely conflicted about my marriage. It was definitely over between me and Charisse, but there was no way I was going to abandon the children we had together. It would never be over between me and my kids.

Tracy understood that, but there was no way she would commit fully to a relationship with me until I manned up and got clear on all those issues. She had her own struggles and healing to do.

"You have to figure out what it is you want," she said. "Nothing's going to happen between you and me until you make up your mind. You let me know when you do."

I felt pulled in all directions, and sometimes I did what I always did in that situation. I'd disappear for two or three days at a time—hole up with some user and get high.

Sometimes I'd call Tracy and make up some excuse for why she hadn't seen me in a couple of days. That was really stupid of me. Tracy wasn't fooled for a second. She'd been there, done that, knew all the tricks and lies. She knew all the deepest, darkest places where I was likely to be hiding—and she did not hesitate to come bang on some-body's door and haul me out of there. I mean, she was fearless. These were some scummy, dangerous spots. I wasn't afraid to be there, but I wasn't a white woman driving and walking in the 'hood by myself. Tracy didn't care. She knew I was backsliding. She loved me. She was willing to risk her own life to help me save mine.

More than one time I'd be getting high with some people, there was a knock on the door, and Tracy was standing there. I'd be stunned.

"Are you out of your mind?" I'd cry. "Do you know where you are?"

"I know exactly where I am," she'd fire back at me. "Do you know where you are? Get in that car right now!"

Man! I can't tell you how impressed I was with her. In my career I'd been around a lot of stud athletes with huge cojones. This woman had them all beat.

It was incredible what she put up with from me. But that's Tracy—all or nothing. She loved the person she knew I could be, and once she decided she was going to help me save myself, there was no halfway about it. She'd turn heaven and hell upside-down if she had to, go into the lowest spots on earth and drag me out by the earlobe if that's what it took.

• ▾ • ▾ •

BUT I PUSHED even Tracy too far. She wanted to start a new career as a real estate agent. It's a good profession in Florida. So she signed up for classes.

On the first day of class, I drove her to real estate school and dropped her off. It was her car—I didn't have one anymore. I borrowed it to run some errands. I'd come back and pick her up at the end of the day.

But I didn't. I drove to a place I knew and got high. When Tracy got out of class and I wasn't there, she had to walk home. Think about that. I let the woman I loved walk home so I could go get high. And it was her car! That's how low and selfish an addict's behavior gets.

She knew right away what I was doing. It broke her heart, and it really infuriated her. She'd been letting me store some stuff at her place. When she got home, she piled all my stuff into the back of her truck. Then she drove right to where I was hanging out. She parked the truck, opened the back, and dumped all my belongings on the lawn. Some baseball memorabilia, shoes, Armani suits from my high-rolling days—she didn't care. It all went on the lawn.

Then she walked up to the door and banged on it. I couldn't face her, so I told the person I was with not to answer.

As usual, Tracy wasn't fooled.

"Darryl Strawberry, I hope you're having fun in there!" she yelled through the door. "Because all your stuff is out here on the lawn, and all the kids in the neighborhood are walking off with it!"

Oh man. You best believe I got out there.

That's just how Tracy was. Even when she was really hurt and angry with me, she loved me, she believed that underneath it all I was a good person, and she was determined not to let me destroy myself. She was absolutely convinced that if I did not clean up my act I was either going to go back to prison or going to die. And she was right.

Little by little, step by step, she dragged me down the path to getting right. It was a huge ordeal for both of us. I really was trying. My wild and stupid behavior was finally sputtering out. I wasn't going out every night, hanging out in clubs. I was still tempted, but I was so tired of my terrible behavior, so exhausted with myself, so ashamed of how low I'd gotten. I knew I had to stop.

"If I can get clean, you can," Tracy said.

She told me I was the strongest person she'd ever met, inside and out. She knew I could do it. She couldn't do it for me.

"I'm leaving Florida," she told me. "I'm moving back to Missouri."

"Missouri?" I said. She might as well have said she was moving to Mars.

"Yes, Missouri. And you're not coming with me. You need to get straight. Go stay with your godparents if that'll help. Do whatever you have to do. I've got to do what I have to do."

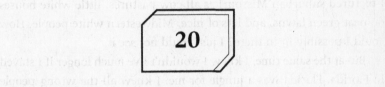

20

THAT WAS WHEN I knew I was done. Tracy was the strongest, most dedicated person I knew. If my behavior was too much even for her to put up with, I knew it had to stop. It was now or never. God had shown me that he wasn't going to let me just crawl off and die. I really had no choice but to end the craziness. I had truly bottomed out, and there was nowhere to go from there but to climb back up.

Tracy was right. I needed to get refocused and recentered and back into church. I knew my roots. So I did what she suggested and went and stayed with Ma and Pa Leonard for a while. Went to Bible studies with them a few times during the week, church all day on Sunday. I got myself grounded in the Word again.

Even though Charisse and I had broken up and she had filed for divorce, Ma and Pa were still my godparents, and they are to this day. I spend a lot of time with them every time I go to California. The sad thing is that because they maintained their relationship with me, Charisse broke off hers with them. They were so huge in her life, they taught her so much about life, but I guess she felt they had to choose between me and her, and they didn't want to. So she broke it off with them.

I spent a couple of months with the Leonards, and when I felt my head was on straight I returned to Florida and went to see Tracy. She had settled all her affairs there, sold her furniture, packed up what was left, and was ready to leave. I asked if I could come with her. She said yes.

Going to Missouri was a huge decision for me. I was a big-city boy. I pictured suburban Missouri as all cow pastures, little white houses on neat green lawns, and lots of nice, Midwestern white people. How could I possibly fit in there? I just could not see it.

But at the same time, I knew I wouldn't live much longer if I stayed in Florida. Florida was a jungle for me. I knew all the wrong people and all the wrong places. There were just too many temptations in easy reach. I was like a person on a diet trying to live in the ice cream section of the supermarket. I was never going to break free if I stayed there. I just did not have the willpower. I was a lot more likely to die if I stayed there.

I had to make a serious change in my life and get far, far away from that environment. I had proven year after year that I did not have the strength to live in that kind of environment and resist its temptations. Even with all my friends around me trying to help, it still came down to me in the end. They were a huge blessing to me and helped me start to get back on my feet, but they couldn't walk the walk for me. You have to do that for yourself. I couldn't do that in that environment.

And I knew I needed to be with Tracy. Even if that meant Missouri. So we rented a small U-Haul trailer, hitched it to the back of her little Toyota Camry, filled the trailer and the car with as much as they could hold, and left the rest behind.

We drove straight from Boca Raton, Florida, to St. Charles, Missouri. Cramped behind the wheel of that little car, chugging along the dull stretches of highway, I thought back to the time when Doc Gooden and I lounged in the backs of stretch limos, sipping champagne and tossing hundred-dollar bills out the windows. Let me tell you, it was very hard to understand how I had gone from that to being stuffed behind the wheel of a Camry. All I knew was I was lucky I wasn't dead.

And the humbling process wasn't over yet. In St. Charles, we moved in with Tracy's parents. Into the basement of their humble suburban home. The basement that had been Tracy's bedroom growing up, and that her parents hadn't much changed. Same old linoleum on the floor, same bed she slept in as a teenager, same lumpy old couch near it. The only difference now was that she'd come back with her six-foot-six, ex-superstar, recovering drug addict, black boyfriend, and filled it up with a lot of boxes of stuff.

I have to say her parents were great about it. They were very warm and welcoming, and once they got to know me they loved me. I know it was an extremely strange situation for them, and nothing they had ever envisioned for their daughter. But they loved her and just wanted things to work out for the best.

So there we were, in the basement. Not just physically, either. We had both been stripped down to our bare essence. We had nothing but each other. If we were going to make our relationship work, we had to build it from the ground up. We couldn't have gotten any closer to the ground.

I remember one morning, sitting on the sofa and looking around at all our boxes of stuff, the worn linoleum floor, that old couch, I just started crying. I felt like such a failure. I had failed at so much. Regardless of what I had achieved in the ballpark, all the fame I had and money I made, I felt that I was a complete loser as a man and a human being. No career, no money, no prospects. Nothing.

Tracy saw me crying and put her arms around me.

"What is it?" she asked, although I knew she knew.

"Look at me," I said. "I'm Darryl Strawberry and I'm living in your parents' basement. I can't even rent us an apartment."

"It's okay," she said. "We don't have anything but each other. I don't know how this is all going to work out, but I know it's all going to work out."

BUT THERE WAS another problem. We were both dedicated to the church and the Word, but we were living in sin. We wanted to have our relationship right with God. It felt like we were starting off on the wrong foot, and neither of us wanted that.

Two people aren't good together unless each of them is whole and strong. I needed to keep working on myself and getting myself right. Then Tracy and I could start out the proper way.

One day I asked God, "What is it? What is it you want from me?"

He said, "Walk away from everything."

Oh man. That's when I realized you better be careful what you ask God, because he doesn't joke around in his answer.

"Give it all up?" I said.

Yes, God said. Let it all go. He told me I had to strip away everything from my life, all my habits, all my ways of thinking and acting, so that I could find out who I really was and what my purpose here was.

So I left Tracy again. We both knew I had to get myself right if we were ever going to have the kind of relationship we wanted.

I flew out to San Dimas and stayed with Regina, in a bedroom in her apartment. She was going through an adjustment period in her own personal life, and had just moved into a new apartment with her kids. I helped her out with that. While she was at work, I looked after the kids. I loved my little nieces and nephews, and it was pure joy to be around them.

I spent six months there, working very hard on myself. For six months I lived like a monk in a cave. Regina and her kids were practically the only people I saw. I barely left my room except to go to church. I read and studied the Bible with the same sort of intense focus I used to devote to playing ball. I read until late at night, and then lay back with the Bible on my chest as I went to sleep, praying, "Lord, let your word breathe inside of me."

I surrendered to God. Surrender means doing a lot of things you don't want to, and not doing a lot of things your desires tell you to. It means standing up to your daily responsibilities, even when you're feeling so depressed you can barely drag yourself out of bed. And it means avoiding the people and places and habits that led you astray, no matter how badly you think you want that drink or whatever it is. It means, "I'm listening, Lord. I hear you, and I choose not to do those things anymore."

I swore off all liquor, all drugs, and all sex. I'm not sure which one of those was the hardest. None of it was easy. I wasn't used to going very many days without wanting a drink, drugs, or sex. I had gotten so used to thinking I needed all those things—needed them to fill the empty places inside me. We live in such a materialistic world. We think we need all these things around us to make us happy. The cars, the flat-screen TVs, the clothes, the bling, the drugs and alcohol. But now, when I put together six whole months of complete abstinence, I found that I didn't need any of them. When you strip all that away, you never miss it. There was no joy in it. God had to take it all away for me to realize that.

I had to teach myself how to pray again. Loving God and living dirty don't mix. I had to relearn how to get on my knees and humble myself before God, ask his help. I pleaded with him, on my knees on the floor.

"God, please help me to do the right thing today. Please help me not to hurt anybody today. Please give me the strength to do right. Take anything you want from me. I don't care about the money and fame and parties and success and women. I don't care about anything anymore except my kids and my loved ones and being the best person I can be for them."

Of course, God was right there and ready to hear me. Like I said, God has a lot of patience with us. He was there waiting for me while I went through all my wicked ways, knowing that the suffering I was causing myself with all that bad behavior would eventually be so severe that I'd turn away from it and come back to him.

God began to heal me. And he gave me the strength to face up to all the wicked things I'd done. I emerged from the fog of pain and confusion I'd been living in for so long. Away from everything and everyone, I was able for the first time to examine all the choices I had made, and the terrible consequences of them. The realization of how much pain and misery and destruction I'd caused the people who loved me fell on me like a ton of anvils. I had to look at it all and say, "I have no excuses anymore. My father is no excuse. My childhood is no excuse. My self-loathing is no excuse. None of that makes what I did okay. It's not okay. I was responsible for my actions. The people I hurt are real."

It was very hard, but I got over my bitterness and anger toward my father, my wives, the press—all the people I had blamed for my own bad behavior. I forced myself to step up like a man and accept responsibility for everything I'd done.

I'd like to say that God finally revealed the Truth to me in a blinding flash of light, but he doesn't usually work that way. I didn't have a dramatic flash of revelation. It was more gradual. I just surrendered. All those years I'd been struggling, struggling, struggling. Hating myself and wondering why on earth God chose me. I had raged through my life like a hurricane. And now, by sitting quietly, studying, praying, purifying myself, I let the hurricane blow itself out.

I finally found myself, and God. This time, when God called, I didn't run away and hide. I answered.

I changed a lot. Everyone around me could see it. I walked differently, talked differently, thought differently. There'd always been a good, kind, peaceful, loving man inside me. I had just never accepted him. Now I did.

And that was when I was finally, truly born again.

That was in 2006. I have not gone back to any of my old ways since then. I'm a different person today. I don't make any claims, promises, or predictions about what kind of person I'll be tomorrow. If there's one thing I learned from surviving cancer twice and surviving all the turmoil I brought into my life, it's that you live today. You're not living in yesterday or tomorrow. Today is all you've got, and how you live today is all that matters.

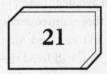

21

I WENT BACK TO Tracy a changed man. She saw it right away, and was really happy for me, and for both of us. We stayed for a little while in her parents' basement, then were able to rent ourselves an apartment.

Now that I was finally facing up to what I had done, the obvious question was, "What am I going to do about it? How am I going to make amends?"

At first I threw up my hands and said, "Where do I start?" There's a long, hard road from wanting to do the right thing and actually standing up like a man and doing it.

One of the first things to tackle was a mountain of bills. In my last few years of spiraling down to the bottom, I let a lot of financial obligations slide. I skipped a lot of alimony and child support payments. I let back taxes, and the interest and penalties on them, pile up. I had to—I was broke. But there was a right way and a wrong to deal with that situation. I could've gone back into court and said, "Look, I'm not the man I was when I agreed to pay all that alimony and child support. I'm not making $4 million a year anymore. I'm in jail trimming the lawn. We need to review these cases, judge, and you tell me how to handle it in the appropriate way. We need to work something out, some partial payments or something."

I didn't do or say anything like that. I just let it all slide as I kept falling down and down.

Now, I could just continue to let it all lie. I had fallen below everyone's radar. I had dropped out of sight. No one knew where I lived or how to reach me to serve court papers on me. I was in suburban St. Louis. I could have stayed incognito and avoided those bills for a long time. Just keep running and hiding from those consequences of my actions.

But you know, you can't run and hide from yourself. Wherever you run, you're still you, you still lived the life you did and made the choices you did. Wherever you hide, the consequences of how you lived will find you. I knew that as I got back out in the world and started my new life, the bill collectors would take notice anyway. If I was going to start fresh, I had to face up to all my obligations. I had to be a man and take ownership of my whole life, the bills included.

When I resurfaced, the bills did in fact start to come in. They came in the mail. Process servers knocked on the door. Man, was it a lot of bills. There was no way I could just sit down and pay them. I wasn't a million-dollar man anymore. Initially, a lot of the financial advice I heard was about how to keep running from the debt, like declaring bankruptcy or using this or that accounting trick.

"No," I said. "I'm not running and hiding anymore. If I'm ever going to be free of my past, I have to pay the dues. If I'm going to own up, I got to pony up."

So Tracy and I dealt with the bills one by one as they came in. She threw herself and her awesome energy into it. She worked her way through the mountains of paperwork, negotiated with bill collectors and attorneys. She was amazing. I did my part, too, working the phones. We got attorneys to handle the cases for us at reduced rates. God bless them, they did what would usually be hundreds of thousands of dollars in services for just thousands.

Friends also stepped up and helped out, including a new

acquaintance, Phil Tavella, who became one of our nearest and dearest friends. I met Phil at a Little League event and we hit it off right away. He could see that the once-mighty Darryl Strawberry had come down a few pegs in his life. We talked for a long time, and I told him about my financial situation.

It turned out that Phil was a financial consultant. He jumped into my financial problems and started swinging. He helped us negotiate with the IRS and deal with my other bills. With Phil advising us, we went before judges, divulged everything about our current financial status, and they rendered their decisions on what would be realistic payment schedules where I could begin to reduce those bills a little at a time. Meanwhile, I was out there making the paid appearances and signing autographs. Whatever I made, some of it got earmarked for the bills.

It wasn't just the bill collectors who came knocking as I resurfaced. I'd been out of the public eye for a few years, and when they heard I was alive and well and living in Missouri, the media came at me from all directions.

"Darryl, where ya been? What ya been doing? How are you? How was prison? What you got planned? What the heck you doing in Missouri?"

I got a lot of book and movie offers. A lot of money was waved under my nose to sell my life story.

I said no. I wasn't ready. I was still working out my life story for myself. I didn't have anything to tell them that they didn't already know. I could tell the stories, but I didn't know yet what they meant. I was still learning those lessons. I couldn't pass them on yet.

When the divorce came through, Charisse dinged me as hard as Lisa had financially. I guess she figured she had to get everything she could for herself and the kids, and that she had earned every penny of it after the fourteen years of pain and suffering I put her through. I was bitter about it, but I couldn't really complain or fight it. I knew she had a right to stand up for herself.

When people ask me if I invested the millions I made as a ballplayer, I say, "Yes. I invested in my first two wives, their divorces, alimony, and child support."

Meanwhile, Tracy started acting as my business manager, too. Out in the world, I was still Darryl Strawberry. Still a star, even if I was a tarnished one. I still had offers coming to me every day. Promoters wanted me to sell autographs and memorabilia. Guys hit me up with all sorts of business ventures. They thought that having Darryl Strawberry as a front man and spokesman would be good for business.

I channeled all the offers through Tracy. She was a good businessperson, smart and tough, and she had fantastic instincts for separating out the good, honest business prospects from the sharks and phonies. And she was fiercely protective of me and my reputation. I can honestly say she's the best manager I ever had, and everyone dealing with us has quickly learned to respect her.

Gradually, we got my financial life and income back in order. We're not wealthy people, and I don't think we ever will be. But we're stable and moving forward and living fine. I don't need a huge house and fancy cars and closets full of Armani suits. I never minded having all that, but I never needed it, either. And I paid for it with more than money. I don't miss it. I've discovered the big difference between living a fulfilled life and living a life that's just filled up with all that stuff. This way is much better.

It's something I wish a lot more people could learn. We make ourselves miserable trying to get a bigger house and newer car and shinier jewelry, because we keep thinking that if we only had this and that and that other thing we'll be happy and feel good about ourselves. And none of it works, so we keep trying to get more.

Things don't make you happy, no matter how big and shiny and expensive they are. They're still just things. Real happiness only comes from getting right with yourself, right in your spirit.

TRACY AND I finally felt we could be together in the proper way. We had already made a great start. We were loving each other, going to church together, and building our life together right, from the ground up. And now we could be properly married.

Phil was having a birthday party in Las Vegas. He and his wife, Shirley, were going to renew their vows. At first, he didn't invite us. I called and asked him about it.

"Darryl, you know why I didn't invite you," he said. "It's Vegas. You're just getting your life back. You don't want to be in Vegas. Talk about jumping into the frying pan."

"But Phil, it's for you," I said. "I'll be all right. Tracy will be with me. We want to be there for you."

"All right," Phil finally said. "I'd love to have you with us, of course. But I'm going to keep an eye on you."

So we made plans to head out there for a long weekend. That's when God put it in my heart: You're going to Las Vegas. Marry Tracy.

I didn't say anything to her until we got there that Thursday night. I popped it on her in our hotel room.

"Trace, you know what? We're getting married while we're here."

She looked at me like I was nuts. "What?"

"No, really. We've got to do this right. We can't keep shacking up. God's never going to bless it."

She agreed with that, but she asked, "What about my family?"

"We'll call them after the ceremony."

The next day we got our paperwork, and on Saturday we went to the Little White Chapel on the Strip. It's a place famous for quickie weddings. It's even open 24/7. Tracy was a little doubtful about it. There's nothing either romantic or spiritual about the place. It's like a 7-Eleven for weddings.

But I said, "You know, hon, I've had the big weddings. I want to do something different. I want to get married in my jeans and tennis shoes." To me it didn't matter where we got married or what we were wearing. It was all about making it official so we were right with each other and with God. And she agreed.

So we got up Saturday morning and got hitched. Phil and Shirley, and Phil's brother Dominic and his wife, Patty, were our witnesses. Tracy called her folks afterward.

"Mom, Dad, I've got something to tell you. We got married."

They were very happy for us. They knew we loved each other and wanted only the best for us.

As it turned out, there was a big party going on at the hotel. Lots of movie stars and sports stars were there. I knew many of them, and they knew me. I won't name names, but a few of them saw me in the lobby and were like, "Yo, Darryl Strawberry! Long time no see! You look great. Where ya been? Come to the party. Lots of old friends there. You want some coke? I got some killer blow on me."

They pulled me into the VIP lounge. I dragged Phil with me. There were a lot of old friends there I was happy to see, but all my old demons were in that room, too.

"Darryl, let me get you a drink."

"No thanks, man. I'm good."

"Darryl, see that hottie over there? She wants to meet you."

"No thanks. I just got married."

Phil hovered at my elbow the whole time, antsy as a cat. After a few minutes I said, "Let's get out of here."

That night Tracy and I went to dinner as a married couple, and on Sunday we flew home.

Eventually we bought her parents' house from them, and that's where we live today, in a normal little house on a quiet street in the suburbs. The neighbors are very cool about having me in the neighborhood. I honestly think a lot of them don't even know who I am. They don't seem like big baseball fans.

People sometimes ask me how the famous Darryl Strawberry, who once tore up New York and Los Angeles, can really be happy living in a suburb of St. Louis. It is very different here. Quiet. Homey. People move at a different pace and are much more polite. Where we go to our church, the Church on the Rock, the whole congregation is friendly and nice. It's definitely a change of pace, and I like it. Life is simple here. I'm a simple guy. All I can say is I have found peace and contentment here, and isn't that what we're all looking for in the end? I know I looked for it all my life. I just looked in a lot of the wrong places.

ONE DAY IN 2006 we went to visit the Center for Autism Education, not far from where we live. It was founded by Amy Buie, a friend of Tracy's since high school, and Tracy's sister Angie worked there. They specialize in working with the most severe cases, kids who were dropped by regular schools because the teachers and staff just didn't have the skills to deal with their behavior, which included outbursts of violence directed at teachers and other students—and at themselves.

"You need to be careful around them," the staff told me when we arrived. "These kids have real trouble dealing with strangers. They won't let anyone touch them, not even people they're around every day. Don't expect them to talk to you or meet your eye. If you get too close to them and they feel stressed, they may act out by hitting you or slapping your face."

I just laughed. "These kids can't hurt me," I said. "I'm six-foot-six and 230 pounds of professional athlete. Besides, if one of them slaps me in the face, it won't hurt me anywhere near the pain I've caused myself over the years."

So we go walking around, and the kids didn't react to me anything like I was warned. They were drawn to me. They came around me, hugged me. The teachers were startled. These kids didn't know me. They weren't reacting to me as Darryl Strawberry, the baseball star. It was a spiritual connection. They could feel that my spirit was real and at peace, and there was no fear in me. They could feel the energy from me. These kids who won't let anyone near them were hugging me. Teachers and staff standing there with their mouths open and tears in their eyes.

That day changed my life. I suddenly knew why God had kept me around, through all my struggles and two bouts of cancer. I looked into those kids' eyes and saw pain, which was something I was very familiar with. And I saw God's purpose for me.

See, I'd always known, even growing up the way I did, even through my struggles, that I had a gift in me. It wasn't baseball. Baseball was just a talent. The gift in me was the capacity to love and care for others. It's a gift I think many of us have, but for all sorts of reasons we don't use it the way God wants us to, to help others and make the world a better place for our being in it.

It couldn't have been more plain to me that this was an opportunity to use that gift. Right away, Tracy and I got busy on creating the Darryl Strawberry Foundation to raise awareness of autism issues and generate donations for the center's great work. Well, Tracy did all the hard work. She sat right down at our computer at home, did all the paperwork you need to do to start a nonprofit organization, figured it all out. She's the president, and we got Phil, Dominic, and some other friends to be on the board of directors. I do what a celebrity and former baseball star does: I'm the spokesperson and front man.

We figured out a great way to do our fund-raisers. Pa Leonard is a big golfer, and he was after me for years to take it up. Back in the day, he'd always say, "D, you live on a golf course. When are you going to learn how to play?"

"Nah," I always said.

"I bet you'd be great," he'd coax me.

"You play, Pa. I'll watch you."

But in 2007, when I was out there visiting with them, he finally got me to try it, and I liked it. It's a sport, and I'm an athlete, so once I got started with it, I was up for the challenge of getting good at it. I love being out on the links, all that green grass and fresh air and sunshine. And, to tell the truth, it's a good thing for me to focus my attention on. I know very well that it's not smart for me to be too idle and inactive. I get bored and restless, and I've learned the hard way that's a dangerous state for someone like me. Learning how to play golf got me on my feet and out of the house, and learning how to play it well engages the champion in me. I'm still just a duffer. I hit me some long, long drives, naturally, but they don't always go where I want them to. Yet.

I hadn't been playing very long when we hit on a way to combine my mission for autism with my new pastime. The foundation organizes golf outings, where people pay a lot of money to play with me and some of my celebrity friends. We hold a shotgun golf tournament, where you have foursomes made up of three paying golfers and one celebrity. Afterward there's a banquet, we give prizes to the day's best golfers, and we auction off memorabilia and other things. My great friend Jay Horwitz in the Mets organization gets us Mets tickets to auction off, and the winners get to take batting practice and meet the team.

I get a lot of my friends to participate—Coney, Ron Darling, Howard Johnson, Bernie Williams. I haven't been able to talk E.D. into it yet. He's never played and says he has no interest in learning. Well, maybe he'll change his mind someday. The rest of us all love it, and the other golfers love to meet us, hang out with us a few hours, get autographs, all that. It's a great event. At the first one in 2007 we raised something like $70,000 for the center.

At the end of the day, I said to Tracy, "We touched lives today. God gave them hope through us today." It's awesome to be able to give that gift to someone. It's the highest high I ever experienced. It's real joy, not the fake happiness I used to try to find.

And it was just the beginning. Our goal is to raise a couple of million dollars so the center can expand. As it is now, the center can only serve kids until they turn twenty-one. It doesn't have the facilities to deal with adults with autism. We're going to raise the funds for an adult program.

When I meet the families of children with autism, I am so moved by their loss. A lot of those parents will never get a hug from their kids. The autism has made it all but impossible for kids to show their parents that they love them. Then I think about all the hugs I missed through my own actions. I threw away what these parents may never have. I thank God every day that I finally came to my senses, and I treasure every second I get to be with my kids now. But I can't bring back what my kids and I missed because of me.

That's why I can't stress enough when I speak to young people, "Think about what you're doing. Think about the consequences. The damage and pain you cause yourself and others can never be undone. It can be healed, but you won't be able to go back and change what you did. The best you'll be able to do is own up to it and try to learn from it, like I have. Believe me, I wish they were lessons I didn't have to learn, at least not the way I did."

ONE SATURDAY IN May 2008, I went out to Shea for the sixth annual Autism Awareness Day. There was a barbecue for a few hundred families in a big tent that was set up in the picnic area behind left field, and part of my job that day was to go greet them. When I walked into that tent, it was like a rock star or movie star had arrived. Every head in the place turned, saw me, smiled, and cheered. Then they flocked around me. Adults, little kids, it didn't matter. They all wanted to touch me, get an autograph, get their picture taken with me. It had been, what, eight years since I played ball in New York, and more like eighteen since I'd played at Shea, but you wouldn't know that from the way folks greeted me and how excited and pleased they were to see me.

New York fans have always adored me, and I've always loved them back. Even when they were booing me we loved each other. People are always telling me about this time or that time they saw me at the plate. It might have been twenty-five years ago and it's still one of their favorite baseball memories.

In 2006, I had thrown out the first ball in game two of the Mets' National League Championship Series against the Cards. When my name was announced and I started to walk out to the mound, everyone in Shea Stadium stood up to give me a standing ovation. To be remembered that way, man, that's some feeling.

My brother Mike and my son DJ have walked around in Manhattan with me on various occasions, and both were blown away by how everyone greets me, waves, calls out, "Yo, Darryl Strawberry! You the man!" I can't get far down any block in the city without a fan coming up to me. Recently I was standing outside a midtown office building having a smoke, when a young black woman in a security guard's uniform came up to me. The first thing she said was, "Sir, you can't smoke here. You have to move out to the sidewalk."

"Yes, ma'am," I said.

She broke into a grin. "Mr. Strawberry, I just wanted to come say hello."

"Hello to you," I said.

And then she put her security guard face back on.

"But you still can't smoke here," she said.

I had to laugh. A classic New York moment. I did as I was told.

Mike likes to say that I'm "an icon" in New York. I guess that's true, but I also think one reason New Yorkers still respond so warmly to me is that I always showed them I'm a human being, too. I may have been a star, but I had my flaws and foibles, just like everyone else. I made mistakes. I got ill. I struggled, and eventually overcame. I think that all makes me more approachable and sympathetic to them.

I believe that's got something to do with why little kids crowd around me, too. They never saw me play. Some of them are so little I know they don't have a clue who I am. I think they're responding to the same energy those kids at the Center for Autism Education did. They know somehow that I love kids and love being around them.

Back when I was still playing, I was always the guy who kept signing autographs for kids long after the rest of the team had gone back to the clubhouse. I'd stand there and sign my name until every last kid got an autograph. My hand might be falling off, but I was not going to be the guy who disappointed a kid that day. Tracy remembers a time we missed a flight at the airport because a bunch of kids recognized me and I just couldn't get on that plane unless I had given every one of those kids an autograph. I would've felt terrible. That kid would remember for the rest of his life the time Darryl Strawberry stiffed him for an autograph. How could I do that to him? I could always catch another flight, but I would never see that kid again.

I'm not telling you that so you'll think I'm a saint. If you've read this far in this book, you know I'm not anything like a saint. I just think it's a very small way for me to give back a little to fans who have given me so very much. I know some ballplayers treat the fans as a necessary evil, and others refuse to give away an autograph or pose for a picture without getting paid for it. I've never been that way. To me, it's pretty obvious that we owe it all to the fans. Without them, we'd all be back playing pickup ball on a sandlot somewhere.

I loved going back to Shea. It was like going home to Mom's cooking. Shea was where I got my start in the majors. I love the Yankees and Yankee Stadium, too, but the Mets were like my first baseball family and Shea was where we lived. I had a lot of memories in that place, and I knew everyone.

The summer of 2008 was a highly emotional time to be going back to Shea, and to Yankee Stadium, too, for that matter. It was the final season for both ballparks. In the spring of 2009, the Mets would move to the new Citi Field next door, and the Yankees to the new Yankee Stadium next door. There were a lot of memorial events at both stadiums in 2008, and I attended several. I threw out the first ball at a game in Shea Stadium, and the fans there gave me a standing ovation, too. The Mets put out a special DVD of Shea highlights that I helped promote. Both ballparks were getting old, and both teams and their fans deserved new ones, but I knew that, like an awful lot of folks, I was going to miss those old parks something fierce.

22

I **'M HAPPY TO** say that for the last few years I've been back in the Mets family in a couple of ways. For one thing, I'm a special instructor for the young players in the Mets farm system. I go down South to visit with the minor league teams and talk to the players, try to inspire them and give them the benefit of my experience.

I wish there'd been a program like that when I was an eighteen-year-old in the minors. Back then, kids like me were just thrown in with everyone else and expected to learn the ropes on our own. You can see how well that worked. The organizations have gotten a lot better about providing young players with advice now, everything from how to manage their money to how to deal with the personal pressures of being in professional sports.

Baseball is hard work. I know some people don't believe that, because players make it look easy. They work very hard to make it look that way. The physical part is just the half of it. It's also a tremendous amount of mental and emotional work. Playing well requires mental discipline, focus, and emotional control.

Discipline, focus, and emotional control do not come easily to any young males. You're bursting with energy and hormones. You're out in the world on your own for the first time, struggling to figure it all out and what your place in it is, insecure and self-conscious. You're hungry for respect, to prove yourself as a man, but you haven't done much yet to be respected for, and you probably don't have a clue what being a man really means. You turn to easy, macho ways to prove your manhood to yourself and other people. Does being able to beat up other guys make you a man? Having sex with lots of women? Showing that you can hold your liquor and drugs? Shooting a gun? Driving a fast car? Hitting home runs?

Later, when you really have become a man, you look back and see that the obvious answer to all these questions is *no*! Of course not, you young fool! But it's a lot less obvious when you're young, dumb, and full of . . . hormones and insecurity.

Now, take that young man, fresh out of high school, still living at home, still a wide-eyed innocent, and toss him into the big leagues. Hand him a few hundred thousand dollars—or these days, a few million. Tell him he's a superstar. Surround him with cameras and reporters. Toss him into an exclusively male society of mostly older guys. Push him out there in front of thousands and thousands of fans. Offer him more free booze, drugs, and sex than he has ever dreamed of having.

And then tell him to grow up, be a man, be focused and disciplined and in control of his emotions and a team player and a role model for millions of kids.

And then, if he struggles, if he fails, if he screws up, condemn him, scream at him, laugh at him, spit on him.

I'm not saying boo-hoo, poor me. I'm just explaining how it was for me, and how it's been for lots of other young athletes and celebrities of all sorts.

The temptations may be even worse for young athletes now than they were in my day. And more dangerous. I think the world has gotten meaner and uglier since my day. Young athletes roll into these nightclubs or strip joints today, showing off their bling, attracting the ladies, and other guys get envious and angry. They're frustrated and unhappy about life, they see you've got it all going on, and they want to take it from you. Fights break out, the guns come out. It happens now.

The drugs are still flying, too. In my day it was speed and cocaine. Lately it's been steroids. All these young athletes want to be fit, look better, be stronger, be faster. If that means shooting themselves up with steroids, you know they're going to do that. It's not hard to spot. You'll see a young player one season who looks like I did at his age, lean and mean. He comes back next season looking like the Incredible Hulk. Where'd he get all that bulk in the four months between seasons? You can't throw around enough weights to bulk up that way.

Over the last couple of seasons there's been a lot of talk about the huge increase in broken bats. Hitters are shattering bats at a whole new rate. Pieces of bats are flying like shrapnel in all directions, injuring players, umps, fans. They say it's because there's a shortage of the good wood bats used to be made from. The new bats aren't as strong. I believe that may be true. I also believe that if every batter is built like Arnold Schwarzenegger and Hulk Hogan, they're going to shatter more bats just with the brute force of their swing.

They're not thinking straight about the consequences a few years down the road. They want to compete and be champions here and now, and if they see other guys taking the steroids, they'll take them too.

Since DJ was drafted by the Phoenix Suns in 2007, I have worried myself sick about him. My first instinct has been to protect him from the media, the vultures, the bad influences, the whole world that surrounds young professional athletes. Who knows better how dangerous that can all be? And on top of all that he has to carry the weight of being Darryl Strawberry's son. He has to struggle not to be overshadowed by my past. He's going to have to live with that his entire life. I did that to him.

What if he follows the terrible example I set? I want to guide him, advise him, help him stay away from all the traps that life sets for a young man. But why should he listen to me now? I wasn't a father to him when he was growing up and needed me most. In my own way I was as lousy a father to him as my father was to me. I created a distance between us. I have cried myself dry thinking about that. If only I could go back and fix that damage.

All my children will have to deal with being Darryl Strawberry's kids all their lives. They're great young people. They're strong and smart. I know they'll handle it—and I know I'll move heaven and earth and all the stars to help them deal with it in any way I can. But the pain I feel over putting that burden in their lives just overwhelms me sometimes. I have cried so many tears over that. If I could go back and undo all the wicked and outrageous things I did in my life, I would do it for them in a second. But you can't. You can only live with the consequences and try to repair what you can.

IN APRIL 2008 I also became a pre- and postgame commentator for SNY, SportsNet New York, the Mets channel. I did eighteen games during the '08 season. The half-hour shows were broadcast live from a studio in the Time-Life Building at Fifty-first Street and Avenue of the Americas in Manhattan, across the street from Radio City Music Hall.

As requested, I'd get there two hours early. I've become very fastidious about that. In my younger, wilder days, there were all those times I was late for batting practice, late for the team bus, and when I was at my lowest, there were a couple of games I didn't show up for at all. I took a lot of heat for that, rightly. These days I make a point of being on time or early for appointments.

So I'd get there early and then sit around the greenroom for a couple of hours. I would read the papers, watch TV, drink coffee. Usually a couple of my New York friends would drop by to while away some of the time with me. A little before showtime, a producer and the show's host, Matt Yallof, would stop in and we'd go over some of the questions Matt would be asking me on-air. Then I'd go into the little makeup room. They'd brush some powder on me to keep my face, and my shaved head, from looking too shiny in the hot studio lights. Then they'd hook me up with a wireless earphone and mic, and it was showtime.

The studio where we did the show was a circular room with windows all around, facing Avenue of the Americas and a pedestrian plaza beside the Time-Life Building. If it was a bright day outside they lowered the shades so people outside couldn't see in. But in the evenings the blinds would be up and we'd sit there doing the show with a lot of people staring through the windows, just like you see folks doing on the *Today* show.

My first week at it got off to a weird start. I was scheduled to give commentary on three games. The first game, on a Monday, was rained out. Tuesday was a night game that went into extra innings. I didn't leave the studio until after midnight, and then back in my hotel room I couldn't wind down enough to fall asleep until three A.M. Wednesday I was back in the greenroom at ten-thirty, not feeling too sharp. That afternoon's game was delayed awhile because of a water main break somewhere in the neighborhood outside Shea. Then the Mets proceeded to lose to the Pirates, 13–1. The starting pitcher got slammed for seven runs before being yanked in only the second inning. When you're down seven runs that early, it can demoralize the whole team. We watched the Mets crumble, making errors and playing like they were asleep and just wishing the nightmare would end. I'd been in games like that, and believe me I sympathized. But that didn't make it any easier to come up with useful commentary. There's just not a lot to say when your team loses 13–1. You just move on.

Once I got used to it, I liked doing those shows a lot. I've been around baseball a long time now. I've got a lot of insider knowledge to impart.

I've become one of the Wise Old Men of the game. Who would've thought it? I even went to Yankee Stadium in August 2008 for the annual Old-Timers' Day. I'm an old-timer in my forties. Well, baseball is a young man's game. And like I said, I'm just happy to be alive.

It was a great afternoon, the sixty-second Old-Timers' Day and, of course, the last one in the old stadium. What a turnout. Something like seventy-two of us were there. My boys Coney, Willie Randolph, and Tino Martinez; and Yogi Berra, Whitey Ford, Joe Pepitone, Reggie Jackson, Goose Gossage, Ken Griffey Sr., Wade Boggs, Bucky Dent, Graig Nettles, Don Baylor, Al Downing, Oscar Gamble, Don Larsen . . . No other organization in the game could bring together that many greats. After we all got called out for applause, we played one inning of old man's ball, just goofing around. It was fun, but a little sad, too, because we knew that when we came back for the next Old-Timers' Day, it would be in a brand-new place.

Then again, like I said, baseball is a young man's game. And I knew that the young men on the Yankees and the Mets would get busy right away making new history and new memories in those two new ballparks.

BECAUSE I WANT to help young people break out of the vicious cycle of self-destructive behavior that spun my life around like a whirlpool for so long, I do a lot of public speaking in places like juvenile correction facilities. I think it's good for them to see somebody like me, who came from the same background they do, who struggled with the same issues they do, who did time himself in a few correctional facilities, but overcame and achieved.

I talk to them about the decisions we make in our youth, and how they can affect the entire course of our lives. I explain that I'm someone who made some really foolish and destructive decisions in my day, and I paid dearly for them.

Young people get so involved in their struggles, they can't see a way out, or even believe one exists. They give up on themselves. I tell them that the way to get out is to get counseling and advice from others who have walked through hell. Listen to people who have experienced it. There's a path through your troubles, but you may not be able to see it. You're too caught up with your current situation. We all need guidance in life, especially when we're young. We all need people to build us up, build our confidence and belief in ourselves, and then we get a glimpse of who we really are. I think that's the most important thing for anyone that's in the midst of a struggle. Get a glimpse of who you are, and all of a sudden the light will come on. The light can be awfully dim when you're in the middle of the forest and can't find the path through it. But there are people who have struggled through that forest before you and came out on the other side. They're your best guides.

Now, in the kind of neighborhood I come from, poor, black, and urban, those guides and role models can be thin on the ground. As I said at the beginning of this book, a lot of the folks from those communities who become successful, the doctors and lawyers and Darryl Strawberrys, move up and out of the 'hood. Young black males look around and the only successful males they see—the only ones who look successful, anyway—are the criminals and pimps and dope dealers. They've got the fancy cars and the bling. Yeah, and they're also running from the cops.

That's why, regardless of what I achieved, I've always gone back to my community to talk to young black males about goals. Your goal really can't be just to hang out on street corners and sell dope. That's not a goal. That's living in a nightmare.

One thing I tell them is to stay in school and get an education. The guys they see slinging dope on the corners may have lots of street smarts, but that street is a dead end. They know how to make money and count it, and that's all they know. That's not going to get them out of the 'hood. What if they channeled that skill into something positive, where they weren't looking over their shoulders for the cops all the time?

Their goal has to be to get up out of the 'hood. Most of us who come from those areas and became successful doctors and lawyers and athletes and such made it our goal early on to get out. If you don't put your mind to getting out of there, you're definitely going to stay stuck there.

I tell them that school is also where I found my own personal role models—the teachers and coaches who motivated me, encouraged me, and disciplined me when I needed it. Church is another place to meet positive examples of what it means to be a man and a good, caring, responsible person.

I hope these young men listen to me and act on what I tell them. It's such a waste for them to give up hope and throw away their lives. I truly believe that everyone has a tremendous gift in them. It's just a matter of how we tap into that gift, and then how we go out and use that gift.

I spent a lot of years with no hope for myself, no faith in myself. I wasted a lot of energy on useless and destructive pursuits. My mind's always on a mission now to do something that's a positive influence in the world. It's not about me. It's not about how great I've been. It's about using the gift that's inside me. When I see someone who's lost, I know how that feels. When I see someone who's struggling, I want to guide them. I'm a strong believer that from everyone to whom much is given, much is required. God gave me a lot in my lifetime. He requires of me that I give back, and I'm happy to do that. It's such a gift for me to go out and help someone.

I'M LOVING MY life now. It's great to be me. There was a long time when I could not say that. But I found myself, I found my purpose, and after all those years in darkness, oh is it wonderful to open your eyes and see daylight.

When people meet me now, I can see the shock. "This is not the Darryl Strawberry I've been reading about all my life." Even my physical appearance is a surprise. "You look amazing," they tell me time and time again. "You never looked better. What's come over you?"

The answer is that for the very first time in my life I'm comfortable in my own skin. But that's taken a huge fight. To get to where I am today, I had to own up to everything I did that you've read about in this book. It was only then that I could find peace and happiness.

I know there are skeptics who will say, "We've heard this from Darryl Strawberry many times before. He was clean and sober, he was on the right path, he was in church and loving God. And he always slid back to his bad old ways. Why should we believe any different now? Is he in AA or NA? What's he doing to make sure he won't fall again?"

Well, that's how skeptics are, and that's okay. I don't have to prove anything to them, convince them, or convert them. Their skepticism is their business, and besides, I can't pretend I didn't earn it in the past.

It's true that I'm not in any programs anymore. I did AA, NA, all of them, and they're great. There's nothing wrong with them. They save lives. I got a lot of knowledge from them and met some wonderful friends through them. But my program now is church, God, and faith.

Besides, for me personally, those AA and NA meetings were a problem. Because a big part of my bad behavior had to do with sex and women, and I have to say a lot of the people who go to those meetings are sex fiends. They give up the alcohol or the drugs or whatever their addiction was, but they haven't dealt yet with the root causes of the addiction. They're still addictive personalities, and a lot of them just switch the addictive behavior to sex. It's their substitute. They used to crave the high they got from drugs or liquor. Now they crave the high of sex.

I'm speaking from firsthand knowledge. I was that way, too. The meetings sometimes were just a meat market for me. I got a lot of play from a lot of women in those meetings, and I took it. Obviously that was holding me back from working on my real issues, so I stopped going. It wasn't a problem with the programs themselves. It was how I and some of the other people in the programs treated them.

I don't drink anymore. Haven't had a drink in a few years. I feel no need for it. I've been down that road. I had all the fun I can have. I'm settled into my life and my mission and my wife and my children. Sure, because I'm still well-known I'm still offered things that are bad for me. Guys slap me on the back and invite me out to a bar or club. But I don't allow myself to go to those places. I don't hang out at nightclubs and flirt around in those fields. I don't have any need for it. What's the purpose of going to them? There's nothing there for me. It's not like a place I ain't never been before. Been there, done that, damn near killed myself. Who am I gonna kid? I'm going to kid myself about it?

Sure, it's still a struggle to stay on the right path and avoid the wrong ones sometimes. For instance, when I'm in New York City, for the Mets or Yankees or SNY, they put me up in nice hotel rooms in Manhattan. Manhattan is where I learned to live the wrong way, and where the demons and temptations are everywhere—what Christians call "the near occasion of sin." One of the big lessons I've learned in my life is that to stay out of trouble it's best to stay away from trouble. If you go looking for it, you're going to find it. Just don't flirt with disaster by putting yourself in any place that tests your weaknesses. If you're a recovering gambler, you'd be crazy to spend time in a casino. If you're a recovering alcoholic, you don't walk into a bar. It's just common sense.

So when I'm in New York, I'll often ask Phil if I can come stay with him and his wonderful family rather than in a hotel. Phil's home in suburban Long Island is a lot like my home in suburban St. Louis—quiet, calm, peaceful. I watch TV with the family. I sleep in the guest bedroom. Phil feels bad because my feet hang over the edge of the bed, but I don't mind at all. I'm comfortable there in ways that don't have anything to do with the bed.

Do I know I'll never fall again? I only know that for today. I just know that every day I wake up and spend twenty-four hours living for my purpose and my dream and my desire. See, when you're doing something for others like I'm doing, that's the gift of giving back. That's what I wake up for every day, and that's what's in my heart. I used to wake up dreading my day, unhappy, unfulfilled, in situations and relationships I didn't want to be in, and I thought my only recourse was to go out and spread my wild oats. I don't have to spread any wild oats anymore. I spread a lot of wild oats. I'm not interested anymore. I have real joy in my life. I have a beautiful wife. We love each other and love God and are dedicated to helping other people. I have my beautiful children and I hope for lots of beautiful grandchildren.

What more could I want?

Acknowledgments

Thanks to all of you who are such an important part of my life:

My brothers, Michael and Ronnie, and my sisters, Regina and Michelle. We have endured hell together. For all of the times you have stood up for me and stood by me, and for always loving me as your brother, not as a superstar. My prayer is for much love, peace, and happiness for us all. Mom would want it that way. I love you guys so much!

To Ma and Pa Leonard, for all the years you have stood by my side, flown to be with me when I needed help, encouraged me in my faith, and loved me no matter what.

To Papa Gerry and Mama Peggy Boulware, who never judged me and just love me for who I am.

To Philip Tavella, my boy, who has gone through hell and high water for me and who is always there for me in more ways than there is room to list on this page! Words can't even begin to say, my brother, how special you are to me!

To Steve Lieberman, who is always positive, always opening up new business opportunities, always has an encouraging word, and keeps me laughing. I cherish you as my true, dear friend.

To Steven Moskowitz, a man of his word and of true character like I've never known. You are amazing.

To Ray Negron, Eric Davis, Eric Grossman, my entire Florida support crew, and the many others who have been through so much with me. My love and gratitude to you all!

To John Strausbaugh, my writer, Dan Halpern, my editor, and Tom Hopke, who got this ball rolling, for all your support in turning this difficult journey for me and my wife into the inspirational story we knew it should be.

May this story touch the lives of many!

About the Author

Darryl Strawberry was born in Crenshaw, California. An eight-time All-Star, a four-time World Series Champion, and a National League Rookie of the Year, he played for the Mets, the Dodgers, the Giants, and the Yankees during his headline career. In 2008, Strawberry began serving as a special ambassador for the Mets. He has five children and lives in Missouri with his wife, Tracy.